Towards a Poetics of
Creative Writing

NEW WRITING VIEWPOINTS

Series Editor: Graeme Harper, *Oakland University, Rochester, USA*

The overall aim of this series is to publish books which will ultimately inform teaching and research, but whose primary focus is on the analysis of creative writing practice and theory. There will also be books which deal directly with aspects of creative writing knowledge, with issues of genre, form and style, with the nature and experience of creativity, and with the learning of creative writing. They will all have in common a concern with excellence in application and in understanding, with creative writing practitioners and their work, and with informed analysis of creative writing as process as well as completed artefact.

Full details of all the books in this series and of all our other publications can be found on http://www.multilingual-matters.com, or by writing to Multilingual Matters, St Nicholas House, 31–34 High Street, Bristol BS1 2AW, UK.

NEW WRITING VIEWPOINTS: 10

Towards a Poetics of Creative Writing

Dominique Hecq

MULTILINGUAL MATTERS
Bristol • Buffalo • Toronto

Library of Congress Cataloging in Publication Data
A catalog record for this book is available from the Library of Congress.
Hecq, Dominique, editor.
Towards a Poetics of Creative Writing/Dominique Hecq.
New Writing Viewpoints: 10
Includes bibliographical references and index.
1. Creative writing--Study and teaching. 2. Authorship. I. Title.
PE1404.T69 2015
808'.042–dc23 2014041290

British Library Cataloguing in Publication Data
A catalogue entry for this book is available from the British Library.

ISBN-13: 978-1-78309-322-9 (hbk)
ISBN-13: 978-1-78309-321-2 (pbk)

Multilingual Matters
UK: St Nicholas House, 31–34 High Street, Bristol BS1 2AW, UK.
USA: UTP, 2250 Military Road, Tonawanda, NY 14150, USA.
Canada: UTP, 5201 Dufferin Street, North York, Ontario M3H 5T8, Canada.

Website: www.multilingual-matters.com
Twitter: Multi_Ling_Mat
Facebook: https://www.facebook.com/multilingualmatters
Blog: www.channelviewpublications.wordpress.com

The policy of Multilingual Matters/Channel View Publications is to use papers that
are natural, renewable and recyclable products, made from wood grown in sustainable
forests. In the manufacturing process of our books, and to further support our policy,
preference is given to printers that have FSC and PEFC Chain of Custody certification.
The FSC and/or PEFC logos will appear on those books where full certification has been
granted to the printer concerned.

Typeset by R. J. Footring Ltd, Derby, UK
Printed and bound in Great Britain

This book is dedicated to my postgraduate students,
past and present

Contents

Acknowledgements

Because of the cumulative nature of this book, I want to thank all those students, colleagues, writers, artists and theorists who have contributed to my understanding of creative writing research and to the sheer enjoyment I have experienced working on this project. A special debt is owed to Elizabeth Colbert, whose honesty and generosity helped me reconsider the design of this work. I am also grateful to Kylie Stevenson for introducing me to the work of Donald Winnicott and its pedagogical possibilities. To Christine Hill, I extend my sincerest thanks for her profound knowledge and wisdom in all things human and psychoanalytical. My thanks also extend to: Linda Weste, for her kindness, breadth of knowledge and sharp intellect; Glenice Whitting, for her warmth and friendship; Marion May Campbell, Jen Webb and Marcelle Freiman for their encouragement and feedback on individual chapters; and Paul Magee for saving me from wild etymological conjectures. Finally, I am grateful to Joan Howard, without whom this book would not have attained the editorial consistency it now has. As always, I am indebted to Luke Murphy and our four boys for their understanding and the interruptions I learned to welcome.

Portions of the book in their earlier versions were tried and tested on audiences at various universities and conferences: the AAWP Conference at the Queensland University of Technology in 2007, at the Royal Melbourne Institute of Technology in 2010, at Deakin University in Geelong in 2012 and at the University of Canberra in 2013;the 1st Global Conference on Writing: Paradigms, Power, Poetics in Prague in 2011;the Double Dialogues conference at the University of Melbourne in 2008, at the University of Toronto in 2010 and at the University of the South Pacific in 2012;and also the Great Writing Conference at King's College London, in 2013. Related papers were also presented at the Lacan Circle of Melbourne on too many occasions to list here and I am grateful for the feedback they received each time. Some of the ideas in this book have appeared elsewhere in print, though usually with a different focus, depending on the occasion and development of the ideas at the stage of writing. The event that crystallised the desire to articulate and interrelate these ideas was the writing of a chapter for *Research Methods in Creative Writing* (Kroll & Harper, 2013), and I am grateful to Jeri Kroll and Graeme Harper for entrusting me with the task. An earlier version of Chapter 9 was published in a special issue of *TEXT* edited by Scott Brook and Paul Magee (Hecq, 2010b). A much shorter version of Chapter 12 appears in the proceedings of the 18th AAWP Conference (Hecq, 2012c), for which I thank Shane Strange. The poems and excerpts from my own longer creative works were also published elsewhere, sometimes in slightly different form. I would therefore like to thank the editors and publishers of the following journals and collections of essays for their support of work in progress: Nigel Krauth, Anthony Lawrence, Enza Gandolfo and Kevin Brophy at *TEXT*; Ann McCulloch and Paul Monaghan at *Double Dialogues*; Justin Clemens and Paul Ashton at Re-press; and Jacques Rancourt at *La Traductière*. Thanks again to Graeme Harper, and to Anna Roderick, Elinor Robertson and Sarah Williams at Multilingual Matters, who have been unfailingly gracious and efficient in guiding this book to completion, and special thanks to Ralph Footring for the proverbial eagle editorial eye and for the conversation.

There are echoes here in French, German, Spanish, Italian and Dutch, mostly of poets and prose writers, but also of philosophers, whose works are duly acknowledged in the text. However, the title of the creative work 'Blue like an orange' in Chapter 11 comes from a poem by the French surrealist poet Paul Éluard and the phrase 'How a single word can kill' in the same chapter is a homage to the late Australian poet Philip Hodgins, whose phrase was 'Words can kill'.

I would like to thank and acknowledge Faber and Faber as well as Farrar, Straus and Giroux (US) for granting me the right to quote from Seamus Heaney's poems 'Alphabet' (*The Haw Lantern*, 1987) and 'Out of the Bag' (*Electric Light*, 2001) under the terms of fair dealing.

Introduction:
The Making of a Poetics

I am a mirror, an echo
Jorge Luis Borges

I never understood those writers who claimed to find in a moment of
inspiration their immortal subject matter. The work finds us, not we the
work, and the most we can do is not to turn and flee from it
Gerald Murnane

This book concerns itself with the subject of creative writing. The word 'subject' refers here to *what* is being studied in the discipline of creative writing as well as *who* is involved in the act of writing. In seeking a poetics of creative writing, the book focuses on creative writing as a subject in universities in the dramatically changing context of practice as research, while taking into account the importance of the subjectivity of the writer as researcher. The poetics at stake denotes neither the study of poetry (in particular the techniques of poetry) nor a general theory of literature, but rather:

> the means by which writers formulate and discuss an attitude to their work that recognises influences, the traditions they write within and develop, the literary, social, and political context in which they write, and the processes of composition and revision they undertake. (Lasky, 2013: 17)

As such, this book is inevitably coloured by my own educational background, life experiences, theoretical interests, pedagogical frameworks and aesthetic preferences. The poetics offered here is a tailor-made one. At no point do I suggest that it ought to be a poetics off the rack, one that would suit all creative writers. Rather, this cumulative work is meant to incite writers to

1

find out about their own *style* in order to design their own poetics – one that suits their interests, preoccupations and generic choices. Beyond the personal, the book's premise is that writers create content, and therefore think and research in a particular way, and consequently need to design a poetics that is suited to the specificity of creative writing as a human activity that partakes of the discipline of creative writing studies (Donnelly, 2012). I am convinced that the Australian poet and novelist David Malouf is right when he says: 'it is the act of writing itself that makes articulation possible' (Malouf, 2008: 78). Here lies the specificity of writing as an act of experiential and academic research. But here also lies the challenge, for writing is an act of representation, even when it wants to be purely conceptual or non-representational, which means that, as writers, we need to be mindful of the metaphorical mesh that privileges the visual in which we are caught up, particularly in Western societies. In other words, our challenge will be to identify the specific mode of articulation in creative writing studies as distinct from other disciplines.

In its brief history, research in creative writing has been considered by many to be highly problematic, fraught with unanswered fundamental questions and lacking in any clear models and concepts. The greatest impediments for conceptualising creative writing practice and research may be the epistemological character of the research itself, coupled with a resistance to theorising creative writing within the constraints of a traditional model of theory formation, expansion and diversification. This resistance has compounded creative writing's perceived inferior status in the academy, condemning it through the romantic binary to the wild feminine epitomised by the rude girl who 'sits in the senate ... out of place amongst all that beige and grey' (Krauth, cited in Sparrow, 2012: 78). For some, the problem stems from the mode of production of creative research and the indivisible link to the subjectivity of the researcher, thus bringing the 'objective' aspect of research into question. Nonetheless, beyond these three factors, the defining characteristic of creative writing research would appear to be its conceptual uncertainty and, perhaps ironically, this incoherency has proved to be the feature around which the debates have found common ground. In this book I will argue that the subjectivity of the researcher is a strength. I will also argue that reading plays a critical role in establishing subjectivity and agency with regard to existent symbolic constellations and therefore that language is not only constitutive of subjectivity but fundamental to experience and instrumental to creativity in our discipline.

Lewis Carroll knew this – or at least Alice did. In *Through the Looking-Glass* (1871), the sequel to *Alice's Adventures in Wonderland* (1865), Alice moves about in the freedom of her daydream, and from the first establishes the unlimited power of the imagination: 'Let's pretend', she says to her cat, 'there's a way of getting through into [the Looking-glass House]' (Carroll, 1992: 173), and the game begins. The game of 'how abouts' and 'what ifs' by which Alice, perched on the mantelpiece, invents a universe beyond appearances, more beautiful than the universe of the everyday, yet still bearing a resemblance to it, as if performing for us an allegory of what we do when we write: 'Why, it's a Looking-glass book, of course! And, if I hold it up to a glass, the words will all go the right way again' (Carroll, 1992: 180).

Even though Alice is delighted to leave behind everything that is familiar, her leap into the unknown harbours its share of hazards. She has to learn another language and discover other behaviours. She finds herself thrown into the middle of a chess party played according to rules she does not know. It is a strange party. The two-dimensional space that has become hers obeys the laws of an inverted geometry. The garden that she is trying to reach retreats each time she approaches; only detours and digressions and regressions allow her to advance. Alice gets lost in this labyrinth and lives in a mode of discontinuity and instability, just as we do when we give free rein to our imagination in the act of writing.

But Alice discovers that she herself exists only as a mirror reflection, as a projection of some other, when her two interlocutors, Tweedledum and Tweedledee, question her (Carroll, 1992: 224):

'[The Red King's] dreaming now … about you! And if he left off dreaming about you, where do you suppose you'd be?'

'Where I am now, of course,' said Alice.

'Not you!' Tweedledee retorted contemptuously. 'You'd be nowhere. Why you're only a sort of thing in his dream!'

It would seem that, from the other side of the mirror, identity is most elusive. It would even seem that a little predisposition to insanity could deteriorate into full-blown delirium. The mirror is this surface between the reality of everyday life and the place of dreams, nightmares and hallucinations we might call voices, images or films in our minds. The creative writer crosses through the mirror but does not go mad because he or she relates the two sides of the mirror by way of a symbolic recuperation, which occurs in the act of putting an experience into words. This is a theoretical ideal for creative writing, of course, because, unfortunately, the history of literature comprises many examples of writers for whom the act of writing has led to madness or suicide. The French author Antonin Artaud may have revolutionised theatre, but some of his poems are but the ravings of a madman and make for very painful reading (Artaud, 2004). Sylvia Plath, too, for all her genius, may have been unwell – certainly her legacy has crossed the borders of literature and lives on in the field of psychopathology (Kaufman, 2001). Creative writing, in itself, is a risky business.

If I pretend I am Alice, I will produce a poem, a story, a play or an academic paper depending on what is at stake when the work finds me; the nature of the work will depend on the decisions I make in that moment. If I get stuck in the labyrinth, I might produce a drawing or a painting – symbolic representations that may lead to subsequent writing. Let us dismiss the possibility that I might get lost in the labyrinth and lose my mind, for even in the labyrinth relationships and symbolic exchanges are paramount.

There are multiple and complex dynamics at the heart of art-making and implicit in the creative writer's work – in the language itself, for its capacity to instigate associations – is the explicit connection to reader perception and reception of the work. However complete or incomplete it may seem, every text invites communication. In the labyrinthine complexities and entice-ments of writing, each reader is potentially an intrepid Theseus summoned to negotiate the pathways of language. Since Jorge Luis Borges used the term 'labyrinth' for a collection of his stories, it has been associated almost as much with the Argentinian writer as with classical mythology. For the sake of telescoping time, for entertainment, and for the purpose of intro-ducing the problematics of identity for creative writers, here is Borges in the labyrinths of his mind, his city, his tradition and his language in translation:

> The other one, the one called Borges, is the one things happen to. I walk through the streets, perhaps mechanically now, to look at the arch of an entrance hall and the grillwork on the gate; I know of Borges from the mail and see his name on a list of professors or in a biographical diction-ary. I like hourglasses, maps, eighteenth century typography, the taste of coffee and the prose of Stevenson; he shares these preferences, but in a vain way that turns them into the attributes of an actor. It would be an exaggeration to say that ours is a hostile relationship; I live, let myself go on living, so that Borges may contrive his literature, and this literature justifies me. It is no effort for me to confess that he has achieved some valid pages, but those pages cannot save me, perhaps because what is good belongs to no one, not even to him, but rather to the language and to tradition. (Borges, 1970: 282)

Borges concludes his parable 'Borges and I' with the words 'I do not know which of us has written this page'. Perhaps we are all, as writers, puzzled from time to time by me-not-me and by me-this-other[1] distinctions. Writers have many roles, none of which cancels all the others. If the writer is in the work, she or he is also outside the work and, increasingly, it belongs not to her or him but 'to the language or to tradition' (Borges, 1970: 282). Creative production is a function not so much of perception as of apperception.

If these diversions into allegorical territory show us something about the creative mind, it also shows us something more fundamental about subjectivity: there is some 'thing' that eludes the mirror, some 'thing' that, perhaps, cannot even be captured by the eye, some 'thing' that nonetheless finds its way into our writing, unbidden. But as we know from life and from re-reading ourselves, there are glimpses of that 'thing' which can be revealing. It always happens after the fact. Every instant and instance is immediately beset with others, those ghostings of memory, desire, fantasy that work by association and become part of our constructions *in* and *through* language. Similarly, it is *in* and *through* language that these acquire significance. Images – visual, verbal or aural – combine in order to create narratives that are not only sequences of images but also sequences of ideas that are charged with emotions and affects. This may explain why the concepts and frameworks pertinent to the visual arts cannot be readily translated for the purposes of creative writing research.[2]

The importance of the mirror image to the organisation of subjectivity was highlighted in the last century by psychologists, who recognised that the construction of the self was progressive and implied the conscious differentiation of the exterior world and other people. The subject, thus capable of objectifying himself or herself and of coordinating exterior perceptions with interior sensations, can then progress from the consciousness of the body to the consciousness of a self. It is precisely this notion of bodily projection, the representation that each person makes of his or her own body in space, which culminates in self-recognition in the mirror that psychoanalysis critiqued, drawing attention instead to the importance of desire and language. The French psychoanalyst Jacques Lacan famously explicated this in his essay 'The mirror stage as formative of the *I* function as revealed in psychoanalytic experience' (Lacan, 2006 [1949]), in which he made the point that the 'I', or ego, is an illusion and the subject a divided subject, as we will see in more detail further on. Nevertheless, the mirror as a matrix of the symbolic accompanies our quest for identity even though we now know that the contemporary Western subject is 'a mixture of the medieval "I" believe; the Cartesian "I" think; the Romantic "I" feel; as well as the existential "I" choose; the Freudian "I" dream' (Ragland-Sullivan, 1987: 10), to which we might add the Lacanian 'I/d' speak, the Winnicottian 'I' relate and, finally, the Joycian 'I' write. To see oneself in the mirror, to identify oneself, requires a mental operation by which the subject is capable of objectifying himself or herself, of separating what is outside from what is inside. This operation can be successful if the subject recognises the reflection as his or her own likeness and can say, *I am the other of that other*. The relationship of self to self and the familiarity of the self cannot be directly established and remains trapped in the reciprocity of seeing and being seen, as needed to be shown to Alice and as Narcissus discovered by himself. Creative writers may be in a particularly good position to elucidate this problem. In fact, they have done so since time immemorial. The *enfant terrible* of French poetry, Arthur Rimbaud, wrote, in a letter dated 15 May 1871, the much coined phrase *Je est un autre* ('I is an other') (Rimbaud, 1966: 105). Rimbaud expresses here the idea that his conscious personality conceals a new being who has to be sought out and who will see anew and express anew. To put it more succinctly: 'A Poet makes himself a visionary' (Rimbaud, 1966: 102). Notwithstanding the Romantic sentiment expressed here, the juxtaposition of these two phrases is not only the idea that the poet, like most of us, has a double,[3] but that he *makes* himself other. I suggest that this is because what eludes consciousness, namely, the unconscious, is creatively active in both the subject and the writing process, thereby changing writing, and changing us, as we write. Would the very existence of the unconscious entail that conscious life is nothing else than a conceit, an exercise in dissimulation – yet without being able to recognise itself as such? For Freud, dreams, parapraxes, forgetting, jokes, namely the stuff of the psychopathology of everyday life (Freud, 2001 [1901]), are in fact telling a truth about ourselves that we cannot face. So we fabulate. Creative writers are notorious for recording this deceit and exposing conceit as they repeat, transform and transgress.

As in all relationships, the relationship that we entertain with our other, or others, is complex and versatile. Rimbaud entertained a querulous relationship with his other and ended up silencing it altogether. So did Samuel Beckett, for whom the other was a voice (Bernold, 1992: 108) that is paradoxically silenced in his work, as in, for example, *Murphy* and *Watt* (Beckett, 1965, 1968). Conversely, the late Nobel laureate Seamus Heaney enjoyed a harmonious partnership with his double (Heaney, 1995: 202). So did the Guyanese writer Wilson Harris, who stated that his other was female (Harris, 1983: 13). For the Portuguese poet Fernando Pessoa, harmony resided in radical separation (Pessoa, 1994). For the Australian poet Kevin Brophy, self and other are strangers, and remain so in the process of creating 'a recognisable and even predictable act of literature' (Brophy, 2009: 68). Brophy explains what is at stake:

> For the writer, as much as for the critic, it is this division and relation between inventiveness and imitation – or between the personal and the

public – that must be negotiated and considered over and over again as poems are written and then read. (Brophy, 2009: 68)

It would seem that, as echo-makers, we are both Narcissus and Echo, inventors and imitators, readers of our own minds and scribblers; script-writers and actors, authors and critics; and when we reflect upon our words, when we carry on our research, the process is no different. Only the mirror is different, possibly already and always flawed.[4]

In the 50-odd years of anti-humanist or post-humanist debate it is certainly the case that the subject has not emerged unscathed. We are certainly more aware of the process of representation involved in the production of images, narratives and discourses. The positivist illusion that we can more or less recreate a subject in his or her totality no longer holds. The modern subject is split, decentred, extimate[5] or scattered, and narrative techniques have evolved according to this unrelenting othering process.

Creative writing as a subject also has its other or others, and in the first half of this book we acquaint ourselves with some of them, those which may help us understand the doubleness of this subject – *what* is studied in creative writing and *who* writes. These others include literature, philosophy, criticism and theory. In the second half I gradually apply and perform some of the ideas and concepts covered in the first half, in order to suggest what creative research in action might look like.

This book takes the progression of the PhD candidate in creative writing as an exemplar of practice and research. It takes the reader on a personal journey through a grappling with creative writing within the context of theory. As such, the book is performative. It defies linearity and conventional modes of argument. Accordingly, the structure of the chapters varies. Some chapters are devoted entirely to theory, some are theoretical but engaged with literature, some weave the personal with theory and some discuss my own creative work in the light of theory. It demonstrates how creative writing can push the boundaries of theory and make new discoveries. It does so in circular fashion: it articulates how poetics may be understood in creative writing and then moves away from poetics towards criticism and theory only to return to poetics via theory. In a sense it performs the constant interaction between creative and analytical discourses, or between practice and research, and delivers various modes of practice as research whereby creative works talk back to theory.

Arguments in this book develop by accretion. It could be said that its anti-method is inspired by Freud's essay 'Creative writers and daydreaming', in which he famously admits that psychoanalysis cannot explain a creative writer's 'innermost secret' (Freud, 2001 [1906–08]: 153). The

French philosopher Paul Ricoeur takes this essay as a prototype to argue that Freud's writings on art are fragmentary in a very systematic way, enacting as they do the process of analytical discovery through association and *Nachträglichkeit* ('deferred action') (Freud, 1991 [1896]: 229). Freud uses the term *nachträglich* – usually translated as 'deferred' – repeatedly and constantly, often underlining it. The noun *Nachträglichkeit* also keeps cropping up, well before he explains the concept in 1914. Thus, although Freud never offered a precise definition of the notion of deferred action, it was indisputably part of his conceptual framework and research method. This concept is particularly useful for understanding creative writing research, as most of the discoveries we make occur after the fact, that is, after the writing is done. Ricoeur shows that Freud proceeds by a series of analogies. Far from being random or reductive, these analogies make up the organising principle of Freud's essay. By a series of displacements he works from the child at play, to the writer's fantasy world, to the novelist's hero, bringing together dream and fiction in their joint function of fulfilling a wish (Ricoeur, 1970: 165–166). But Freud, as Ricoeur rightly points out, also distinguishes daydream from artistic creation, by including the role of play – which goes beyond hallucinatory wish fulfilment – and by stressing that the daydream makes use of the relation of fantasy to time. It does so by taking 'an occasion in the present to construct, on the pattern of the past, a picture of the future' (Freud, 2001 [1906–08]: 148). Freud also suggests we gain pleasure as readers from the writer, from 'what we are inclined to take to be his personal day-dreams' (Freud, 2001 [1906–08]: 153). Since this pleasure is intimately connected with the dynamics of the work, Ricoeur sees it as the systematic aim of what might be called Freud's poetics.

The reader may wonder why Jacques Lacan is a looming presence in this book. This is both deliberate and inevitable. It is deliberate because I believe that for theory to be useful we need to immerse ourselves in it. Indeed, mere exposure to it is futile. It is also inevitable, for I have been reading Lacan since 1985. As a result, some other theorists receive much less attention or hardly any. Hélène Cixous, Julia Kristeva and Luce Irigaray, for example, deserve a more thorough treatment. But, as I explain in the Afterword, they have joined the conversation in oblique ways and further creative research will be devoted to their work. Jacques Derrida and others are mentioned only in a historical context, and this is because, being true to the immersion argument, I can engage with their ideas only at an intellectual level.

A poetics is always a work in progress and as such it is necessarily selective. Any project starts with a cluster of questions. This project starts with: What does 'poetics' mean? What is the productive tension between poetics and creative writing at this point in time? Inevitably, I refer back to the etymological root of the word *poesis* and the ambiguity it contains for modern readers. One of the abiding questions of the discussion is: What is the process whereby discourses and artefacts are constructed and keep changing? How are they incited? What are the dynamics at their core, in all their intricate, aesthetic and emotional minutiae?

As intimated in Chapter 1, characteristic of the contemporary creative arts scene – as overtly deployed in universities – is a false dichotomy between theory and practice. In the larger field of literature, this is most obvious in the polarisation of literary studies and creative writing. Yet the tension between criticism and the arts, or theory and practice, is not new. It was Northrop Frye who perpetuated the New Critics' misconception in viewing the mode of existence of the literary work as wholly self-enclosed and inaccessible to language by saying, no doubt ironically: 'Criticism can talk, and all the arts are dumb' (Frye, 1957: 4). Chapter 2 sets out from the hypothesis that such a false dichotomy is predicated upon the tension between intellectual and emotional elements in our aesthetic response to texts. I postulate here, with others in the field, that writers are first and foremost readers and hence can learn from their reading processes. The chapter offers a brief history of the tension between intellect and emotion through the course of literary criticism and points to ways of using reading paradigms that may be further informed by psychoanalysis to enhance an understanding of writing praxis.

Chapters 3 and 4 are a twin set, or mirror images of an old argument that reconsiders the problematic relationship between creative writing and theory, one that is arguably based on mutual neglect and one that is complicated by the alleged death of one of the partners. Chapter 3 looks into the motives for creative writing's distrust of theory, while Chapter 4 reconsiders the significance of theory *for* creative writing as research. It aims to remedy the misperception of theory instated by creative writing scholars and practitioners, and hence to counter theory's marginalisation from within creative writing circles in the academy. In Chapters 5, 6 and 7 we acquaint ourselves better with what I call 'theories without credentials'. 'Styling the subject of creative writing' and 'The ego in the mirror' concern themselves with psychoanalysis, while 'Between thought and the real in creative writing and philosophy' revisits philosophical discourses that offer ways of apprehending subjectivity in relation to aesthetics. Chapter 5 offers key concepts from the work of Freud and Lacan that are of particular import for creative writing, and Chapter 6, in a conversation between precursors and detractors of these two major thinkers, confronts the mirror that is so central to our understanding of human subjectivity. Although Chapter 7 reassesses the importance of philosophy for creative writing for the 21st century and hints at patterns that are emerging in the contemporary *Zeitgeist*, it also shows the limitations of philosophical discourse, namely its repression or sanitisation of the unconscious.

In Chapters 8 and 9 we turn to the practice of creative writing and ask the question: What is writing? 'Inking the *in-between*' seeks answers to this question in personal experience and in the teachings of psychoanalysis, complicating the argument by tackling two subsidiary themes, namely the *why* and the *where from* of creative writing. It begins with a meditation on writing as a mode of being *in-between* – life and death, sanity and madness, self and other – and then turns to Lacan's seminar on Joyce to address these questions from a theoretical angle (Lacan, 2005 [1975–76]). 'On experiential knowing as creative writing research mode' tackles similar questions and themes, but with pointed reference to research in creative writing. By focusing on the work of metaphor and methexis as well as on Kristeva's concept of the semiotic chora, it questions the relevance of the paradigm of practice-led research.

The three concluding chapters of the book stage creative writing *as* research in a gesture whereby the creative work talks back to criticism and theory. Having demonstrated one way of immersing oneself in theory, I utilise, rehearse and perform the concepts that have stuck in the process of creating a poetics and validate the argument put forth in Chapter 1 and developed in Chapter 4, 'Craft, knowledge, theory, and the designing of poetics'.

Notes

(1) Otherness is a necessary category in the process of self-definition and cultural defini-tion within a social system, however reduced it may be. I use the term 'other' to define the hypothetical complement entering into play in the formation and under-standing of identity in intersubjective relationships. Depending on the context, it may refer to an object of desire, identification or rivalry in psychical, existential and political terms.

(2) I would argue that an analogous mode of articulation is activated in the production of research, even though a certain amount of objectification occurs in the research process.

(3) Lacan (1978 [1954–1955]: 17) cites Rimbaud's phrase in relation to his claim that the speaking being is ex-centric to consciousness.

(4) Another Nobel laureate, the Australian Patrick White, exposes his self and its many others in his autobiography *Flaws in the Glass* (1981), as well as in all of his novels, but perhaps most irreverently so in his hilarious *Memoirs of Many in One* (1986).

(5) The adjective 'extimate' derives from 'extimacy', a late Lacanian neologism derived from, yet not opposed to, 'intimacy'. As such, it denotes phenomena that impinge on the self–other, inside–outside boundaries. *Extimité* is bound up with the real as that which cannot be said.

1 What Poetics for Creative Writing?

Best would be to think in a form one had invented.
Paul Valéry

Inherent in practice-led research is the dialectic between practice and research. For some time, this dialectic has been problematised in varying ways and to varying degrees across the creative arts in terms that are reminiscent of Deleuze and Guattari's 'disjunctive synthesis' (Deleuze & Guattari, 2004: 14).[1] Nowhere is this more obvious than in the discipline of creative writing, which often defines its position within the paradigm of practice-led research and the theoretical associations linking practice and research with models historically defined by the visual arts, consequently obliterating its own 'domain specificity' (Baer, 2012). Creative writing is a craft. But its writerly component also highlights that it is a way of apprehending, knowing and being in the world. More specifically, creative writing functions simultaneously as a perspective, an epistemology and an ontology specific to *writing*.

This chapter makes the case for a new – though old – discourse which distinguishes the discursive frameworks used in discussions about what the future will understand as 'creative writing studies' (Donnelly, 2012), or more broadly 'writing studies' (Fisher, 2012). I argue that our conceptual tools need to be made over in order to fit creative practice in *writing*. These tools should enable us to deal specifically with writing in relation to the experiential and to subjectivity – that is, from the inside out. I ask what the epistemological thrust of creative writing might be and propose a poetics which takes into account the process of knowledge production from within an experiential practice that mobilises intellectual, emotional and unconscious processes. I do so by pointing out that creative writing is in thrall to a regime of images and by seeking answers to this question in a dialogue with philosophy regarding text and image. I then explain why creative writing needs its own poetics, highlighting its affinities with, but also difference from, criticism and philosophy.

Mirror, Text, Image

Creative writers in the academy have been seriously debating the relationship between theory and practice for over a decade, and the deployment of practice-led research has both extended and restricted the boundaries in considering how practitioners contribute to research inquiry. The debate has been vigorous in the UK and in Australia, particularly since the publication of Paul Dawson's influential study *Creative Writing and the New Humanities* (Dawson, 2005). In the USA, the issue has been reluctantly and sporadically addressed, although the Association of Writing Programs has been more alert to the state of the arts in that domain in recent years due to a more global conversation in response to cross-national demands and incentives. In that regard, Dianne Donnelly's *Establishing Creative Writing Studies as an Academic Discipline* (Donnelly, 2012) has been a major contribution. Journals such as *New Writing* in the UK and *TEXT* in Australia have been critical to this debate, as they have brought practitioners from diverse backgrounds into the conversation and paradoxically focused the debate more sharply on creative writing. This is also reflected in essays which have appeared in collections with an increasingly international appeal (e.g. Harper & Kroll, 2008; Krauth & Brady, 2006; Kroll & Harper, 2013; Smith & Dean, 2009; Webb & Brien, 2012). However, what is striking from this now global debate is how much creative writing has been linked to the visual arts in terms of theorising the relationship between practice and research. Perhaps this is due to the impact of studies written by scholars or practitioners with a background in aesthetics, the visual arts, design and architecture (e.g. Barrett & Bolt, 2007; Biggs & Büchler, 2007; Bolt, 2004; Chalmers, 1996; Sullivan, 2005). Nevertheless, as creative writing continues to grapple with the appropriateness of the term 'practice-led research', highlighting the relevance of other topoi (Brook, 2012; Magee, 2012; Williams, 2013), it is clear that the dominance of the visual field in research paradigms hinders the way we think about creative writing research.

The apparent effacement of writing does not necessarily betray cultural biases. After all, Western culture has long privileged written representation over images. There are deeper psychological and philosophical reasons for this uncertain state of affairs, and these reasons are translated by the linguistic choices that we make. As Freud showed, the eyes carry an unusually high affective charge for human beings (Freud, 2001 [1915b]). The eyes also regulate perception, our way of understanding and interpreting the world and, if one were to interpret Lacan's mirror stage rather literally, access to the symbolic order of language (Lacan, 2006 [1949]). The eyes are close to the brain, by virtue of their location in the body; they may even control or structure the secondary process. But as Martin Jay has shown in *Downcast Eyes* (Jay, 1993), vision is by no means the prevailing sense in comprehending Western culture. Instead, Western culture comprises a plurality of scopic regimes (Jay, 1993: 48), particularly in postmodern discourses. If Jay is right, Western culture is in fact dominated by a certain 'antiocularcentrism' (Jay, 1993: 27) from Plato through to modernity and postmodernity – Plato himself being responsible for this development due to his profound ambivalence towards images (Jay, 1993: 29).

There are those who argue that writing is also a visual phenomenon. The British linguist Roy Harris is a case in point (Harris, 1986). Harris urges us to take a harder look – consider the visual metaphor I cannot help but using – at the nature of writing as visual sign. He designates writing as 'scriptorial sign', and image as 'pictorial sign', going on to say:

> Where the boundary between pictorial and scriptorial signs falls will patently be one of the contentious issues to be resolved. Consequently, it will also be necessary to have a term which is neutral with respect to that particular distinction; and for this purpose it is proposed to adopt the term *graphic* sign as referring to pictorial signs, scriptorial signs, or both. (Harris, 1986: 56)

Fair enough, but the kind of writing Harris has in mind is all a matter of surfaces; it neither addresses the *experience* of writing or writing as *discourse*. What Harris is interested in is how we *perceive* writing. But writing and visual image actualise antithetical views of perception in Western culture.

'Well, Protarchus', Socrates tells his interlocutor in *Philebus*, 'the alphabet which was the basis for your education is a clear example of what I'm talking about, so use it to see what I mean' (Plato, 1982b: 61). Plato proposes the alphabet as a model for teaching abstract moral principles, and not simply as a utilitarian means of communicating. Images in *Philebus* have a much more ambiguous, even negative character, and they are secondary to writing. Socrates says:

> When memory coincides with perception, it and other faculties relevant to these experiences seem to me to write words, as it were, in the soul. When this experience writes the truth, it gives rise to true belief.... [There is] another member of the soul's work-force on these

occasions…. An artist, who turns the secretary's words into images in the soul. (Plato, 1982b: 100)

Writing here is a substitute for, a flight from, visual image. By its rhetorical tropes – ekphrasis, description, hypotyposis, metaphor and other figures of speech – writing attempts to substitute itself for visual images. Yet this occurs only after having despatched some profound truth.

Writing, it must be said, also elicited suspicion from Plato. In fact, it elicited suspicion from others as well, right through the Middle Ages (Stock, 1983). A close look at some of the famous passages denouncing writing is highly entertaining, especially when the focus is on the graphic quality of writing and its putative status as a picture of the spoken word. In *Phaedrus*, for example, Socrates remarks:

> You know, Phaedrus, that's the strange thing about writing, which makes it truly analogous to painting. The painter's products stand before us as though they were alive, but if you question them, they maintain a most majestic silence. It is the same with the written words; they seem to talk to you as though they were intelligent, but if you ask them anything about what they say, from a desire to be instructed, they go on telling you just the same thing forever. And once a thing is put in writing, the composition, whatever it may be, drifts all over the place, getting into the hands not only of those who understand it, but equally of those who have no business with it; it doesn't know how to address the right people, and not address the wrong. And when it is ill-treated and unfairly abused it always needs its parents to come to its help, being unable to defend or help itself. (Plato, 1982a: 521)

The ambivalence towards the image, and towards writing as image, reveals a certain distrust of texts and their authors. It also signifies a deep cultural cleavage at the heart of writing itself.

The cultural cleavage between word and image is responsible for the rupture between the pictorial and the linguistic in a text. Socrates helps us understand why. In the *Phaedrus* excerpt above, he says that rendering ideas in graphic form liberates words from their discursive context. Meaning may not be controlled since anyone may have access to the words to interpret at their own whim. What Socrates offers here is a concept of the image as an indeterminate sign whose meaning may be discontinuous from the discourse in which it is meant to participate. Instead, the image detaches itself and 'drifts all over the place', at the risk of falling into the wrong hands (Plato, 1982a: 521). Socrates, then, identifies a rogue property of the image, a transgressive element capable of turning back on the discourse that produced it, to propose new, unsettling meanings by exposing what the narrative has repressed.

Having referred back to philosophy, let us pause before turning to poetics. To be fair, it must be acknowledged that Aristotle had a more optimistic view of writing than Plato. This optimism is matched by Part II of John Carey's controversial book *What Good Are the Arts¿* (Carey, 2005).[2] In it, Carey argues that literature is the only art capable of argument and criticism, including self-criticism (Carey, 2005: 177). This, he suggests, is because writing is an art form that has reasoning accessible to it in a way that the other arts do not. While it is true that literature makes use of reasoning's tools, that is, words and the art of putting them together, it is rather contentious to say that it is closer to reason. But would it be so of thinking¿

If, as I suggest in the Introduction to this volume, David Malouf is right in saying that 'the act of writing ... makes articulation possible' (Malouf, 2008: 78), then creative writing has nothing to do *with* thinking. Creative writing *is* thinking. Psychologists Keith Oatley and Maja Djikic demonstrate this with aplomb in their paper 'Writing as thinking' (Oatley & Djikic, 2008). In it, they analyse writing *as* thinking that utilises paper or other media to externalise and manipulate symbolic expressions. They explore four methods to identify how established writers externalise thoughts and interact with them, namely laboratory experiments involving two groups of writers, interviews, biographical analysis and exegeses of notes and drafts. They find that writers often use paper to extend their thinking and to devise frameworks of cues that establish forms of communication between authors and readers. They conclude that creative writing augments thinking and promotes empathy:

> Imaginative prose fiction, the product of long and deep thought by its authors, has enabled empathetic understanding of emotions, the honing of irony, and possibilities for the growth of consciousness, that we suggest would have been far more difficult to accomplish without the augmentation of thinking by writing. (Oatley & Djikic, 2008: 24)

Thinking is language – embodied language, and it takes place as we write. It is an experience 'situated between perception and consciousness' (Lacan, 1986 [1964]: 45) because creative writing is an experiential form of practice involving an intertextuality which is first and foremost *intratextual*, that is, played out from within.

Having located the significance of the word, what are the implications for creative writing¿ I argue here that we need conceptual tools tailored to the domain specificity of writing rather than taken off the rack of a germane domain such as the visual arts. We need a poetics of creative writing which enables us to articulate the experiential nature of writing; a poetics that underscores the aesthetic and human subject of creative writing in its historical, conceptual and social dimensions. In what follows I consider the tools that may be useful to that effect; these tools are conceptual and theoretical frameworks paired with an attitude of self-consciousness or self-reflexiveness.

Paratextual *Poesis*

But what poetics? Traditionally, 'poetics' is an overarching term used to incorporate multiple discourses in literary theory. As such, it encompasses the theory of literary forms and literary discourse. It may also refer specifically to the theory of poetry and poetic techniques or, as used by the French literary theorist Gérard Genette, it may refer to theory itself (Genette, 2005: 14). This definitional breadth is, as we shall see shortly, due to the etymology of the Greek term *poesis*, meaning making, and thus allowing for a certain confusion between what we now distinguish as 'poetry' and 'poetics', with the latter term still being applied to other arts or cultural practices.

Aristotle's *Poetics* (c. 335 BC) is considered to be the first work of dramatic theory and the first treatise to attempt a general theory of literature. As a consequence, poetics has comprised prose, drama and poetry from Plato through to the 19th century. But it has been discussed in various discursive ways, including as a sub-set of rhetoric and philosophy, as an artistic practice and as a cultural practice. In the field of literary studies, poetics has long been appreciated as a sub-set of rhetoric. Since Aristotle's conceptualisation of rhetoric as the art of persuasion, poetics has evolved to include the prescriptive manuals of rhetoricians such as Cicero (1952), Quintilian (1921) and Nicolas Boileau (Boileau-Despréaux, 1966). In modern usage it extends to the rhetorical hermeneutic and structural linguistics of the late 20th century. From Russian formalism, the Prague school, French structuralism and poststructuralism, there was a certain appeal for a science of literature which would devote itself not to the piecemeal criticism or interpretation of specific literary works, but to identifying the general properties which make literature possible (Culler, 1975). The focus thus shifted from 'literature' to 'literariness' in the quest for general laws underlying texts (Das, 2005: 78). The contemporary global condition of poetics tends to be experimental, usually offering theoretical frames for looking at the continuities and discontinuities between print and digital forms (Armand, 2007). Today, the word 'poetics' seems to promise some sort of systematic analytic rigour, a kind of afterglow of the structuralist interest in systematising, universalising and scientising poetics, not only as it applies to the study of poetry but also as a general intellectual principle capable of laying bare the semiotics of the whole of human culture, indeed human activity (see for example Jimenez, 2012). So why use the word?

Through its etymological and historical origins, the term 'poetics' implies not only scientific rigour but its putative complement – emotional sensitivity, aesthetic self-consciousness and an acknowledgement of the constructedness of all human cultural artefacts and discourses. This, especially the last, is the sense in which scholars in the field of literary and cultural studies, in reaction to the atemporal stasis of the structuralist model of poetics, came to use the word 'poetics' to mean precisely the plasticity, changeability and dynamic, interactive nature of social and cultural phenomena.

Moreover, poetics takes care of the formal and the affective realms of a subject under inquiry. In contradistinction to the structuralist association of poetics with analytic rigour, poetics nowadays implies a somewhat different engagement. Poetics becomes the interactive aspect of the researcher's task – how do researchers handle and make explicit the relationships *informing* the work assumed by their discipline, especially with regard to their subject matter, their own subjective spin on things and their subjects, for example the characters they make up or the subjects they interview? This kind of poetics, it seems to me, occupies the complementary role of self-reflexive soul-searching with respect to the creative writer as fabulator and fabricator: how am I making this up as I go along, how do my structuring of my insights and prior knowledge create meaning within the genre I am participating in and, most significantly, what are the implications of this meaning-making process?

What is particularly important to remember is that 'poetics' originally came into being from practice. As an understanding of practice, poetics has consistently concerned itself with the art of putting a text together, and subsequently with the act of analysing how this was accomplished. Poetics has, of course, evolved from its early normative character to a more empirical study of how figures of speech are used in writing. Poetics, like rhetoric, is therefore first and foremost akin to criticism, understood as the close reading of texts which privileges the examination of speech acts and figures of speech. As I write these words I am struck that this is a task that many creative writing students with no background in literature struggle with. And yet, as Kim Lasky makes clear, poetics is 'integral to composition' (Lasky, 2013: 25). Perhaps we need to go back to the text and urge our students to do so. Perhaps we need to examine its surface and then go through it as if it were a looking-glass text. Perhaps we would come back from our adventure somewhat other and ready to tell the tale with a critical spin on it. This would certainly facilitate all exegetical endeavours.

Aristotle's principles of rhetoric are still relevant today, for they 'move back and forth between criticism and theory' (Pappas, 2005: 15). Most students of creative writing would know that rhetoric involves the presentation of a self that is persuasive to a given audience and the construction of an audience that will empathise with that self. In fact, as Desmond Barry demonstrates in his paper 'Wrestling with Aristotle' (Barry, 2013), rhetoric is at the very communicative heart of creative writing. Underestimating rhetoric may downplay the materiality of the text at the expense of its dominant themes and ideas, thus erasing the significant differences that arise because of an author's engagement with the craft and with the world at large, including culture and politics. However, overestimating the rhetorical dimension of a given text may downplay the unconscious dimension of the creative process and product. A single-minded approach to rhetoric and poetics would reveal only 'a deep commitment to question/ response formations as more fundamental than concepts of referentiality in discursive exchange' (Struever, 1998: 155), for rhetoric notoriously thrives where ideologies fail (Meyer, 1993).

From the Greeks to Alain Badiou, France's leading contemporary philosopher, poetics has also been viewed as akin to philosophy, and hence a potential harbinger of truth and knowledge. In this light, the main purpose of a text is to convey knowledge or to formulate truths. But, oddly, this is not the view taken by philosophers who read creative works, for questions of form and genre often recede into the background (Badiou, 2003). Perhaps the appropriation of poetry by philosophy was, and remains, necessary for philosophy, if only to articulate anew the old problem of the meaning of life. But for this aspect of poetics to be useful to creative writers, the critique of philosophy needs to be articulated from a practitioner's point of view. In this respect, a book like John Calder's *The Philosophy of Samuel Beckett* (2001) speaks volumes.

The assimilation of poetics by philosophy is problematic, for it disparages the poetic. To read a text as an illustration of some philosophical premise is to smooth it out and to negate both its depth and heterogeneity, as the French philosopher Alain Badiou tends to do in his analysis of poetry, even though he has written creative works himself (Hecq, 2014a). This no doubt applies to other fields of knowledge as well. But, here, the key to understanding how poetics might work is explained in Chapter 4, where we come to understand that for any theory to be useful it requires the creative writer's full immersion in it.

From Aristotle to the present, poetics has also been defined as one of the aesthetic frameworks for the arts. In this configuration, poetry, for example, was placed in the context of the visual arts, music, dance and architecture. This in itself complicates matters: not only does it highlight the ambiguity at the core of the term 'poesis', it also radically sets apart literature from all the other arts. The definitional breadth of the term is allowed by its etymology, which closely allies it to poetry (as noted, 'poesis' means 'making' in Greek, in verse or not). The contrast invoked is between that which is constructed and that which is natural. Traditionally, 'poetry' has been narrowed to the sense of a verbal making, as opposed to *poesis* in the other art media, but it is still more general than 'verse', hence obscuring the distinction between metred and unmetred language which discursive theory (Easthope, 2003) and common usage actually supports. Poetics thus comes to mean the general aesthetics of literature as opposed to other arts and, more particularly, litera- ture seen as a particular kind of discourse. This means that a novel can be a poem and, again, the verse criterion for poetry disappears.

In the *Ion*, Plato argues that the practice of poetry involves *techné kai episteme*, with *techné* denoting both a practical skill and the knowledge or experience underpinning it. 'The resulting range of application', Stephen Halliwell points out, 'is extensive, covering at one end of the spectrum the activity of a carpenter, builder, smith, sculptor, similar manual craftsman, and, at the other, at least from the fifth century onwards, the ability and practices of rhetoricians and sophists' (Halliwell, 1998: 44). Thus *techné*, meaning 'craft,' 'skill', 'technique', 'method' or 'art', coupled with *episteme*, meaning 'knowledge', has been to some extent the domain of the arts ever since. However, the discourse *about* poetry, Plato suggests in the conclusion to the *Ion*, does not seem to have sufficient *techné kai episteme*: unlike the shipbuilder or carpenter, critics demonstrate no special skill in speaking about Homer, and hence their ability to do so must be a matter of inspira- tion. Owing to this account, criticism is no more than a metalanguage, an awkward echo of what a given artefact says. But the theory that poetics is a metalanguage need not lead to such an impasse. To conceive of poetics as a framework for articulating the *why* and *how* of creative writing also implies that it is a form of discourse inherently other, exposing the alterity of its own foundations.

Having learned from the lessons of structuralism and poststructuralism, we could say that, for the cultural critic, the *raison d'être* of poetics is that artefacts perform cultural work. From this perspective, a text is essentially understood as a symptom of the larger culture to which it belongs (Hart, 2013) or as an index of particular historical or cultural factors (Wallis, 1984) or, more recently, as an agent of social change (Bourriaud, 2002). In this viewpoint, creative practices are seen as no different from other social or cultural practices. A play or poem or novel or script is discussed not for its inherent qualities or as expressive of some subjectivity or truths, nor for its powers of persuasion, but for its function in exposing a society's historical, ideological or political make-up. Accordingly, questions of technique and craft become irrelevant in the reception process. Why, for example, would the novels of Ian McEwan be deemed a better index or symptom of the cultural aporias of our times than the best-sellers of J.K. Rowling? Such an understanding of poetics is problematic for creative writers unless their chief motivation is to make a political statement.

Poetics as rhetoric, as philosophy, as artistic framework, or as index of cultural production – what is at stake in adopting one of these discourses to the exclusion of the others? Perhaps these are not mutually exclusive, for the first three in fact incorporate the fourth, in that they examine the history and cultural position of the different poetic, rhetorical, philosophical and generic forms, as well as the history and culture of their philosophical reception. Paul Dawson (2003) proposed an account of creative writing poetics as a practice-led strategy for inventing and organising discourses about cultural production, suggesting that creative and critical discourses are interwoven with social, political and aesthetic discourses. In a similar vein, Shane Strange (2012) proposed a reconceptualisation of creative writing as a radical subjectivity based on a Marxist definition of creativity whereby critical and creative practices reveal the human content of seemingly autonomous artefacts, inscribing himself by default more firmly into the cultural studies understanding of poetics.

It is, however, the uniqueness of the artefact that such an approach to poetics downplays, an aspect which is addressed, albeit with restricted focus, by Stuart Glover (2012). Applying terms from classical rhetoric, though useful for sharpening our vocabulary, ignores an artefact's distinctive articulation as well as its emotional quality. These characteristics do not operate independently of each other, but they do allow us to distinguish the different components of a text. Such an approach to poetics also ignores the vexed issue of subjectivity, process or even 'subject in process' (Kristeva, 1984: 28), as it does all that which is between the mirrors of perception and consciousness, or beyond. For example, it leaves unexamined the pleasures, anxieties and motives at stake in the act of writing. And yet, the pleasure of representation is a fundamentally human disposition that can be observed in infants and young children who, like Alice, 'pretend' to be someone else – an observation that is not lost on philosophers (Wittgenstein, 1953) and psychoanalysts of different orientations (Freud, 2001 [1906–08]; Winnicott, 1971) – who make up a story and pass it off as 'true'. It is the double pleasure of *logos*: the twin pleasures of recognition and its mirror image, the pleasure of taking in the impersonations, fictions and language creations of others and recognising their relevance. This insight leads us to refine our conception of a poetics of creative writing, whereby creative writing research is a triangulation of two seemingly mutually exclusive discourses, one recognising the importance of rational and critical processes, and the other the reality of the unconscious.

Such triangulation encompasses (tacit) *knowing* and (explicit) *knowledge*, or, in classical terms, *techné* and *episteme*. This conception breaks down the distinction Jen Webb (2012) makes, perhaps unwittingly, when she argues for the recognition of creative practice as either 'creative representation' or 'theoretical investigation' within the contemporary university system. Webb's distinction, of course, reminds us of the spurious, albeit useful distinction between practice-based and practice-led research (Candy, 2006). An alternative topos – that of 'beyond practice-led research' – was explored in a special issue of *TEXT* (2012), a journal that continues to foster a re-examination of the relationship between our scholarly arguments and the modes of expression we adopt to record, represent and communicate them (Kroll & Harper, 2013). In this book, I want to invite academics and creative practitioners as well as students to think through ideas developed in that issue. I believe that, as writers staking a claim for our practice to be regarded as a form of research, we have to consider the consequences of our chosen mode of expression, its appropriateness to our inquiry, its generic assumptions and its epistemic implications. Such issues resonate far beyond practice-led research in creative writing, raising a number of central questions for the wider scholarly community at a time when the epistemological foundations of knowledge have been shown to be provisional at best. For example, such questions relate to a broader question concerning 'material thinking' (Carter, 2004) or practical knowledge – namely, how do we integrate theory and practice by way of devising a poetics that suits creative writing today within the problematic framework of practice-led research?

Before we address this question, two related questions need answering: what is the core concept of practice-led research, and why is it problematic for creative writers?

Critical Reversals: Towards Creative Writing Research

The core concept of practice-led research is communication, for if this were not the case, practice would remain practice and would not evolve into research, whose purpose is to be disseminated and shared with a community of scholars and professionals. In that regard, practice-led research is comparable to rhetoric as an art, which contributes to shaping individuals and communities. Yet creative writers, unlike rhetoricians, often lack the capacity for critical evaluation. They also often lack the capacity for self-reflection. One result of this is that creative writers find it difficult to express their judgements about purpose, methods, methodology and quality, thereby obstructing the research process itself. If, to a certain extent, creative writing may be understood 'as communication' (Sarrimo, 2010), its core concept is closer to articulation than communication, one that at first involves making tacit knowledge explicit. Not only does this involve the 'pre-conscious' processes Christine Sarrimo (2010) invokes in her paper 'Creative writing as a communicative act', but also unconscious processes.

Practice-led research values data creation over data collection, which means that research and practice are reciprocal. There is no doubt that these ephemeral qualities are what make 'practice-led research' and its cousin 'research-led practice' such appealing paradigms for understanding art-making, due to their limitless possibilities. At their core, the common goal of these paradigms is to disrupt the known, and thus move us inter-rogatively to the borderline of the unknown. Finding methods for creative writers to examine their own practice has the potential to open new avenues of 'knowledge' and may, in fact, assist in redefining exactly what knowledge is. The description of practitioners' methods provides a unifying framework, but utilising existing methodologies, which are regulated by form and vocabulary, appears to be problematic. Two recent publications have highlighted these issues: namely, *Practice-Led Research, Research-Led Practice in the Arts* (Smith & Dean, 2009) and *The Routledge Companion to Research in the Arts* (Biggs *et al.*, 2012). In the latter, Jen Webb and Donna Lee Brien explain why the term 'practice-led research' is problematic for creative writing: 'while creative writers do draw on the main body of literature on practice-led research, [they] have to adapt and adopt other methods and modes of approach' (Webb & Brien, 2012: 193), which means that 'much of the recent discourse around practice-led research lacks a comfortable fit with the methods and approaches that suit writing' (Webb & Brien, 2012: 193). Importantly, existing approaches, 'with their focus on the critical, and often *a posteriori*, investigation and interpretation of textual content' (Webb & Brien, 2012: 193), do not offer a satisfactory research methodology for creative writers. This, I speculate, may be precisely because creative writing practice and research *are* reciprocal, thereby *creating* a third element, which covers the spectrum from *knowing* to *knowledge*.

If only we could map out the nature of this reciprocity, perhaps we could begin to approach the idea of a common idiom in order to speak of creative writing research and, in turn, artistic research which would underscore rather than erase 'the domain specificity of creativity' (Baer, 2012). The premise of this chapter is that creative writing research is first and foremost an 'experiential knowing' (Lakoff & Johnson, 1980: 19), whereby affects and emotions interact with rational processes. An understanding of subjectivity is critical to this reciprocal process (Mullin, 2012: 185), though I acknowledge that the notion of subjectivity itself needs revision, as Shane Strange quite radically demonstrates (Strange, 2012). Of course, one can survey situated knowledge in order to define the specificity of knowledge in creative writing. This would entail identifying forms of practice that demand more than the formal properties of communication – and therefore rational language – by assuming strategies, methods and concepts from other discursive regimes, such as those of literary studies, including criticism and theory, philosophy and, at their intersection, psychoanalysis. Literary concepts and rhetorical practices would offer the practical as well as conceptual tools required for creative writers to become not only better scholars and critics, but also better writers. The account of writing in both its research and creative dimensions in fact positions writing as an essential tool for articulating practice-led research. As such, far from being antagonistic to the tacit knowledge of practitioners, writing – creatively, critically and reflexively conceived – takes on an integral role and integrated function within practice-led research. Therein lies the potential for literary studies, philosophy and theory to extend our way of being, seeing and experiencing as creative writers.

One way of understanding the reciprocity between creative writing practice and research is through focusing on criticism, with its embedded aspects such as poetics and rhetoric, at a micro level. In particular, I want to redefine one of poetics' prime tropes, namely metaphor, through the prism of linguistics in order to link it with theories of subjectivity, to throw light on what happens in writing, for 'human *thought processes* are largely metaphorical' (Lakoff & Johnson, 1980: 6, original emphasis here and below). I briefly draw on Lakoff and Johnson's *Metaphors We Live By* (1980) to assist in defining the triangulation I have in mind, which is one that concerns the interplay between *knowing* and *knowledge*. Knowing would denote grasping a situation or event using prior (unconscious) knowledge and synthesising as well as integrating new information, affects or stimuli into a personal knowledge base. Knowledge, on the other hand, would include identifying and evaluating new (rational) knowledge and making decisions about what the next steps or possible course of action might be.

From the experientialist perspective, say George Lakoff and Mark Johnson, 'metaphor is a matter of *imaginative rationality*' (Lakoff & Johnson,

1980: 235). Because metaphor as a linguistic expression is part of a person's conceptual system, it enables 'an understanding of one kind of experience in terms of another, creating coherences by virtue of imposing gestalts that are structured by natural dimensions of experience' (Lakoff & Johnson, 1980: 235). This is why new metaphors are capable of creating new under-standings and, therefore, new realities, as is 'obvious in the case of poetic metaphor, where language is the medium through which new conceptual metaphors are created' (Lakoff & Johnson, 1980: 235). For, as Lakoff and Johnson rightly point out, metaphor is not merely a matter of language:

> It is a matter of conceptual structure ..., [which] involves all the natural dimensions of our experience, including aspects of our sense experiences: color, shape, texture, sound, etc. *These dimensions structure not only mundane experience but aesthetic experience as well. Each art medium picks out certain dimensions of our experience and excludes others.* (Lakoff & Johnson, 1980: 235, my emphasis)

This conjures up the words of Webb and Brien quoted above, to the effect that 'much of the recent discourse around practice-led research lacks a comfortable fit with the methods and approaches that suit writing' (Webb & Brien, 2012: 193). Although it is not what they suggest, I think that 'our sense experiences' are dominated by the scopic field and associated dualistic paradigms of what constitutes knowledge and research. In order to examine the relationship between 'mundane experience' and 'aesthetic experience', or 'language' and 'conceptual structure' (Lakoff & Johnson, 1980: 235), creative writers need to pay attention to the specificity of their craft and to the slippery nature of subjectivity. I address this nexus from different perspectives in the following chapters, invoking the relationship between creative writing, criticism, philosophy and theory, focusing on theories – for lack of a better word – which illuminate different aspects of human subjectivity and creativity.

To return to our question, how do we integrate theory and practice? The answer may be by means of a discursive manoeuvre that would highlight the function of criticism within a poetics of creative writing.

Criticism exists to examine, more or less systematically, aesthetic differ-ences among human creative artefacts and processes. If we seek to improve such artefacts and processes, and also enrich creative writing discourse, our critical practice must be informed by method, so that we can explain why we think the way we do. Norms of criticism come from a history of system-atic reflections about the principles, techniques, tastes and readerships that guide practice – in other words, theory, although it remains to be seen 'what theory?' (Harris, 2009). However, both individual and collective judgements shape the process of inquiry in creative writing research. As such, it must acknowledge traditional belief systems and propose alternative, contradictory or even competing belief systems that overtly or tacitly inform their practice (historically, culturally, aesthetically and intimately). In this sense, creative writing research may serve not only to deconstruct systems of logic underpinned by a process of self-validation for their support, but also to reconstruct the question of how we might investigate, make comparisons and judgements, and thereby devise our own 'poetics', one predicated upon a highly subjectivised use of language, perhaps. Accordingly, I propose here an account of creative writing research as a strategy for inventing and organising discourses about cultural production in a way that such discourses intermingle with discourses about aesthetics centring on reader, writer and process. Unlike other attempts to broach a poetics of creative writing, however, my focus will not be on the interwoven discourses of social, political and moral discourses (Dawson, 2003), nor will it be aimed at identifying pedagogical frameworks and teaching strategies (Lasky, 2013: 14–33). My focus will be on the triangulation between practice and theory at the point where it interacts with subjectivity.

Applying terms from classical rhetoric, creative writing research comprises three elements: *logos*, or linguistic articulation of an artefact; *ethos*, or its character; and *pathos*, its emotional quality. These elements do not operate independently of each other, but they do allow us to distinguish between the different elements in a piece of creative research. *Logos* may thus denote the way in which words are used to solve practical problems in both theory and practice. *Ethos* refers to the voice or style employed in the writing, as well as its capacity to suggest a set of values. *Pathos*, or emotion, would refer to the engagement with the scene of writing as well as with the audience. These terms may help us focus on how we investigate, research and report on our practice without having to engage with spurious dichotomies between various avatars of theory and practice. For it seems that we may have forgotten any written text's capacity to interrogate, as well as represent, practice as research.

It is often as though the pretence in creative writing studies of an absence of connections with literary history, literary studies and literary styles has become so established that few wish to acknowledge the validity of a philosophical debate on these issues. It is, in fact, as if the lessons of deconstruction were lost here. Consider, for instance the implications of Derrida's observation that a philosophical debate is also a contest of imposing discursive modes, demonstrative procedures, rhetorical and pedagogical techniques: 'Each time philosophy has been opposed, it was also, although not only, by contesting the properly, authentically philosophical character of the other's discourse' (Derrida, 1995: 219).

A focus on the relationship between philosophical, literary and creative modes of writing would allow us to identify some of the rhetorical characteristics of philosophical inquiry and to discern how these shape relationships to readers and the formation of engagements with the world. The conventional means of writing, by which I mean language, including vocabulary, rhetoric, syntax and grammar, have no more to do with what is written than do the further literary possibilities exemplified by individual style, with its particular marks betraying the author's voice. All that counts philosophically is the *what* that is asserted, not the *how*, by means of which the what puts in an appearance. In creative writing, such characteristics include sensory details, anecdotes and examples, characterisation and personification, story and tension, as well as the subliminal undertow of the text; in philosophy, they typically involve abstract, impersonal, dis-embodied and schematic articulations and positions. But if we consider the distinction between creative and critical practices as one of role-playing – of the capacity to shift positions – writing expertise would consist of moving between creative and critical writing conventions, genres and strategies, as required by a particular project. This would mean that one has agency over choosing 'ways of seeing' rather than being subdued by culturally legitimised perspectives and discourses. This would also enable a better articulation of the tension between knowing and knowledge.

To some extent, this is what Kim Lasky proposes in discussing the present challenges encountered in research in creative writing (Lasky, 2013). For Lasky, 'one of the key challenges of creative writing research lies in suc-cessfully articulating the relationship between the creative work and the critical context, thinking, and outcomes associated with its production' (Lasky, 2013: 14). She considers the history and background of poetics, but also its applications, by drawing on examples of creative writers speaking about their practice, and finally by proposing a model based on the metaphor of the triptych, whose three interlinked panels allow the two outer panels to hinge, 'folding over the central panel in a dynamic movement involving close touching' (Lasky, 2013: 15). Poetics, she argues, is the middle piece, between, on the one hand, 'critical and theoretical inputs and outcomes' and, on the other, 'creative work' (Lasky, 2013: 22). As Lasky demonstrates in clear and practical fashion, literary concepts and rhetorical practices can furnish the practical as well as conceptual modes that promote not only better scholarship and research but also better writing. This account of writing – both scholarly writing and exploratory writing of the research and creative kind – positions writing as an essential tool for research. As such, far from being antagonistic to the practical (or tacit) knowledge of artists, writing, critically and creatively conceived, assumes an integral role in research. One important aspect of this concerns the capacity of poetics to explain the *what* of our subject. Another task will be to identify the *where from* and *why* of writing, a task all writers and aspiring writers grapple with at one stage or other of their trajectories, especially if engaged by the artefact and exegesis model. This is where psychoanalysis may be helpful, for, as will become clear in the next chapters, the unconscious is creatively active in both the subject and the process of creative writing.

The traditions of theory would soon fade without some connection with praxis. This is equally true of creative writing and psychoanalysis, a theory, or set of theories, of human mental development and functioning established by Freud's clinical *practice* at the turn of the 20th century and constantly revised in light of clinical experience ever since.[3] This partly explains my interest in defining creative writing research as distinct from practice-led research. Practice, in this context, helps us revitalise, refine and redefine the concepts underpinning our research methods and aims. Practice highlights the experiential dimension of research. Therefore I suggest that, in our discipline, the term 'creative writing research' may be more appropriate than 'practice-led research', if only because creative writing entails seeing, knowing and being in the world: as such, creative writing is a perspective, an epistemology and an ontology, which all dissolve the boundaries between 'practice-led research' and 'research-led practice'.

I have shown that creative writing is akin to a primary form of criticism we call rhetoric, in that it shapes language, affects individuals and com-munities and sets patterns for new directions. It is necessary because creative writers, unlike rhetoricians, often lack the capacity for critical evaluation of their practice. This may be an example of 'trained incapacity', a term Kenneth Burke used in another context to convey the idea that any way of seeing is also a way of not seeing (Burke, 1966: 28). The paradox goes back as far as Plato's *Theaetetus*, where he repudiates the account of knowledge as justified true belief because a justification that will yield new knowledge requires that the justifiers themselves be known, and this raises the question of whether these justifiers identify themselves as being justified. Plato does not offer any account of how one might avoid the problem, but there is no need for creative writers to persist in resisting an engagement with theory.

What I have outlined above, and will continue to explain and perform in the next chapters, is a hybrid genre of poetics, a fusion of creative, critical and theoretical strategies which operate dynamically at the level of inquiry, thereby provoking and producing creative knowledge rather than evaluating aesthetic representations in light of situational and yet discipline-specific knowledge. Such an endeavour based on paratextual *poesis* will display uncertainty and ambivalence grounded in a simultaneous love for and distrust of language, theory and traditional aesthetic conventions.

Notes

(1) In their book *Anti-Oedipus* (2004), Deleuze and Guattari distinguish between three types of synthesis: connective, disjunctive and conjunctive. These syntheses perform three functions: production, recording and enjoyment, respectively. In keeping with the poststructuralist thrust of their argument, the subject has no agency, but is rather produced by these syntheses. Deleuze and Guattari's position is materialist and radically opposed to that of psychoanalysis. The main characteristic of the 'disjunctive synthesis' is that it is based on an either/or logic. As such, it is 'restrictive rather than inclusive' (Colebrook, 2006: 130).

(2) Thanks to Jen Webb for making the connection and for enlivening my holiday reading.

(3) Assuming that most readers of this book are acquainted with psychoanalysis, I define its project only in Chapter 4. What I want to stress here is the importance of practice as informing theory.

2 Critical Antecedents, Theoretical Directions

We are, at the core, reading animals and ... the art of
reading, in its broadest sense, defines our species.
Alberto Manguel

The novelist is God in his own interior world. Commonly, men make God
in their own image.... Let us add our quota of inadequate description
and say that he is of all things an artist who labours under no compulsion
but that of his own creativity. Are we, in some sense, his novels¿
William Golding

Characteristic of the contemporary creative writing scene – as it is deployed
in universities and colleges across the world – is the enduring nature of
the spurious dichotomy between theory and practice. This divisive stance
remains most obvious in the academic separation of creative writing from
literary studies despite rigorous scholarly attempts over the last 10 years to
create a foundation for a better integration of these disciplines. One reason
for such persistence is that the tension between criticism and the arts,
or theory and practice, is not new. Northrop Frye may have perpetuated
this tension by asserting, most likely tongue in cheek, that 'Criticism can
talk, and all the arts are dumb' (Frye, 1957: 4). And the phrase may have
stuck. Although the New Critics established a new theoretical construct
through which to view creative works, they may also have created new
misconceptions by viewing the mode of existence of the literary work as
wholly self-enclosed and inaccessible to exegetical endeavours. Peter Elbow's
influential book *Writing with Power* (1998) may also have contributed to the
polarisation with his 'self-help' approach to writing. David Morley and
Philip Neilsen, however, assert that there is a new paradigm emerging:

> In recent years, the development of creative writing as a discipline
> in higher education has changed the shape of literature departments

in universities across the globe. It has also changed the development
of literary studies through creative reading ('reading as a writer') and
through practice-led teaching.... Creative writing is a rearrival at a
balance in which the practice of writing is placed on an equal platform
to its study. (Morley & Neilsen, 2012: 1)

Although this might be the case, the problem is far from being resolved, as
the diversity of questions raised in *Key Issues in Creative Writing* (Donnelly
& Harper, 2013) attests. In fact, the problem has become even more complicated now that universities are facing quite radical changes because of the
economies of which they partake.

This chapter revisits old quarrels in oblique ways. It sets out from the
hypothesis that this spurious dichotomy is predicated upon the tension
between intellectual and emotional elements in our aesthetic response
to texts. It also postulates that writers are first and foremost readers and
hence can learn from their reading processes, as Prose (2006) and Boulter
(2007) have argued before. By offering a brief history of this tension
between intellect and emotion through the course of literary criticism it
points to ways of using reading paradigms, informed by criticism, and more
particularly reader-response criticism. It also suggests ways in which these
paradigms may be enriched by theory in the practice of writing, thereby
integrating cross-disciplinary knowledges. This move anticipates the search
for understanding theory in Chapters 3 and 4, for selecting psychoanalysis
as a 'theory without credentials' and for applying it in different ways and
to varying degrees in the remainder of the book, zooming in, as it were, on
Lacanian psychoanalysis and its possible rapport with creative writing.

Aggrieving Antecedents

The discomfort experienced in universities and colleges which expresses
the false dichotomy between, on the one hand, literary studies and creative
writing and, on the other hand, theory and practice is coterminous with the
rise and growth of the latter discipline (see e.g. Dawson, 2005; Donnelly,
2012; Harper, 2010; O'Rourke, 2005; Wandor, 2008). More importantly,
though, debates arising because of this false dichotomy reveal that it
continues to affect both teaching and research in negative ways. Not only
does this determine how teaching and research are continuously redefined
in an academy in constant flux – as best practice ought to be – it also affects
the ways in which research is assessed in terms of financial returns. For
example, while the title and focus of the 15th Australasian Association of
Writing Programs (AAWP) conference, 'Strange Bedfellows', epitomises the

former dichotomy, recent collections of essays which discuss this dichotomy with reference to the academic environment – where employment, government funding, promotion, enrolments and other factors are all dependent upon the question of value and how it is captured in a metrics-dominated system (Donnelly & Harper, 2013; Turcotte & Morris, 2012) – exemplify the latter, that is, the ways in which research is assessed. Consequently, if 'evidence of critical understanding is as important as a demonstration of creative capacity (Pope, 2005: 130), we need to re-examine the nature of this dichotomy, no less because it is inherent in the tension between intellectual and emotional elements in our aesthetic response to texts.

The enduring assumption by some within the academy that the activities of literary criticism (or theory) and creative writing are 'strange bedfellows', with criticism and theory the scholarly forms of literature and creative writing their sloppy cousin (see exemplars of this sentiment in Boulter, 2007: 1; Donnelly, 2012: 4; Elbow, 1998: 9), is not new, nor is it the province of the academy. Just think of *The Paper Men*, William Golding's parody of the literary world in the mid-1980s, a moment of theory we will revisit in the next two chapters. *The Paper Men* is a comedy, an indictment of the literary industry to which creative writers serve as raw material and willy-nilly find themselves trapped. 'No novelist in the second half of the twentieth century', Golding had said some time earlier, 'can be anything but part of a wide literary world that stretches from journalism into academia'. He went on:

> The academic world, the literary world, the world of journalism and that Bohemian world once called Grub Street, are now inextricably mixed, not just in the same country or city but, more often than not, in the same person. (Golding, 1982: 154–155)

Wilfred Barclay, the protagonist and I-narrator of *The Paper Men*, is such a confused person. He serves as a link, or gap, between the two 'voices' of the novel. He is at once an artist involved in the parodied literary world and an image of the modern subject as defined by Foucault (1966), who is the object of study for Tucker, the critic deprived of critical sense because of sheer academic pressure.

The Redress of Reading – *With Feeling*

While I want to stress the tension between creative writing and criticism, including its germane branch, theory, I want to highlight that these disciplines share a common heritage, as Lauri Ramey (2007) demonstrates in an essay from *The Handbook of Creative Writing* (Earnshaw, 2007). Moreover, expertise from these disciplines can be used to engage with creativity, the role of the writer and the practice of writing within the academy. Andrew Melrose (2007), who tacitly endorses psychoanalysis in his 'Reading and righting: Carrying on the "creative writing theory" debate', rightly suggests that creative writing is a form of thinking enmeshed with the act of reading, even though writing and reading might be 'analytically distinct' (Wandor, 2008: 147). Since this form of thinking is both creative and critical, Melrose rightly argues in favour of making connections rather than undoing them (Melrose, 2007: 113).

If, as human beings, we are first and foremost readers (Manguel, 2010: ix) and if many of the best critics in the Anglophone tradition were and are writers (Bate, 2012), reflecting upon our own reading habits and processes can only be beneficial. The act of articulating and conceptualising the writing process, with all the conflicting factors that this entails, is indeed one of the crucial goals of writers – including students, teachers and researchers. These factors, I want to emphasise, are those which play not only on our intellect, but also on our emotions, desires and affects. Combining the rigorously objective methods of Iser's aesthetic response (Iser, 1980) with psychoanalysis, I want to argue, is an excellent match for writers interested in exploring the *subjects* of creative writing.[1] Although I speak of psychoanalysis in very general terms here, different psychoanalytic orientations of particular relevance for writers will be explored in subsequent chapters.

Our aesthetic response to writing is informed by both emotional and intellectual processes. The emotions described depend on both the communicative and evocative functions of language: emotional attitudes instigated during the reading process are partly engendered by textual strategies. Yet these strategies are not always identical to those that pre-structure the intellectual processing of the text, but are akin to it by way of a metaphorical operation which involves both condensation and displacement (see Chapter 9). This conjures up the enduring clash between, on the one hand, creative writing and criticism and, on the other hand, theory and practice in literary studies, a clash which may just be a restaging of the old conflict at the heart of the term 'poesis' or of the more recent 'two cultures' debate (Snow, 1963; Wandor, 2008: 64) which divided the sciences from literature only half a century ago. What I want to argue here is for the merging rather than the separation of the two areas.

Literary critics have always known that feelings influence our reception of art. Plato and Aristotle, of course, immediately spring to mind. While Plato banished the poets from society in his *Republic* because of some reactivity akin to madness due to the pleasure it induced (Naddaff, 2002), Aristotle saw the arousal of pity and terror as the function of tragedy, generating a cleansing release of those dangerous emotions, which he felt to be disturbing, as Plato did, albeit more acutely so (Stanford, 1984). Whereas for Plato the response of pleasure is entirely inappropriate – logically, ethically and psychologically (Naddaff, 2002: 115) – it has the merit of being psychologically relevant for Aristotle. The *Poetics* may in fact, as some have suggested, be read as a critique of the Platonic indictment of drama for stirring up inappropriate passions, since in Aristotle's view the audience's subjective participation in fictional events had – at least potentially – a positive value. Since this 'ancient quarrel' (Webb & Brien, 2012), generations of writers and critics have returned to the question of whether responding emotionally to art is desirable or not. Evaluating the subjective elements within art is an integral part of all aesthetic theories, whether this is seen as desirable or not (Badiou, 2005). Readers' emotions are usually related to the philosophical foundations of a particular aesthetic theory, and are judged within this frame of reference – logically, ethically and psychologically. For example, although emotion received a fair amount of attention from the New Critics, pleasure was almost always limited to the enjoyment of cognitive harmonies or tensions, thus both abrogating Plato's ambivalence towards poetry and perpetuating his rejection of pleasure. Any mention of the power of the text to induce sensation, indeed to arouse pleasure, stimulate desire or provoke distaste was conspicuous by its absence.

Susan Sontag spoke up against this state of affairs when, in *Against Interpretation* (1966), she insisted on an erotics of art. Her emphasis not only anticipated but, along with Julia Kristeva's *Σημειωτική* (1969), may have prepared the way for the reception of Roland Barthes's *The Pleasure of the Text* (1973). In different ways, and to varying degrees, both works also brought into fashion a more playful and performative style of literary criticism. A critic should not simply register pleasure, Sontag and Kristeva implied, but also relay it. In short, the question of what the literary was good for was emphatically reopened by a generation at once highly politicised (after May 1968) and attuned to philosophical upheavals, as well as increasingly ethnically aware and focused on the body. This celebration of Eros, needless to say, died a spectacular death with the rise of 'high theory', for reasons that will be invoked in the next chapter. Despite the recent resurgence of interest in emotion itself in fields as varied as neuroscience (see e.g. Damasio, 1989; Hopkins, 2000) and the humanities (see e.g. Cunningham, 2005; Harpham, 2005; Janicaud, 2005; Mousley, 2010), the fickle history of emotions in the history of aesthetics has yet to be written.

However, the effect of literature cannot be founded on a single principle. Aristotle's theory of catharsis is not comprehensive. It does not account for the fact that many texts have, for example, a frustrating or stimulating effect for both writer and reader; our intellectual interaction with the text plays a crucial role too, one that must not be overlooked. Aristotle reduces the broad spectrum of possible responses to art to catharsis. Thus, his theory cannot provide a convincing explanation of the complex fascination that proceeds from reading or writing, because this fascination arises from the fact that the rational and the irrational both participate in the receptive and reflexive processes inherent in these two activities, that they often come into conflict, and that tensions may arise due to an interplay of identifications with the material which is being deployed. Consequently, erratic and unpredictable responses can occur. Both reading and writing, I claim, are psychological affairs in which intellect and emotion as well as conscious and unconscious processes interplay.

The New Critics were aware of the tensions between intellect and emotion. They even went so far as to claim that certain cognitive processes are instigated by emotions. For example, the authors of 'The affective fallacy' postulate that 'Emotion … has a well-known capacity … to inflame cognition, and to grow upon itself in surprising proportions to gains of reason' (Wimsatt & Beardsley, 1972: 349). The emphasis laid on the subjective dimensions of the cognitive process in the writings of the New Critics is significant inasmuch as they drew up the manifesto of axioms to which all the divergent trends in literary theory have been reacting until recently (Ayers, 2008). Frank Lentricchia describes the New Critics' concept of literature as: 'Another shibboleth of the New Critics – one worth remembering, given recent attempts to portray them as life-denying formalists – was that literature gives a "special kind of knowledge" of non-literary, non-linguistic phenomena' (Lentricchia, 1980: 18). Although the New Critics recognised the importance of the tensions between the rational and the irrational, and there was even a place for non-verbally communicated knowledge in their concept of literature, they were unable to make statements about this phenomenon. They had no theory whereby non-linguistic phenomena could be conceptualised. They did not discuss, draw upon or assimilate theories like phenomenology or psychoanalysis. Therefore, the New Critics had to limit themselves to intrinsic textual analyses on the one hand and devastating polemics on the other. They constantly spoke out against the use of psychological terms in discussing reading processes. René Wellek and Austin Warren, in their *Theory of Literature*, tell us:

> The psychology of the reader … will always remain outside the object of literary study – the concrete work of art…. Psychological theories must be theories of effect and may lead in extreme cases to such criteria

of the value of poetry as that proposed by A.E. Housman, ... [who] tells us, one hopes with his tongue in his cheek, that good poetry can be recognized by the thrill down our spine. This is on the same level as eighteenth-century theories which measured the quality of a tragedy by the amount of tears shed by the audience or the movie scout's conception of the quality of a comedy on the basis of the number of laughs he has counted in the audience. Thus anarchy, scepticism, a complete confusion of values is the result of every psychological theory, as it must be unrelated either to the structure or the quality of a poem. (Wellek & Warren, 1956: 147)

According to Wellek and Warren, even the slightest deviation from the assumptions of the New Criticism would necessarily end in anarchy. Would one be too close, perhaps, to the reality of the unconscious? And given the slippery nature of the term, what unconscious would that be?

Northrop Frye, an immediate successor of the New Critics, rightly criticises them for their inarticulateness: 'Here criticism is restricted to ritual Masonic gestures, to raised eyebrows and cryptic comments and other signs of an understanding too occult for syntax' (Frye, 1957: 4). Frye pleads for a democratisation of literature. In his *Anatomy of Criticism*, he attempts to initiate this democratisation by proposing a strict system of classification into which all literary and critical phenomena are to be integrated. But even Frye perpetuates one of the New Critics' misconceptions in viewing the mode of existence of the literary work as wholly self-enclosed and inaccessible to language: again, 'Criticism can talk, and all the arts are dumb' (Frye, 1957: 4). Consequently, Frye postulates two different kinds of processing of reality, one *verbal* and one *pre-verbal*: 'Criticism ... is to art what history is to action and philosophy to wisdom: a verbal imitation of a human productive power which itself does not speak' (Frye, 1957: 12). This human productive power consists, for Frye, in what C.G. Jung problematically describes as the 'collective unconscious', that is, a reservoir of symbols and archetypes which is timeless and accessible to all humankind. Frye bases his comprehensive system of literary typology on Jung's psychology. However, that does not make the pre-verbal area, in which he situates literature, any less cryptic, since Jung's terms and concepts rest on inadequate foundations too, ignoring, as they do, the libidinous and linguistic aspects of human subjectivity.

In his radical rejection of Freud's metapsychology, a term coined by Freud to describe the theoretical dimensions of psychoanalysis, Jung not only subverts the Freudian theory of sexual drives by taming the threatening and chaotic sexual energies, he also confines himself to that genetic concept of an unconscious which, temporally speaking, originates in a realm preceding ontogenesis, and therefore exists independently of the individual human being. Whereas Freud answers the question of how the unconscious comes into being dualistically, as we shall see in more detail further on – seeing a phylogenetic and an individual conception as being on equal terms, with an unconscious developing in the latter only because of repression (Freud, 2001 [1915b]) – Jung's unconscious is entirely pre-given. According to Jung, every single conscious impulse arises from far-removed unconscious areas (Jung, 1997 [1916]). Speech processes are ego functions (and thus reside in the conscious mind); they have nothing in common with the collective unconscious, which Jung considers to be non-verbal and mystical. Freud's conjecture is that some unconscious impulses are indeed akin to the structures of language, and form patterns in speech. Jung's unconscious, however, eludes cognition itself. More particularly, it eludes the fact that we are 'reading animals' (Manguel, 2010: ix), subjected to language, as Freud intimates (Lacan, 1978 [1954–55]: 257) – a reality that even Descartes's 'cogito ergo sum' acknowledged long before (Descartes, 1974: 110). Like Descartes, in Lacan's account of Freud's unconscious, the latter, certain of doubt, locates through it a subject who thinks (Lacan, 1986 [1964]: 37). The difference between Freud and Descartes is that for Freud the subject is, in fact, synonymous with fundamental (unconscious) doubt (de Klerk, 2009: 71).

Even though Frye distances himself from Jung (Frye, 1957: 111–112), his theory is based on Jung's concept of a collective unconscious, and thus proves unsatisfactory for mapping out both the pre-verbal (or proto-verbal) area which supplies creative energies (see the discussion on Kristeva in Chapters 6 and 9) and the reading process. For Frye, both author and reader receive impulses from a collective unconscious, impulses that will be more effective the less they are influenced by the content of the individual unconscious concerned. Frye's model of the individual unconscious is that of a filter: as soon as too much sediment settles on it, it will inevitably muddy the clear, pure current of symbols emerging from the collective unconscious. According to this model of unconscious processes, emotions have the status of smudges. Affects, incidentally, do not even exist. Yet, as we shall see in the later chapters of this book, affects can powerfully colour our responses to texts.

The manifestos of the New Critics and their successors have proved to be as inadequate as Aristotle's theory of catharsis to describe the role of emotions in reading, let alone writing. Despite Wellek and Warren's (1956) fervent dictum that any attempt to construct a theory of *effect* will necessarily end in anarchy, one of the aims of this chapter is just that: I want to account for both the rational and the subjective elements in reading, so that, as a writer, I can understand what effect I may have on the reader and how this, in turn, might affect my own writing process. In sketching out my concepts, I draw on what Wellek and Warren (1956) call 'the structure of the poem', that is, on the textual strategies, schemata and divergent perspectives contained in a literary text. I also use phenomenology and psychoanalysis, the very theories that the New Critics neglected to assimilate. I address the following questions: How can the actual process of reading texts be conceptualised? To what extent are readers' responses pre-structured by what they are reading? Are reactions to reading contained in the text?

'Experiencing' Reading

Let me first reconsider the question of *reading*. For a long time, reading was regarded as an innocent enough and perfectly straightforward activity; thus this concept did not seem particularly problematic in its application to literary theory, as Patricia Meyer Spacks still seems to hold (Meyer Spacks, 2011), ignoring that, in the latter half of the 20th century, the reader moved closer to the centre of critical attention. Audience-oriented criticism, by focusing on the reader, brought a long-ranging development within literary theory to an end with the emergence of Russian formalism, Prague structuralism and the New Criticism – all critical schools which have been themselves criticised for being interested only in the formal aspects of texts. The very neglect in which the reader, as a significant component in communicating with literature, used to be held did however exercise a stupendous effect towards the end of last century, which led to intensive critical research and theorising. Unfortunately, today, reader-oriented criticism no longer presents itself as a lively and controversial field. This is a shame, for in hindsight it comprised a multitude of different reader constructs that may assist writers to be better writers, by which I mean self-critical or, rather, 'self-reflective' writers (Hunt & Sampson, 2006a).

Describing the various reader constructs developed in the late 20th century is a possible first step towards mapping out this rather complex area. They comprise the contemporary reader (Jauss, 1982), the ideal reader (Culler, 1982), the super reader (Riffaterre, 1971), the informed reader (Fish, 1980), the intended reader (Wolff, 1971), the empirical reader (Holland, 1975) and many more (Iser, 1980: 27–38). In comparing the philosophical assumptions that guide these heuristic constructs, it soon becomes clear that decisions about the ultimate cognitive aim of the theory in question lurk within all the different models.

Thus, the contemporary reader would seem to embody that conglomerate of scientific, philosophical and literary knowledge which constitutes the horizon of expectations against which a text is read. With the help of this construct, a work's history of receptions can be conceived of as a sequence of differing interpretations conditioned by the connections between the changing horizons of reader expectations and the text concerned (Jauss, 1982).

However, as soon as literature is regarded as a grammar-based system analogous to language – as in structuralism – an ideal reader is required, one whose comprehensive reading competence enables him or her to decode all the conventions and potentials of meaning in the text. As Jonathan Culler argues:

> To read a text as literature is not to make one's mind a *tabula rasa* and approach it without preconceptions; one must bring to it an implicit understanding of the operations of literary discourse which tells one what to look for. Anyone lacking this knowledge ... has not internalized the 'grammar' of literature. (Culler, 1982: 176)

Magpies that writers are, they read with a view to enriching their data – by which I mean themselves, their subject matter, stylistics, poetics and so on – and understanding their creative process. Culler's statement speaks volumes. I would, however, be inclined to emphasise that for this quote to be wholly relevant to the work of creative writers, 'implicit understanding' needs to become 'explicit' and 'internalised' and subsequently 'externalised' through a process of self-reflection (Bolton, 2010; Hunt & Sampson, 2006a).

In contradistinction to the magpie analogy, Riffaterre's 'super reader' would assist writers aiming at consolidating an already conceptualised poetics; the 'super reader' consists of a 'group of informants' and is able (in the sense of deviation stylistics) 'to recognise the specific character of the style' (Riffaterre, 1971: 178) at certain crucial points in the text, that is, its patterns, its breaks and discontinuities. In other words, studying the super reader aims to make statements about poetic language. This hypothesical super reader might appeal to writers who regard themselves as both critics and theorists, if only because they were trained in the discipline of literary studies – as is often the case with creative writing teachers and practitioners.

In his early work, Stanley Fish employs the model of the informed reader, who has the character of a construct – she or he must have linguistic and literary competence – but also actually exists, and whose reading experiences should therefore lend themselves to empirical examination (Fish, 1980: 44). Fish writes:

But what reader? When I talk about the responses of 'the reader', am I not really talking about myself, and making myself into a surrogate for all the millions of readers who are not me at all? Yes and no. Yes, in the sense that in no two of us are the responding mechanisms exactly alike. No, if one argues that because of the uniqueness of the individual, generalization about response is impossible. It is here that the method can accommodate the insights of modern linguistics, especially the idea of 'linguistic competence', 'the idea that it is possible to characterize a linguistic system that every speaker shares'. This characterization, if it were realized, would be a 'competence model', corresponding more or less to the internal mechanisms which allow us to process (understand) and produce sentences that we have never before encountered. It would be a spatial model in the sense that it would reflect a system of rules pre-existing, and indeed making possible, any actual linguistic experience. (Fish, 1980: 44)

For this very reason, the informed reader is too unsystematic an entity to be of value to readers. Consequently, in his later phase Fish finds himself obliged to abandon this concept. Instead, he takes his own reading processes as the norm and preaches subjectivism – he contends that a text can mean anything (Fish, 1980: 305). However, this weird entity, or conglomerate of entities, might be useful to writers, particularly in examining the process of identification between writer and reader, as well as its vicissitudes, in problematising the competence model with respect to creative writing.

In Norman Holland's work, on the other hand, the personality profiles of actual readers, their individual 'identity themes' (Holland, 1975: 814), provide a fixed and rather static framework within which these readers read and interpret (Holland, 1975: 816). Holland writes:

As readers, each of us will bring different kinds of external information to bear. Each will seek out the particular themes that concern him. Each will have different ways of making the text into an experience with a coherence and significance that satisfies…. The overarching principle is: identity recreates itself. That is, all of us, as we read, use the literary work to symbolize and finally to replicate ourselves. We work out through the text our own characteristic patterns of desire and adaptation. We interact with the work, making it part of our own psychic economy and making ourselves part of the literary work. (Holland, 1975: 816)

Thus, although Holland seems to advocate singular reading experiences, just as each writing experience is singular in creative writing and in psychoanalysis, Holland's reader never meets with anyone but her- or himself in dealing with texts (see his conclusion, emphasising 'the same overarching principle: identity recreates itself' in Holland, 1975: 818). Given this limitation, it is difficult to see how creative writers can fruitfully apply Holland's ideas, except, perhaps by sourcing Mark Bracher's ideas on how to increase self-knowledge and self-reflexivity in composition workshops (Bracher, 1999, 2006).

The individual features of reader constructs are determined by their respective philosophical foundations, as well as by the specific cognitive aims of the reader-response theory in question. The fact that emotions play an important part in our interaction with literature is scarcely *ever* reflected. Moreover, all the reader constructs presented so far are essentially deterministic: the reader either is dominated by the text (as in Culler's and Riffaterre's theories) or has unlimited power over the text (as in Fish's and Holland's).

A way out of this dilemma is provided by Wolfgang Iser's 'implied reader', a concept that brings into view not any specific reader, but reading, the process upon which the dynamic interaction between reader and text relies. For Iser, meaning is neither pre-given nor arbitrary, but is constituted only in the *act of reading*. One of his basic notions is that a text has two poles, one artistic – created by the author – and the other aesthetic – the 'concretization' accomplished by the reader. These poles interact with each other (Iser, 1980: 21). In his model of the reading process, Iser draws on phenomenology, particularly the theories of Roman Ingarden (1973: 276ff.), to sketch out the text's mode of existence, on hermeneutics to conceptualise the way in which the literary strategies contained in the text are decoded, and on Gestalt psychology to outline the interactions between text and reader.

According to Ingarden, a literary work consists of several layers, each comprising a sequence of schemata, positions, perspectives and strategies. His concept of literature is informed by the notion that the noblest task of art lies in the symbolic representation of some inorganic whole. The role that Ingarden therefore assigns to the 'schematized aspects' in his model is that of chiming in 'polyphonic harmony' (Ingarden, 1973: 276ff.). The concept of polyphonic harmony, in turn, serves him as criterion for distinguishing between true and false concretisations: the reader has to process the separate strata in a way that makes them merge. A lively interaction between text and reader is thus hardly possible, and reading remains an activity which is to a large extent dominated by the text.

On the other hand, the literature of the modernists and postmodernists (e.g. James Joyce, Virginia Woolf, Samuel Beckett, Thomas Pynchon), upon which Iser's textual theory is based (Iser, 1980), is characterised by the very fact that any attempt at creating polyphonic harmony is, from the outset, doomed to failure. In his theory of aesthetic response, Iser draws upon Ingarden's model, but emphasises the blanks, gaps and vacancies within each of the text's several layers. Iser highlights the difficulties in linking the individual schematised aspects into a harmonious whole. Contoured 'places of indeterminacy' reinstigate and limit a reading process whose aim, first and foremost, is to build consistency. Through an interplay of 'retensions' and 'protensions' (Iser, 1980: 23) – the information provided by what the reader has already read, which subsequently gears his or her expectations as to what might follow – the reader attempts to convert open Gestalts into closed ones, a process which the contradictions and negations in the text are constantly trying to undermine. Thus, the structure of the reading process is an essentially dynamic one which cannot be separated from its temporal dimension.

The 'implied reader' is a concept which embraces both the formal structures contained in the text and the reader's acts of concretisation. The reader's responses are written into the text and the aesthetic effect of a text therefore results from a decoding of its many layers, each layer having a double aspect: layers are verbal structures, on the one hand, and, on the other, the very conditions which allow the text to be affectively and mentally activated (Iser, 1980: 21). The idea of a 'correct' concretisation such as Ingarden – and later Culler and Riffaterre – has in mind as an ideal is not present in Iser, but the idea of an adequate one is: Iser by no means leaves the act of consistency-building entirely open – as do Fish and Holland. Rather, Iser conceives of the interaction between text and reader as a process which – within a range of possible variations – describes certain patterns and movements.

If we classify the various reader-response theories according to whether they not only acknowledge but also conceptualise the tensions between the emotional and the intellectual elements contained in the reading process, they fall into two groups. On the one hand, we have critics like Holland, who entirely deny that there are intellectual components involved in reading. The individual reader's personality profile is of greater interest to these critics than questions relevant to the study of literature, such as analyses of a text's formal structure, or of the function of emotions stimulated by reading literature. The methods applied by Holland are just as subjective as the ultimate aim of his studies; they do not stand up to close examination. On the other hand, there are the works of Iser and Jauss, which limit themselves mainly to analysing our intellectual interaction with literary texts. Neither the theory of aesthetic response as developed by Iser, nor Jauss's reception theory, can be accused of moving too far away from the text as the proper object of literary criticism, or of employing subjective methods. However, Iser and Jauss are almost exclusively interested in the cognitive processing of a work of art; the fact that emotions play an important part in our interaction with literature is scarcely ever reflected in their work. Thus, Culler's polemic attack against reader-response criticism is – to a certain degree – justified:

> The experiences or responses that modern reader-oriented critics invoke are generally cognitive rather than affective: not feeling shivers along the spine, weeping in sympathy, or being transported with awe, but having one's expectations proved false, struggling with an irresolvable ambiguity, or questioning the assumptions on which one had relied. (Culler, 1982: 39)

'Shivers along the spine' are difficult to conceptualise with the methods developed by the theory of aesthetic response or by reception theory.

Textual Clandestines

No text can ever be fully permeated by conscious intention.
Anthony Easthope

Characteristic of the reading processes contained in all texts are the tensions between intellectual and emotional elements. These tensions are mirrored in the two opposite schools of thought within reader-response criticism: theorising is exclusively about subjective factors and conducted with subjective methods, on the one hand; or it is entirely about intellectual factors and conducted with rigorous objectivity, on the other. As a result, problems and tensions arise within academia which are staged in attacks on the philosophical bases of the positions in question. These tensions derive from the subject matter, from the specific nature of the reading process, which consists in ever-changing relations between various modes of perception. Obviously, the structured field of dynamic interactions between the two cannot be analysed with the methods of reader-oriented literary criticism alone. Were we to adapt the concepts uncovered by reader-response criticism to understand what happens in the drafting process, the shortcomings of these methods would be even more salient.

However, as Hunt and Sampson demonstrate in their book *Writing: Self and Reflexivity* (2006a), subjectivity, including emotions and affects, should by no means be equated with irrationality. Subjectivity can be understood perfectly well by rigorous and objectifiable methods. Psycho-analysis has provided us with objective descriptions of seemingly erratic subjective events. In Freud's writings, the categories of the rational and the irrational, the intellectual and the affective, are subjected to a fundamental reassessment, for in all manifestations of the unconscious it is the apparently irrational that is the most significant. As we saw in the introduction when we reacquainted ourselves with Alice, identity is most inconsistent on the other side of the mirror. The mirror, however, no matter how flawed, is the surface between the reality of everyday life and the place of dreams, creation and insanity. As such, it bears the trace of what we may have forgotten, preferred to ignore or unwittingly turned a blind eye to. Freud insisted that all human behaviour could be understood as meaningful or significant, and that the meanings are often unknown (consciously) because they are repressed. He also claimed that the most frequently repressed wishes and desires were sexual ones: these sexual wishes or desires are forbidden in our everyday conventional lives and for a variety of reasons are generally unacceptable to the conscious mind. They are excluded or repressed from consciousness and become 'unconscious'. In other words, because we do not want to acknowledge them and live with them in our conscious life, we attempt to disown them. But they nonetheless continue to exist, unbeknownst to us. To uncover these wishes was Freud's project and we will explore this later on, when we look into psychoanalysis and examine what happens when primordial desire gets directed into social goals, when bodily needs become subject to the mores of culture. Through language, desire becomes subject to rules and yet, as we know, language cannot define experience accurately – can it adequately define body, mind, subjectivity and relationships? Does language perhaps get in the way? We will see that what is of particular interest to psychoanalysis is that aspect of experience which has been ignored or prohibited by the rules of language. Words fail to match it but *id* is there, nevertheless. Now the energies of this desire become directed outside conscious awareness, attaching themselves to particular ideas and images which represent unconscious wishes – *Wunsch* in German, which refers to desire associated with particular images or word presentations, as distinct from desire, which refers to underlying energies not yet bound to specific aims, later known as drives.

For the time being let us say that our conscious and unconscious reactions are always discontinuous; they lack coherence. The unconscious, though containing material which is repressed by the conscious mind, cannot be simply equated with what is repressed. The unconscious is not an objective entity, but a dynamic process that involves mind and body, knotting together signifiers, silences and traces, which can be perceived only through their effects, namely through dreams, slips of the tongue, jokes, repetitive and compulsive actions, symptoms and so on. These effects form patterns which allow certain conclusions to be drawn about the very nature of the conflicts on which they are based. Psychoanalytic methods permit a conceptualisation of the enmeshing of the conscious and the unconscious. In order to do so, however, one must also examine the hinge between the conscious and the unconscious, that is, affects. Psychoanalysis thus opens up the opportunity to elaborate on the seemingly erratic and apparently irrational elements contained in the reading process and, hence, in critical and creative processes.

For psychoanalysis, the act of writing always presupposes that the text transmutates the loss into a fictitious positivity. Thus it would be fair to say that we all write out of the need to negotiate anxiety. But we seem to do this in different ways. This will be the object of Chapters 8 and 11, which unpack and illustrate some of the concepts introduced here. Combining the concepts of reader-response criticism and psychoanalysis may help us articulate our own writing processes, define our own poetics and articulate these in terms of contemporary speculations and debates, thus disproving that 'Criticism can talk, and [that] all the arts are dumb' (Frye, 1957: 4).

Note

(1) It is heartening to see, as this book heads for publication, that others share this view. See Luke Johnson's PhD thesis, 'Literary subjectivity', which combines Lacanian psychoanalysis and reader-response criticism to redefine subjectivity and authorship in the context of creative writing (Johnson, 2013).

3 Obituaries, Contestations, Proclamations: The Theory Question

I want to suggest that to write to your best abilities, it behoves you to construct your own tool-box and then build up enough muscle so you can carry it with you.
Stephen King

Think of the tools in a tool-box: there is a hammer, pliers, a saw, a screw-driver, a rule, a glue-pot, nails and screws. The functions of words are as diverse as the functions of these objects.
Ludwig Wittgenstein

Why does creative writing need theory if it has the tools to go about its business? After all, it could carry on in its shed in the backyard of literary studies, as it has mostly done since antiquity, using the tools of prosody to perfect its own craft. Unfortunately, particularly in the Anglophone world, creative writing met theory at the least opportune time: when it was emerging as a discipline and struggling to define itself as such, some 25 years ago (Dawson, 2005). But the seeds of the disagreement had been sown long before. Paul Dawson locates this momentous seed in the soil of the 1980s (Dawson, 2008). Like most unlikely couples, creative writing and theory have been arguing with each other ever since. Perhaps this argument has been unnecessary, owing to the death of theory (Eagleton, 2003, 2012) and the apparent self-sufficiency of the craft – a self-sufficiency which in fact seems for some to have been brought about by the death of Theory itself (Royle, 2013). Are we perhaps going around in circles, trying as we may to make a point?

Let us briefly define this word 'theory', as it has often been blamed for the dysfunctional relationship between the creative and critical components of writing, if not for its 'traumatic impact' on the 'discipline of English' (Royle, 2013) and, worse, for the 'educational costs' in the humanities (Kitching,

2008). Let us also investigate theory's project – so we are able to ground the discussion about the influence of theory on academic discourse and the historical difficulty of integrating theoretical concepts into 'creative writing studies' (Donnelly, 2012) – before considering why we might need theory, or perhaps a plurality of theories.

Theory's Obituary

Although allied to literary criticism, theory should be distinguished from it, since theory concerns itself with the analysis and judgement of *concepts* rather than *creative works*. Currently, theory, without a capital 't', refers to an 'embedded presence' (Dawson, 2008) in creative writing, one that encompasses a plurality of theoretical approaches to writing spawned by Theory, with a capital 'T'. As such, 'Theory', or 'high theory', was essentially a 'moment' (Hunter, 2006) in the history of literary criticism, spanning the 1960s and 1970s, which saw society as the undesirable product of the Enlightenment. This moment drew together a series of philosophical developments evolving in the mid-1960s from within the university discourse in continental Europe, even though the philosophical premises and ideological foundations underpinning it have a much longer history and, indeed, continue into the present. Theory then reached the USA, where it was reconceptualised and later disseminated across borders of time, geopolitics, linguistics and poetics. Rumours about the death of Theory reach back to the early 1990s and were probably initiated by Theory itself. The French philosopher Jean-François Lyotard had no doubt written its proto-obituary when he announced the death of the 'grand narratives' (Lyotard, 1984), those large-scale theories and philosophies of the world, such as the progress in history. But it is in the 1990s that the death of Theory was most loudly proclaimed. Thinkers as versatile as Pierre Bourdieu (2000), Terry Eagleton (2003) and Valentine Cunningham (2005) are among those who later wrote about this opportune death, only to anticipate the richer, though no less problematic, topos of *Life.After.Theory* (Payne & Schad, 2003). More recently, some commentators have welcomed this passing, bemoaning the 'damaging effects [of] a certain kind of poststructuralist or postmodernist theorising' (Kitching, 2008: 4) or the philosophical and aesthetic problems that arise in connection with the appreciation and evaluation of literature (Royle, 2013).

Thus, as a general term, Theory formally originated in the Anglo-American academy in the 1970s, with works by Jonathan Culler (1975) and Terry Eagleton (1978). Theory denotes the Critical Theory associated with the Frankfurt School and the work of thinkers such as Walter Benjamin and Theodor Adorno. It also conjures up the philosophical and psychoanalytic theories of signification associated with poststructuralism, the so-called 'French Theory' that has its roots in the work of linguists such as Ferdinand de Saussure and Émile Benvéniste, as well as colleagues from the Prague School. French Theory usually refers to the work of Roland Barthes, Hélène Cixous, Jacques Derrida, Michel Foucault, Luce Irigaray, Julia Kristeva, Jacques Lacan, Jean-François Lyotard as well as Gilles Deleuze and Félix Guattari, and the relevant philosophical traditions they draw upon. The writings of Pierre Bourdieu and Jean Baudrillard complement this core definition of theory, as do the works of Fredric Jameson and Hayden White, for their emphasis on its social and political ramifications. Today, however, cultural theory has in many ways replaced structuralism and poststructuralism as the main discourses to which many turn for cross-disciplinary, cross-cultural, multicultural, postcolonial and geohistorical ventures.

Nonetheless, it remains true to say that theory has long had affiliations with different modes of critique instigated by theory – lower-case 't'. Towards the end of the 18th century the German philosopher Immanuel Kant published a series of critiques aimed at discovering the nature and limits of human understanding. He asserted that the answer was to be found in what he described as the mind's fundamental structures. In a similar vein, romantic theories of the imagination attempted to assign the origins of literature to a faculty located between a human and a divine mind (Frye, 1957; Wellek & Warren, 1956). For at least the last 50 years, the different modalities of critique – such as Marxism, feminism, linguistics, structuralism, poststructuralism, psychoanalysis and postcolonialism – have all, in concert or separately, produced critical theories which are concerned not only with the analysis and evaluation of creative works, but also with their conditions of existence, whether these are encountered in the structures of culture or language, in the laws of narrative, or in the ideologies produced by gender, class and race divisions inherent in societies. This has made it possible to distinguish between forms of criticism which have some affinity to academic critique, and others which do not bother with reflexive thought but rather entertain a literary canon that is not subjected to inquiry. But there are still other, and equally important, types of distinction to be made, for example between those types of critique which question forms of power, and those which locate more fundamental questions outside the political sphere, namely in properties of culture, language or the human mind – both conscious and unconscious. Perhaps the distinction between the political and the apolitical is a false dichotomy, as feminism demonstrated by proclaiming the personal to be political. Creative writing is at the nexus between the personal and the political. It therefore needs to be self-reflexive and engaged with theory to understand how it is positioned within socio-political and institutional discourses, just as writers need to be self-aware in order to articulate what their praxis is about and how it is situated within these discourses.

Contestations: The Question of Representation

It must be said that even during its heyday Theory received some serious condemnation. Critics of poststructuralist theories – often themselves critics of postmodern trends in writing – have argued that these discourses are apolitical and in the end amount to a total denial of the existence of reality outside of discourse. This is, of course, a serious generalisation and an oversimplification, as we will see shortly. However, David Lodge stated, somewhat disingenuously perhaps, in the context of Hayden White's ground-breaking *Metahistory* (1973): 'History may be, in a philosophical sense, a fiction, but it does not feel like that when we miss a train or somebody starts a war' (Lodge, 1977: 109). We could retort that while missing a train may be a non-discursive phenomenon, wars are the products of competing versions of history, and for those of us who are not on the firing line, these wars are experienced through the agency of political, economic and technological forces which in turn have very real impacts on events in war zones, past, present or future. In the context of the so-called 'War on Terror', for example, there is little doubt that storytelling was politically motivated. It is now a cliché to say that life is mediated through representations. Nevertheless, it makes a great deal of difference which version of the real we choose to believe in, and whether we take the stories we are told as truth or recognise their fictionality and the motivation behind the fictionalising process, particularly if we are to turn these stories into 'recognisable and even predictable act[s] of literature' (Brophy, 2009: 68).

There are no simple deaths in literature, no simple births and no simple truths. Just as well. Otherwise, what would be the point of reading? Of writing? What would be the point of dreaming in-between reading and writing – writing and reading? Alice shows us a way through this hall of mirrors. We owe it to Theory to make the flaws in the glass of representation obvious to all, and by extension to illuminate the limits of literature. The case of deconstruction is particularly relevant in this regard. The logic that marks a deconstructive reading is interwoven with the very logic that sustains writerly, and therefore logocentric, readings – in the plural. Deconstructive strategy cannot work by means of an absolute distinction between what we might call the logic of speech and the logic of writing, the one articulated on the principle of non-contradiction and the other contravening this principle. Rather, each is seen as the precondition of the other. There can never be a situation, for example, in which a text can be read either grammatically or rhetorically, for the conditions of textuality are such that a text is the warp and weft of both grammar and rhetoric; and the text's apparent claim to univocality is deconstructed, in that grammar and rhetoric fail to work in concert and thereby promote positive or negative disjunctions, when univocality would require conjunctions. In a sense, deconstruction construes both experience and consciousness as texts. In citing Rousseau's dictum 'There is nothing outside of the text' (Derrida, 1976 [1967]: 158), Derrida is making an epistemological rather than ontological claim: not that everything is only a text, but that everything is also a text. This move does not destroy the world or the possibility of thinking about the world; however, it does question any appeal to a natural, unhistorical or unpoliticised framing of the world.

Although this is not the focus of this book, the fact that poetics is often identified with politics merits some notice, because in creative writing circles there is still a tendency to see poststructuralist theory and postmodern practice as simply replacing representation with the idea of textuality. Yet, paired with politics, poetics specifically concerns the formal and affective realms of a subject under inquiry: it explicitly and reflexively becomes the socio-political aspect of a writer's work. A quick glance at this intersection reveals hugely influential books such as *Writing Culture: The Politics and Poetics of Ethnography* (Clifford & Marcus, 2010) and *The Politics and Poetics of Transgression* (Stallybrass & White, 1986). The problematic nature of this intersection led the Canadian theorist Linda Hutcheon to complement *A Poetics of Postmodernism* (Hutcheon, 1988) with *The Politics of Postmodernism* (Hutcheon, 1993). First published in 1989, the latter draws substantially on Robert Siegle's *The Politics of Reflexivity* (Siegle, 1986), which may explain why Hutcheon considered titling her book *Re-presenting Postmodernism* (Hutcheon, 1993: x). In *The Politics of Reflexivity*, Robert Siegle quotes the novelist and critic Umberto Eco, now famous for his theory of semiotics: 'to change semantic systems means to change the way in which culture "sees" the world' (Siegle, 1986: 10). Having learned the lessons of deconstruction, Siegle explores reflexivity's potential for challenging the supposed transparency of representation. Reflexivity, he argues:

> is a permanent revolutionary dimension of literature that persists in resisting the yoke of any paradigm that attempts to obscure its own self-transforming qualities. (Siegle, 1986: 247)

Siegle refers to the ideological dimension of reflexivity in specific political terms: it is 'revolutionary' (Siegle, 1986: 247), it fosters a 'proletarian theory' (Siegle, 1986: 244) and it pits itself against 'both the aristocratic and the capitalist modes of organising society' (Siegle, 1986: 243). No doubt aware of these theoretical contexts, Hunt and Sampson, in *Writing: Self and Reflexivity* (Hunt & Sampson, 2006a), propose a concept of reflexivity associated with the creative process, not the reception of artworks. Their model draws on theories of subjectivity, not politics. But the two are not necessarily mutually exclusive. Marion May Campbell shows us the way when she argues for radical conceptions of subjectivity embedded in subversive textual practices (Campbell, 2014). Paying attention to the reflexivity of texts and to the modes of representation of subjectivity these enfold offers a rich avenue to do so, as it flaunts the politics that is 'driven by representation' (Campbell, 2014: 292).

Challenging the supposed transparency of representation is what poststructuralist theories and postmodern practices do: they resist being framed in terms of 'either–or' and play a double game of 'neither–nor' and 'both–and', which recalls Friedrich Schlegel's aphorism 'It is just as deadly for the mind to have a system as to have none at all. So, one has to make up one's mind to have both' (see Todorov & Porter, 1983: 123). This brings us to an interesting twist: theory against theory – that is, if we consider, as I do, philosophy as partaking of theoretical discourse, especially when it straddles philosophy and literature, as does deconstruction.

The Attack on Theory's Dead Body

The Trouble with Theory (Kitching, 2008) was published well after the death of Theory. The author, British-born Gavin Kitching, is a philosopher, expert on Wittgenstein, and currently emeritus professor of social sciences and international relations at the University of New South Wales, Australia. With its claim that 'postmodernist theory is damaging the minds and intellects of good students' (Kitching, 2008: 15), *The Trouble with Theory* is, at best, a rant against the ideas discussed in literary studies, cultural studies and philosophy since post-Saussurian theories demonstrated that the relationship between language and reality can never be one of simple mirroring or imitation. Wittgenstein himself was acutely aware of 'the functions of words' being 'as diverse as the function of … objects' in a toolbox (Wittgenstein, 1953: 11). *The Trouble with Theory* systematically dismisses all attempts at problematising truth, reality and representation – indeed, the very idea of such an attempt. Worse, for a philosopher trained in the epistemological tradition, there is no account of what postmodernism and poststructuralism might mean. These two terms are used interchangeably as 'labels, or sledges to "criticize" and "close off" other serious issues in the academy'

(Marshall, 2009: 244). Now that we have established that a toolbox is not all that it is cracked up to be, let us finally address our question.

Why has the relationship between creative writing and Theory, like its relationship with the academy, been problematic for so long? And by 'so long', I mean since the inception of creative writing courses in English departments. In Australia, Paul Dawson contextualises this problematic relationship in his analysis of the 1990s literary studies crisis and explains creative writing's resistance to theory in terms of an artificial split between theory and practice, or professional writing and literary criticism, as a series of pedagogical responses to a longer-standing crisis in literary studies (Dawson, 2005: 161). But this relationship remains fraught to this day, despite the vigorous intellectual debate that it has spawned. The issue is now exacerbated by creative writing's need to redefine itself in the context of research and excellence in the academy.

It was in unlikely surroundings – in Prague – and in the unlikely company of colleagues from an interdisciplinary network, at the First Global Conference on Writing, that I was again struck by the enduring, persistent and pernicious nature of the whole argument. From the USA, author and academic Sigi Leonard (2011), for example, deplored that creative works are often considered to be in direct opposition to critical thinking. At the same time, UK-based literary theorist Joanne Metevier (2011) attributed the struggle of authorship in different writing contexts to a lack of engagement with theory, making a case for Lacanian psychoanalysis and discourse analysis. Meanwhile, focusing on composition classes in the USA, composition teacher Michele Ninacs (2011) lamented the fact that courses are often perceived to be 'skills-based service courses' and she advocated a critical pedagogical stance steeped in the theories of Freire, Giroux and the New London Group. It was that conference in Prague, 2011, which, unbeknownst to me, was to rekindle an old quarrel with Mike Harris, which had begun at the 13th annual conference of the Australasian Association of Writing Programs (AAWP) in 2008.

Harris (2009) exemplifies an anti-theory stance in creative writing circles which is still prevalent in some circles, particularly in the UK and the USA; and as Cassandra Atherton points out, it also typifies the 'inflammatory nature' of the debate, fuelled by 'emotive terms' (Atherton, 2010). While 'emotive terms' should not be ruled out on principle, the metaphors used to convey emotion also convey ideologies that may not be appropriate. Dismissing the broad gamut of literary theory on the grounds that writers may prefer 'that old recipe, the meat-and-two-veg of creative writing: one part realism, one part romance and one big dollop of neo-classical craft-based formalism' (Harris, 2009), Harris overlooks that some writers and readers may be vegetarian or vegan, either by necessity or by choice, which might dispose them to a diet of experimental fiction, non-representational poetry or fictocriticism, in which case 'cherry-picking from different theories' might not necessarily end up 'a dog's' dinner' (Harris, 2009), but prove to be a carefully planned menu ready for informed selection. To be fair, however, Harris does suggest one theoretical approach to creative writing, one that concerns itself with elucidating creativity, in particular Mihaly Csikszentmihayli's psychology of creativity (1997). As stated previously, in the Australian context this resistance is typically ascribed to some spurious dichotomy between theory and practice, itself an effect of the 1990s literary studies crisis (Dawson, 2005: 160–161) which has persisted in the ongoing and continuously restaged debate concerning whether creative writing needs to concern itself with theory in terms of both curriculum and pedagogy, as Nigel Krauth and Tess Brady provocatively asked in one of the first books to address the issue head on (Krauth & Brady, 2006). Indeed, the issue was pointed out in 1999, when Jeri Kroll declared creative writing and theory to be 'uneasy bedfellows' (Kroll, 1999). In universities the world over, the debate is now enlivened by the need to define what research by creative writing means in comparison and contrast with the so-called 'hard disciplines'. In some quarters, this debate is now increasing the divide between creative writing and literary studies, particularly in the UK, where it is perceived to be 'a contentious, [and] in many ways divisive, aspect of literary studies' (Royle, 2013). This complex argument is not likely to abate, particularly if the rise of creative writing courses is seen in conjunction with 'a quiet but deluded triumphalism', which 'affects the media and the publishing industry as well as the ethos of English in universities' (Royle, 2013).

However, it needs to be stressed that, for creative writing, theory remains a question more intimate and urgent than the above suggests, particularly for doctoral students, who often have to grapple with the question for more than three years in order to satisfy the requirements of the degree. No doubt like many other supervisors, I am faced with protest and resistance from PhD students and I have captured some of the sounds of their frustrations, exasperations, even profanations denoting sheer infuriation. Consider the following poem:

Theory

(For Mark Carthew)

To hell with Lacan and his linguisteries, **says** one
Next time I hear Barthes I'll puke, says the other

That makes bullfighting sound appealing
I'd rather take up ballroom dancing

And so they do – after a fashion

It's rhetoric in the eye and in the ear
with the expert conjugation of limbs
of fabulous form playing on the I
as guitar strings strum
and spangled jargon turns
to stunning sentences
with prepositional grace
and grand structure – all
in perfect rhyme and the present tense
they announce their favoured metaphors:
Paso Doble, Fox Trot
the Samba and Rhumba

they enhance their grammar
with fluid ornament. The mood

of this discourse is periphrastic and muscles up
into lyrics of glamorous freight

silken transitions resonate in the air

to meter and flair and love of words.

(Hecq, 2011b)

The poem, 'Theory', is dedicated to a former doctoral student who came to detest theory and who, like many others, made me reassess the importance of it. The sentiment expressed in the opening stanza of the poem would no doubt be familiar to many creative writing students and academics who have experienced or witnessed some crisis brought about by theory, especially French theory conveyed in poor translation (Atherton, 2010). For those of us who are teachers as well as practitioners, I think that such expressions of frustration, resistance or exasperation need to be taken seriously.

As the poem makes clear, the discomfort about theory extends to pedagogy and interpellates students, teachers and supervisors. The voice of the poem first expresses ambivalence, if only amused, towards the sentiments expounded against theory and theorists, but then adopts these to question the (main) speaker's own stance. Although the poem ends in jest, in some actual cases of supervision I have urged doctoral students to argue against the usefulness of theory, indeed against the usefulness of writing an exegesis. And we know now that there are confirmed divergences of opinion on that particular topic (Magee, 2012). More broadly, though, returning to our original question, Lauri Ramey points out that, in her experience:

> A common reaction to the idea of introducing critical theory in creative writing is 'It will take away my creativity' or 'If I know too much, I won't be able to write "naturally".' (Ramey, 2007: 47)

But Ramey rightly points out that this resistance is counterproductive and even 'detrimental' to the acquisition of 'new knowledge' (Ramey, 2007: 47). While this is true at both undergraduate and postgraduate levels, what is most concerning at postgraduate level is that dissertations which refuse to engage with theory often end up being 'navel-gazing exercise[s]' instead of 'considered reflection[s]' (Skrebels, 2007). In anticipation of my defence of theory in the next chapter, I take Paul Skrebels's point seriously that:

> the strategic application of theory, particularly in its explication of the notions of creativity and praxis, can turn the exegesis ... into a considered reflection by students (and their supervisors) on the social, historical and cultural circumstances of the writing process, and of the place and role of the writer within those contexts. (Skrebels, 2007)

But in this book the emphasis will be on one of Atherton's observations:

> Without an understanding of creativity and how to harness imaginative ways to express new ideas and theories, students may imitate rather than create theoretical texts and commentary. (Atherton, 2010)

Theories of creativity alone, though, are not sufficient: they often draw on psychology – a case in point is Csikszentmihalyi's *Creativity: Flow and the Psychology of Discovery and Invention* (1997) – and therefore often obfuscate the questions of *where* creativity comes *from*, and *why*, which touches on the reality of the unconscious. I will argue in the next chapter that in order to be useful to writers, theories of creativity need to be paired with other theoretical approaches, for example those informed by psychoanalysis, which enable a deeper understanding of praxis.[1]

Other arguments invoked by writers against theory include a distrust of the impact of 'fashion' on creative writing. Australian poet and academic Andrew Taylor has long maintained that creative writing should not be 'theoretically informed' (Taylor, 2006: 225), preferring instead to call himself 'old-fashioned' (Taylor, 2006: 227), which suggests that some older fashion was divorced from links to theory. This is a common sentiment among authors in Australia and elsewhere, even when these authors have but the most remote relationship with academia. In his work *A History of Books*, Gerald Murnane (2012), once an academic himself, writes:

> At some time during the 1970s, or it may have been earlier, the phrase *magical realism* became fashionable among the sorts of person who are paid to write comments on published works of fiction.... The persons seemed to believe that the authors mentioned had devised a new way of writing fiction. The authors themselves seemed mostly followers of fashion and ignorant. In their fiction, they reported things becoming other things or persons becoming other than persons as though such reports had not been included in works of fiction since so-called classical times. The phrase *magical realism* later fell out of fashion, and most of the works of fiction by the so-called magical realists seem nowadays forgotten. (Murnane, 2012: 3–4)

Murnane is here seemingly condemning fashion. But isn't he at bottom bemoaning the labelling and pigeonholing which comes with fashion? He himself had previously disclaimed an interest in theory and criticism (see Salusinszky, 1993: 93), while it is obvious from his well stocked bookshelves and many books of fiction that he has, at least during the heyday of Theory, immersed himself in many theories of writing (Genoni, 2009: 96). In one of his essays, he even refers to himself as the 'breathing author' (Murnane, 2005: 157), no doubt a foil to Wayne Booth's 'implied author' from *The Rhetoric of Fiction* (Booth, 1961), a work Murnane often evokes with praise, but also elusiveness (see e.g. Murnane, 2005: 85).

It is, of course, not uncommon for writers to pretend that they have no interest in theory. In his preface to *The Art of the Novel* (2002), the Czech novelist Milan Kundera, often singled out as a prime example of post-modernism, states: 'The world of theory is not my world: these are simply the reflections of a practitioner' (Kundera, 2002: iv). But is this genuine? The question did not fail to cross the mind of one PhD student who, in the first footnote to his doctoral thesis, writes:

This is a rather spurious claim on Kundera's part insofar as, to the present date, in his career he himself has published some four non-fiction works dealing with such matters; namely, *Testaments Betrayed* (1996), *The Art of the Novel* (2000), *The Curtain* (2005) and *Encounter* (2010). (Bos, 2014: 6)

While both Kundera and the PhD candidate dispute that creative writing and theory should be studied simultaneously, the candidate needs to be commended on having examined the antagonism between theory and practice and admitting that he (the candidate) has learned a great deal from theory and that this has made him a better writer.

More radically, perhaps, the arguments invoked against theory also include a scepticism about the usefulness of creative writing courses as deployed in universities. In a review of *A World of Other People* (2013), a novel by Steven Carroll (previously a winner of the Miles Franklin Literary Award) in which T.S. Eliot and his poetry figure prominently, author, critic and former academic Don Anderson has this to say:

> Anyone familiar with Eliot's critical prose as well as his poetry will note that Carroll has done his homework and that, in a manner of which Eliot would approve, has kept his research invisible, unlike some novels that emerge from university creative writing schools and all too publicly declare their indebtedness in supplementary essays and bibliographies. It seems at times as if universities cannot trust, or indeed believe in, the imagination. (Anderson, 2013: 20)

What these comments imply is not only that research should be 'invisible', but also that a commitment to questioning the so-called transparency of language, as do poststructuralist theories and postmodern approaches to writing, ought to be discouraged. It also reflects a lack of understanding of the creative process and the variations that occur in a creative work's relationship with theory.

Most of all, I think the resistance to theory from writers within the academy, and even more so from those outside, comes from fear: fear that it will stop them in their tracks as creative people – or, to repeat Ramey's expression quoted above, that 'it will take away [their] creativity' (Ramey, 2007: 47). Perhaps this is because, for some, writing is always a journey into unmapped territory, an event always about to happen, above all, an event about to be experienced, and also about to disappear, to be checked by conventional thought, policed by critics and either illuminated or obscured by theory.

Writing, the act of writing into the unknown specifically, may present itself not so much as a rational choice as a compelling urge. As such, it comprises no 'royal road' but rather many avenues, narrow paths and dead ends. With each word, what will be written or said next becomes determined, and perhaps arbitrarily controlled, by usage or tradition or rebellion against these. What the writer experiences is a jubilant recognition that he or she has been drawn into a territory made of words that resonate with some 'magical turning' propitious to the poetic articulation of new knowledge. Theory may be perceived as a stop sign before this magical turning, a barrier to this enjoyment that can happen only in a state of *rêverie*, somewhere *in-between* language in its spoken and unspoken manifestations, before it terminates in the words of death. But more of this in Chapter 8.

Theory's Legacy: Discursive Forays into Pedagogy and Canonicity

From an institutional point of view it may be that the antagonism between creative writing and theory boils down to what the sociologist Basil Bernstein called, with respect to the structures through which educational institutions shape ways of knowing, the three 'message systems' (Bernstein, 1977: 85), except that today it would have to be a four-message system, not three. If the curriculum defines what counts as knowledge, pedagogy what counts as valid demonstration that knowledge has been transmitted and assessment what counts as valid demonstration that the knowledge has been acquired, then, according to some, we now need to make sure that knowledge is not only transmitted and assessed, but also validated by financial gain or other 'esteem measures' (Australian Research Council, 2012). Like the market, these esteem measures are conservative. They certainly discourage any attempt to challenge the apparent transparency of language and representation.[2]

If we ignore the lessons of Theory and its proliferation into new theories, are we in danger of electing a new master? Are we unconsciously seeking one? By which I mean a market, or a tradition-driven canon for creative writing. Are we perhaps seeking, or condoning, a reinstitution of the Western canon? And if so, why would this not be desirable?

Some of the problems with any such hierarchies were pointed out as early as 1957 by Northrop Frye, when he observed that 'every deliberately constructed hierarchy of values in literature ... is based on a concealed social, moral or intellectual analogy' (Frye, 1957: 23). Frye also pointed out that this practice was already exemplified in the 19th century by the 'touchstone' theory of Matthew Arnold, 'where we proceed from the intuition of value represented by the touchstone [namely some passage deemed to embody literary excellence] to a system of ranking poets in classes' (Frye,

1957: 21), a matter later complicated by the politics of gender, class and race. In any case, Frye went on in hilarious satirical fashion:

> There is no question of accepting the whole of literature as the basis of study, but a tradition (or, of course, 'the tradition') is abstracted from it and attached to contemporary social values. The hesitant reader is invited to try the following exercise. Pick three big names at random, work out the eight possible combinations of promotion and demotion (on a simplified, or two-class, basis) and defend each in turn. Thus if the three names picked were Shakespeare, Milton and Shelley, the agenda would run:
>
> 1. Demoting Shelley, on the ground that he is immature in technique and profundity of thought compared to others.
> 2. Demoting Milton, on the ground that his religious obscurantism and heavy doctrinal content impair the spontaneity of his utterance.
> 3. Demoting Shakespeare, on the ground that his detachment from ideas makes his dramas a reflection of life rather than a creative attempt to improve it.
> 4. Promoting Shakespeare, on the ground that he preserves an integrity of poetic vision which in the others is obfuscated by didacticism.
> 5. Promoting Milton, on the ground that his penetration of the highest mysteries of faith raises him above Shakespeare's unvarying worldliness and Shelley's callowness.
> 6. Promoting Shelley, on the ground that his love of freedom speaks to the heart of modern man more immediately than poets who accept outworn social or religious values.
> 7. Promoting all three (for this, a special style, which we may call the peroration style, should be used).
> 8. Demoting all three, on the ground of the untidiness of English genius when examined by French or Classical or Chinese standards.
>
> (Frye, 1957: 21–22)

If notions about canonicity and tradition seem somewhat remote from the antagonism between creative writing and theory, these are nevertheless at the core of what knowledge means. The very concept of 'canon' implies conformity and compliance with some authority. It is difficult to see how such a conservative model is conducive to creativity. Besides, the existence of a canon presupposes a model of knowledge as consumption, not production. Nearly 50 years ago, the Brasilian pedagogue Paulo Freire, whose insistence on the political character of education led him to draw a sharp distinction between two models of teaching and learning, in terms of their political implications, criticised what he called 'the banking concept of education' (Freire, 1970: 46). By this he meant the notion that a student is a kind of container into which knowledge is to be placed by the teacher. In this view, the process of education is a kind of depositing, and the only criterion of its success is the efficiency with which knowledge is deposited and the security with which it is stored. Of particular importance for Freire were the implications of this model for the relationship between learner and teacher. As he put it: 'The teacher teaches and the students are taught. The teacher knows everything and the students know nothing. The teacher thinks and the students listen – meekly' (Freire, 1970: 46). His list goes on, but this is enough to show its general tendency: Freire is describing a situation in which the learning of one person is wholly under the control of another person. The teacher decodes what is to be learned, determines the mode of instruction and assesses the outcome. The student, or rather the successful student, can only submit to this authority. Freire sums up:

> It is not surprising that the banking concept of education regards men [*sic*] as adaptable, manageable beings. The more students work at storing the deposits entrusted to them, the less they develop the critical consciousness which would result from their intervention in the world as transformers of the world. The more completely they accept the passive role imposed on them, the more they tend simply to adapt to the world as it is and to the fragmented view of reality deposited in them. (Freire, 1970: 47)

The consequences of the banking concept come through clearly; these are psychological, social and political. In his conclusion, Freire stresses that the same problem can be found in other areas of social life. The point he wants to make is that a tendency to conservatism has a certain basis in the concepts in terms of which people understand themselves and their world.

Interestingly, it is philosophy which enables Freire to rebuke the banking concept of education. He uses Jean-Paul Sartre's concept of intentionality to do so: 'The objects which surround me are simply accessible to my consciousness, not located within it. I am aware of them, but they are not inside me' (Freire, 1970: 49). Both Shoshana Felman (Felman, 1982) and Mark Bracher (Bracher, 2006) approach a critique of education along the same lines as Freire, but these authors rebut the 'banking' model by using Lacan's theory of the four discourses and his critique of the university discourse in particular (Lacan, 2007 [1969–70). They show how the university discourse partakes of the master's discourse, and Bracher suggests ways of countering the oppressive consequences of this discourse in composition classes. We will see in the next chapter how these theoretical critiques can be applied to the practice of creative writing.

Out of this rather eclectic, if not roundabout approach, I will say that notions about representation, canonicity and tradition concern not only the pedagogy of creative writing but also the definition of our discipline, the methods we use to investigate it and the vocabularies we use to review it. This is something worth pondering, as French philosopher Jacques Rancière recently made clear in the broader realm of aesthetics. In his book *Aisthesis* (2013), he shows how a regime of artistic perception and interpretation was constituted and transformed by erasing the specificities of the different arts, as well as the borders that separated them from experience. Further, notions about canonicity and tradition have serious implications for how research and excellence are understood and for how creative works are received in the larger culture.

What Was the Question?

In the context of poetics, the real question, however, is to ascertain how useful an overview of theory is to writers, especially as the conditions that produced the heyday of 'high theory' have waned. If Derrida told us that reading – in the sense of a univocal meaning – is impossible, it is in part because the drives towards life and death are more complex than we may have supposed. For if deconstruction pronounced the death sentence of philosophy and poststructuralism the death of Theory, the step beyond can only be a 'working otherwise' (Derrida, 1978: 83) in which we have 'participation without belonging – a taking part in without being part of, without having membership in a set' (Derrida, 1980: 206). It would seem that, at this point in time, creative writing ought to concern itself with the remains of theory, paying particular attention to the excesses of signification that mark the remainder in and of texts sometimes audible only in their echoes.

In the 21st century, theory is indeed multifarious, yet it is not always obvious how deep-rooted it can be. Moreover, it often has a thematic or political focus on matters of identity, ethnicity, transculturation, globalisation and, increasingly, sustainability, in both its political and its ethical dimensions. Of course, this does not mean that creative writers should not be exposed to theory, with or without a capital letter. But as we shall see, mere exposure is inadequate. For a body of knowledge to be useful, arts practitioners need to engage with it at a deeper level. An ideal model for creative writing would be based on a dialectic between practice and theory that would engage writers at an unconscious level, but also make them actively conscious of this dialectic integration. This means that we are talking about a false dialectic, as it really entails a third term, and therefore a process of triangulation. This requires reflexivity, itself calling for a reassessment of subjectivity, praxis, creative process and creative writing research.

The World, Theory and Creative Writing

The notion of universal man has received extensive critiques, from Freud's discovery of the unconscious to the moment of Theory and beyond. We therefore cannot invoke this concept quite as easily as writers in previous eras (Eagleton, 2008, 2012). As we know, the concept of a transcendent unified subject as the origin of meaning dates back to Descartes's *cogito*, a point made by countless commentators, and the Enlightenment. In the last three decades, philosophers who predicted the death of Theory, such as Jean-François Lyotard, have defined the episteme of the postmodern as involving incredulity towards 'grand narratives' or meta-narratives (Lyotard, 1984). This follows in the wake of Jacques Derrida's analyses of Western metaphysics as based on a metaphysics of presence and a logocentrism in which writing is valued over speech (Norris, 1982). As we will see in the next chapter, this point was in fact made even earlier, by Lacan, to be precise in 1966 (see Lacan, 2006: 9). But here is what Foucault said, more generally, that same year, in *Les mots et les choses* (*The Order of Things*):

> Man is a recent invention, a figure not yet two centuries old, a simple wrinkle in our knowledge, and he will disappear before he has found a new form. (Foucault, 1966: 15, my translation)

For Foucault, the curious project of knowing man was born in the epistemological soil of the end of the Enlightenment. It is at that time that the human sciences such as psychology and sociology were established. For Foucault, the object of the human sciences is not man himself, but the representation that man gives of himself. However, since the discovery of the unconscious, the representation that man gives of himself must be considered a deception. For Freud, the very existence of the unconscious entails that conscious life must be nothing else than a conceit, an exercise in dissimulation – yet without being able to recognise itself as such.

Foucault concludes that the human sciences are not even false sciences: they are not sciences at all. Western culture, he says, 'has constructed, under the name of man, a being who ... must be a positive field of knowledge and who cannot be an object of science' (Foucault, 1966: 378, my translation). Against the human sciences, Foucault opposes what he refers to as the 'counter-sciences': the psychoanalysis of Lacan, to whom Foucault alludes but whom he does not name, and the ethnology of Lévi-Strauss, for their having in common the use of structural linguistics. 'We can say of both', remarks Foucault, 'that which Lévi-Strauss said of ethnology: they dissolve man' (Foucault, 1966: 390–391, my translation). In the place of man, Foucault proposes the notion of the subject – the subject not as the fundamental and original form, but the subject formed by a number of processes, not of the order of subjectivity as such, but of an order more difficult to name and make appear, more fundamental and original than the subject itself, the subject who has a genesis.

The proliferation of theories of representation and subjectivity spawned by 'high theory' have made visible centrist preoccupations in dominant ways of thinking. The corollary is that it has exposed those elements that had hitherto been excluded, or on the margins – the conditions which make dominant patterns of thought possible. While Marxism's critiques of class contributed to a radical rethinking of Western philosophy, feminism's analyses and deconstructions of patriarchy were among the first critiques to take advantage of the 'linguistic turn' in philosophy. In Genevieve Lloyd's work, for example, the concept of reason revealed itself to be predicated upon a masculinist model (Lloyd, 1984). The analysis of 'white' dominance by writers, critics and theorists involved in 'black studies' (Dyer, 1988) was a further example of such critiques. In Australia, analyses of the marginalisation of indigenous and non-Anglo-Celtic Australians have also benefited from this turn in philosophy. *The Empire Writes Back* (Ashcroft *et al.*, 1989) is considered the germinal study in what has become known as post-colonial theory. One of Lyotard's meta-narratives concerns the apparently paradoxical notion of the universal history of Western civilisation (Lyotard, 1984). This supposed universal account, which is of course quite culturally specific, has provided the model for a variety of narratives of national culture, including our own personal ones. Paradoxically, once again, certain specific national cultures, such as the USA, the UK and France, have been seen traditionally as being emblematic of Western civilisation. It is thus not surprising that they are all still regarded as colonial powers and that one of the most productive areas of critical and theoretical analysis in the last three decades has been the examination of the links between various transnational projects and their starting points. A shift in discourse on local issues brought about by the third phase of globalisation (Wolton, 2009) has resulted more recently in an increase in studies of ethnicity and ethnography, including the popular area of auto-ethnography.

It turns out that the fictions or narratives with which we make sense of the world are subject to all the contradictory codes inherent in textuality (Said, 1979). Not that there is no reality outside textuality, as we saw in the previous chapter, but all our perceptions come via textuality and therefore representation. A plethora of answers have been provided by Edward Said, Homi Bhabha and Gayatri Spivak, whose work, as well as that of their followers and detractors, reaches back to the mid-1960s and the contested notion of universal man. The question of representing alterity has indeed dominated the fields of poststructuralist and postmodernist thought, particularly in its relationship to political agendas, yet it should be noted that although there are points of contact between postmodernism and postcolonialism, the two should not be conflated.

Notes

(1) I am aware that psychology and psychoanalysis do not *necessarily* draw on different models of subjectivity. But my point is that we need to distinguish between theories that describe behaviour and those that seek to understand it beyond behavioural patterns and conscious motivations.

(2) If separating creative writing from Theory produces a spurious dichotomy, so does the resultant separation between the creative and academic components of creative writing within the university discourse. These two dichotomies have nevertheless dominated the academic environment, where employment, government funding, promotion, enrolments and many other factors have revolved around the notions of research value and quality as these are evaluated in a metrics-dominated system. The question of how to measure and rank academic and creative output has immediate consequences for the arts, creative arts and humanities, as has been reviewed by Gerry Turcotte and Robyn Morris (Turcotte & Morris, 2012). These authors rightly point out that 'research measurement exercises' are global (Turcotte & Morris, 2012: 66). They point out that Australia, for example, mirrored trends in the UK when it trialled the Excellence in Research Australia (ERA) scheme in 2009, with a full roll-out across all university clusters/disciplines in 2010. In fact, in the UK, the Research Assessment Exercise (RAE) was replaced by the Research Excellence Framework (REF). Hong Kong has its own RAE and New Zealand has a Performance-Based Research Fund (PBRF). In the Francophone world, France leads the way with an equivalent of the British model, which is overseen by the Agence d'Évaluation de la Recherche et de l'Enseignement Supérieur (AERES) and affiliated to the H-Index. At the time of writing, Belgium and Quebec are lagging behind, dealing as they are with more pressing political questions, some predicated on long-term linguistic problems. In any case, this trend towards metric assessment of research quality has fed into the global university context of the past two decades, whereby universities and associated funding bodies have undergone extensive restructuring, along with an extensive re-evaluation of what constitutes intellectual or scholarly practice. Questions as to how to undertake and how to evaluate the products of creative practice as research have figured prominently: many universities now offer doctorates in practice-led research and many researchers incorporate a considerable amount of creative work into their research. Although this remains a contested field of research, it need not be so.

4 Craft, Knowledge, Theory and the Designing of Poetics

Creative writers are valuable allies and their evidence is to be prized highly, for they are apt to know a whole host of things between heaven and earth of which our philosophy has not yet let us dream.
Sigmund Freud

... there is no discipline, no structure of knowledge, no institution or epistemology that can or has ever stood free of the various sociocultural, historical, and political formations that give epochs their peculiar individuality.
Edward Said

This chapter reconsiders the significance of theory for creative writing studies in the wake of the death of Theory. It revives the debate about the perceived incompatibility of these two fields of investigation and reinvigorates this debate in the contemporary global climate. In particular, it urges writers to reconsider their understanding of the usefulness of theory to practice and argues for a plurality of theories that enable a deeper understanding of subjectivity, creativity and knowledge production, as well as of their ideological underpinnings. It examines what I call theories 'without credentials', with a particular focus on psychoanalysis. It proposes a case for a 'designer theory' which disrupts our certainties rather than consolidates them, by suggesting how a psychoanalytically informed approach can enrich other theories. It singles out postcolonial theory as an exemplar because although the discourses these two theories espouse seem to respond to different ideologies, they do in fact share philosophical antecedents and discursive affinities; both being counter-discourses, they share an awareness that language shapes human beings, cultures and societies. As will become clear, the constellation of discourses embedded in postcolonial theory have points of contact with 'theories without credentials' through their engagement with 'otherness'.

While a psychoanalytic understanding of subjectivity enables writers to gain insights into their own creative processes, an alertness to the ideological positions of postcolonial theory enables writers to become aware of the insidious influences at work in their own socialising processes. Both psychoanalysis and postcolonialism owe a debt to the work of Swiss linguist Ferdinand de Saussure and the critique of representation associated with the 'linguistic turn'. Since the publication of *The Empire Writes Back* (Ashcroft *et al.*, 1989), postcolonial theories have incorporated concepts from linguistics, psychoanalysis, Marxism and feminism that are still useful for unpacking the poetics and politics of representation.[1] This is particularly obvious from postcolonialism's ongoing problematisation of the 'other', itself brought about by existentialism[2] and philosophy's critique of modernity. This is worth pondering, as it signals why we need to continue utilising theoretical tools to scrutinise our own psychological motivations and socialising processes in order to recognise and accept at a deeper level the fact of difference.

The Art and Science of Craft, or Why Creative Writing Needs Theory

Arguments against the use of theory often hinge on the claim that creative writing is a *craft* and therefore does not need to bother with theory. However, if we take a closer look at the etymological meaning of 'craft' we are in for a few exciting surprises. Granted that creative writing is a *craft*, it encompasses notions of 'skill', 'art' and 'occupation', but also the now obsolete meanings of craft as 'artifice' and 'device' (Brown, 1993: 539). This provides a point of entry into the problem of representation and opens up areas for investigating the place of subjectivity in the creative process.

Possibly taking his cue from the sentiment expressed by Freud in the epigraph to this chapter, Jonah Lehrer's project *Proust Was a Neuroscientist* demonstrates that art, and creative writing in particular, often precedes science, especially in relation to knowledge about the life of the mind (Lehrer, 2007). Nicholas Zurbrugg makes a similar argument in *Art, Performance, Media* (Zurbrugg, 2004), where he documents innovative ideas that emerged first in artworks and only later came to be validated as scholarly or scientific work. Such ideas are increasingly, though timidly, finding acceptance within national research frameworks. In the UK, for example, the Research Assessment Exercise (RAE) recognises creative outputs as research, as do the New Zealand Performance-Based Research Fund (PBRF), the RAE in Hong Kong and the Excellence in Research for Australia (ERA). These frameworks are still evolving and the challenge for all these initiatives will be to demonstrate how creative practice functions as a mode of knowledge and a valid source of knowledge production. Theory in such instances is often called upon to legitimise practice in the guise of methodology, knowledge transfer or performance.

Across continents and disciplines, scholars who are also creative arts practitioners have recently turned again to theory in order to explore the epistemological and practical frameworks involved in deploying creative practice as a form of research. In the UK, Carole Gray (1996), Graeme Sullivan (2005), and Michael Biggs and Daniela Büchler (2007) have paved the way by drawing on theories of aesthetics; in Australia, Estelle Barrett and Barbara Bolt (2007), Paul Magee (2008, 2009), Kevin Brophy (2009), Jen Webb (2008, 2009) and others have been actively engaged in reconceptualising aspects of theory from the vantage point of practice. These authors have sought inspiration from 'theories without credentials', such as psychoanalysis, philosophy and social theory, to analyse aspects of practice-led research, including its very definition and relevance. As intimated in the previous chapter, there is also a renewed interest in theory from pedagogical circles in the UK and the USA (see Donnelly, 2012). In Australia, Joshua Lobb has been engaged with reconciling theory and pedagogy since 2008 and is now conducting a major international review of the field across universities (Lobb, 2008, 2012). On reflection, it is ironic to think of such tremendous research activity from a national angle, for scholars from different countries are increasingly working together. Harper and Kroll come to mind (Harper & Kroll, 2008; Kroll & Harper, 2013), as do Biggs, Brophy, Magee and Webb – the latter are currently working on a project funded by the Australian Research Council, 'Understanding Creative Excellence' (Webb *et al.*, 2013–15).

This renewed interest in theory is currently producing exciting work in the wider field of practice-based research. Creative writing, however, still needs 'to answer the critique of authorship and of the category of literature offered by Theory, rather than simply rejecting this critique as unhelpful or deleterious to literary culture' (Dawson, 2005: 161), for writing presupposes 'an active engagement with knowledge producing creative results that embody levels of understanding and communication' (Harper & Kroll, 2008: 4). As such, it needs to be documented, articulated and theorised, as Harper, Kroll, Hunt, Sampson, Wandor and Donnelly have been doing with regard to the larger field, and Brophy, Magee and Webb with regard to poetry. In doing so, they are reminding us of arguments previously put forth in books such as *Creative Writing: Theory Beyond Practice* (Krauth & Brady, 2006), *Creative Writing Studies: Practice, Research and Pedagogy* (Harper & Kroll, 2008) and, more recently, *Research Methods in Creative Writing* (Kroll & Harper, 2013). Clearly, creative writing not only needs to engage in the 'theory debate' in terms of both curriculum and pedagogy, but also of poetics.

It may well be that in the twofold paradigm of practice-led research (Smith & Dean, 2009: 6) the emphasis is on data creation and analysis rather than data collection and analysis. Here, indeed, research and practice are reciprocal (Haseman, 2006: 104). However, one of the key differences between creative writing and other fields of inquiry is the emphasis it places on process (Nelson, 2008). Another key difference is the emphasis on 'the self-in-process' (Hunt & Sampson, 2006a: 17), or what I have called less elegantly the *processor* (Hecq, 2013a: 75). Before going any further, we need to redefine the object of creative writing inquiry as twofold: it entails the creative process *and* the subject in the process of writing. Even writers who resist poststructuralist theories recognise that the process includes 'activities such as thinking, researching, planning, writing drafts, consciously revising, consciously manipulating the unconscious and being unconsciously driven by it' (Harris, 2009). What specifically interests me regarding this process are the questions of how one accesses the unconscious, how one 'consciously' manipulates it and how one transforms the outcome of this process into aesthetic forms. In order to answer these questions, we must first take into account the reality of the unconscious. As we shall see, it is at this point that psychoanalysis becomes useful in terms of the insights it provides into the workings of both subject and world, because the process of critically composing a text cannot be completed without a simultaneous critical assessment of the self in relation to the larger world. But let us first gauge where psychoanalysis fits within the broader field of theory.

Theory for Creative Writing

From my own experience of grappling with theories, the most useful ones to writers are those grounded in poststructuralist theories of language, including those which draw on psychoanalytic theories in order to enhance understandings of creativity or to honour 'the other', as is the case with post-colonial theories and some strands of feminism. While theorists like Terry Eagleton now reject such positions, their value for creative writing research is that they are self-reflexive (Eagleton, 2012). Theoretical concepts grounded in poststructuralist theories of language are by definition self-reflexive and hence enable writers to reflect upon their ideas about subjectivity, identity, the creative process and communication, as well as further to develop their craft or articulate their own poetics. Theories that highlight 'otherworldly views' in turn draw attention to a writer's ideological positioning and social conditioning. Thus, while theories grounded in poststructuralist theories of language do alert us to the fact that writing is a *making* – a construction using language, imagery, sound, silence and rhythm created by a subject who is also a complex construction – an alertness to ideological positions enables writers to become aware of the underlying influences of their own socialising processes. This awareness in turn will allow writers in the academy to examine the concept of knowledge production as it relates to their creative praxis within the discourse of the university.

This stated, perhaps we need to think more broadly about the meaning of theory and refuse to equate one theory, or set of theories, with the act of theorising itself. Theory is not only 'a systematic statement of rules or principles to be followed' (Brown, 1993: 3274), it also signifies a mode of thought that stems from the particular and reaches out to the generalisable while transferring knowledge from the known to the unknown, or vice versa.

However, for creative writers, there is a difference between theory that *triggers* or produces creative work and theory that *informs* creative work. In certain contexts, theory can inspire a creative process that takes form in a painting, a sculpture, a building, a ballet or a simple melody; but that is not the same thing as utilising theoretical constructs in creative work in a way that allows for the possibility of producing new knowledge.

In order to inform the creative work and produce new knowledge, theory needs to resonate with the emotions as well as the intellect. In other words, theory needs to 'hook up' with something in the unconscious through the researcher's or creative writer's immersion in theory.

All readers construct meaning out of their own conscious and unconscious interests. As readers of theory, we bring to it not only our own understanding but also our unconscious experience, which inevitably shapes and determines how we interpret and in turn make use of it. It seems to follow that theoretical constructs that are grounded in theories of language – including, in some countries, postcolonial theory, which draws heavily on the work of de Saussure and Lacan – would be appealing to creative writers. However, although we are all subject to our own unconscious agendas, it is important to recognise and understand that creative writers read, think and research differently. One key difference between theorists and creative writers is indeed the status of affect and the body, and therefore of the unconscious, in relation to thought. One example is that creative writers immersed in active reading are always on the lookout for writing material, even though they may not be aware of this. Reading crystallises elements around a question, an obsession or an affect (a mood, or pre-emotion) – all of which produce effects for both reader and proto-writer.

Research itself proceeds from this crystallisation, as thoughts are organised more consciously according to what I have called a methodology of 'active consciousness' (Hecq, 2013a: 175), whereby new knowledge emerges in three steps: inductive, deductive and retroactive. It could be said that new knowledge is hence produced out of step from a dialectical process between consciousness and the unconscious. This new knowledge may concern concepts and how these evolve by accretion or hybridisation, for example. It may also be centred on poetics and issues of style and composition (Magee, 2009). Or it may focus exclusively on meanings of language and subjectivity, on the *making* of language and subjectivity, or on the ideologies which underpin such making.

Psychoanalysis: Why is it Relevant to Creative Writing?

Psychoanalysis developed in the 20th century as one of the major explanatory frameworks for human mental development and functioning. Founded by Sigmund Freud (1856–1939), it has been extraordinarily influential in many fields of human endeavour. Emerging from the neurological institutes of the 19th century, psychoanalysis soon influenced medicine, psychology, philosophy, literature, politics and the arts – indeed, all practices that integrally involve human subjectivity. Today, after more than 100 years since Freud's discovery, there are numerous rival psychoanalytical orientations, all with their own theoretical frameworks, emphases and vocabularies. Nevertheless, there is one concept that they all share: the concept of the unconscious. In the following chapters we will encounter different definitions of this unconscious and the differing ways in which the concept may be of use to writers.

Psychoanalysis is a psychological and psychotherapeutic theory building knowledge in a dynamic way through a continuous connection to the insights drawn from clinical experience and therapeutic work. As such, it is a continuous process. Therefore, what is called 'psychoanalytic theory' is work in progress radically different from both Theory and other theories because it makes the unconscious its organising concept. The unconscious, however, is largely inaccessible to us. We can only catch glimpses of it in dreams, slips of the tongue or pen, in jokes and in symptoms. To a certain extent, though, we can also access it through self-examination or reflection on process. For Freud himself, the way to the discovery of the unconscious had been shown by writers, especially Sophocles and Shakespeare and poets of the late 18th and early 19th centuries. Had not Freud seen Sophocles' *Oedipus Rex* in 1899, the way we think about human sexuality may have been radically different, even if the French psychoanalyst Jacques Lacan later called the Oedipus complex 'Freud's dream' (Lacan, 2007 [1969–70]: 117). Freud was also inspired by poets such as Friedrich Hölderlin and William Wordsworth, who wrote about the long-lasting effects of childhood experiences on adulthood, and showed how these experiences continued to determine adult modes of behaviour and thought despite most people being unaware of their persistence. Indeed, it is this fundamental lack of awareness – an unconsciousness about oneself – that Freud turned into what he himself considered a scientific theory of the human mind. He achieved this not by holding up a mirror to what could be seen, but by listening to the distant echoes of the human heart.

Freud showed that the unconscious, despite being inaccessible to consciousness, has its own laws, and that these affect everyday behaviour in all sorts of ways, from the most irrelevant slip of the tongue, forgetting of names or things, bungled actions and dreams to mental breakdowns. What was shocking at the time was not so much that Freud thought that the origins of all such phenomena were unconscious, but sexually driven. Freud observes:

> Two of the hypotheses of psycho-analysis are an insult to the entire world and have earned its dislike. One of them offends against an intellectual prejudice, the other against an aesthetic and moral one. (Freud, 2001 [1916–17]: 21)

The first of these hypotheses is that most mental processes are unconscious; the second is that sexual drives, as these are encoded in language, play a determining part in the psyche, including its creative propensities and psychological disturbances.

For Freud, it is the very 'insult' that psychoanalytic propositions offer to the everyday, conscious modes of belief that highlights intrapsychic conflict and so contributes to the symptoms of creative and physical states that might manifest as mental illness.[3] For unconscious wishes are often precisely what cannot be admitted to consciousness, as they are too strange, obscene or disturbing. Yet, because these wishes are founded in infantile experiences and biological drives, they cannot be dismissed. It is how these experiences continue to live in our psyche that psychoanalysis attempts to uncover. Creative writing has tapped into this vein of investigation as it probes into the enigma of creativity, an enigma that Freud, his followers and detractors have been keen to solve.

The work of artists and creative writers holds a prominent position for the articulation of psychoanalytic discourse. Jacques Lacan indeed remarked that, for Freud, 'the artist always precedes him, ... he does not have to play the psychologist where the artist paves the way for him' (Lacan, 1986 [1964]: 192–193). Lacan was to follow Freud in this regard. His Écrits and his seminars are replete with literary quotations and the centrality of literature to the corpus of his writings has been noted (Marty, 2005: 11). Poetry held a particular place for him. He even called himself a poem, and what is more, 'a poem that is being written' (Lacan, 1986 [1964]: viii). In fact, Lacan's later teaching scandalously identifies psychoanalysis with poetry, namely, to a game whose meaning is always doubled by the signifier: literal meaning and figurative meaning, lexical meaning and contextual meaning are what poetry exploits in order to wreak violence on language. What the later Lacan exploits, from 1970 onwards, is language's excess, the part of language that 'escapes the linguist's attention' (Lecercle, 1990: 5) as well as the philologist's attention, because this extreme dimension of language hinges on what Lacan calls the real, namely, that which is beyond representation, by way of the letter. But more of this later in the book.

Psychoanalysis, History, Politics

Although psychoanalytic theory provides the basis for the therapeutic practice of psychoanalysis out of which it emerged, it also provides a structural theory for the construction of subjectivity. As such, it is a theory that shakes up our certainties about what theory is, and disrupts our preconceptions about what the self is. In doing so, it opens up 'designer' possibilities that can be theorised. By focusing on unconscious processes, psychoanalytic theory has made it possible to analyse both the unconscious and the conscious meanings which contribute to the complexity of our identities and the world in which we live, as well as to the question of the very meaning and status of consciousness and language. Lacan's conceptualisation of the unconscious as the driving force of language is particularly relevant to writers, as it demonstrates that language has an integral role in the construction of consciousness and culture. Further, in explaining the unconscious construction of ideology, Lacan shows that language, and therefore discourse, can no longer be seen as transparent, neutral or objective (Lacan, 2007 [1969–70]), which means that, in a psychoanalytic light, neither culture nor society, and not even history, can be seen in apolitical terms. This was, in fact, the driving force of Lacan's seminar XVII, 'The other side of psychoanalysis' (Lacan, 2007 [1969–70]), where he showed not only how discourse governs the laws of politics and history, but also the foundations of psychoanalysis itself. It is in this seminar that he dismissed his own Law of the Father after repudiating Freud's concept of the Oedipus complex as a mere 'dream'

(Lacan, 2007 [1969–70]: 117). Indeed, in this seminar Lacan concerns himself with 'the place of politics in psychoanalysis' and, hence, with 'the (im)possible power of psychoanalysis itself' (Hecq, 2006b: 216).

As a paradigm, psychoanalysis is conducive to an alliance between theory and creative writing, for here 'information and imaginative writing are different forms of knowledge, demanding different skills and wholly different attitudes to language' (Alvarez, 2005: 15). Indeed, for many creative writers, the text is itself a research statement and the knowledge it gestures towards is often beyond words.[4] This knowledge is in fact intimately related to the truth of the subject, namely the truth of the subject's relation to the world as mediated through language. To be useful, theory should enable creative writers to articulate this previously unknowable knowledge. It should also enable them to deviate from what might be called a familiar poetics in order to approach new forms of knowledge, or new ways of knowing the world. In order to achieve this, however, they need to be taught a relation to language that empowers them.

Again, this is tackled from a pragmatic point of view here as elsewhere, when I contest the university discourse for endorsing hierarchies and power structures designed to maintain the position of the intellectual as socially superior and as a result relegating those in our classrooms to the position of student instead of learner, writer or scholar. For significant empowerment of students to occur, teachers need to relinquish the position of master. As Felman puts this:

> Psychoanalysis as teaching, and teaching as psychoanalysis, radically subvert the demarcation-line, the clear-cut opposition between the analyst and the analysand, between the teacher and the student (or the learner) – showing that what counts, in both cases, is precisely the transition, the struggle-filled passage from one position to the other. (Felman, 1982: 38)

From out of my own experience grappling with theory and pedagogy has emerged a form of knowledge which I have called 'interactive narrative pedagogy' (Hecq, 2009a). This type of pedagogy hinges on the importance of transference as an automatic response in all human relationships. Here the focus is on a complicated series of relationships, however: those between student and teacher, student and work, and student and teacher and institution. Both teachers and students are encouraged to develop self-awareness by reflecting upon their master signifiers and the relationship they entertain with their own work (Hecq, 2013a: 185). This philosophy discards Freudian models of a simply repressed subjectivity in favour of the

Lacanian subject, to allow for an examination of multiple aspects of subjectivity (symbolic, imaginary, real) – all of which struggle for expression in
any extended discourse.[5]

It is, however, relevant to creative writing as a self-reflexive practice
(Hunt & Sampson, 2006a). The knowledge produced by way of such
practice in the act of journaling, for example, concerns investments in the
symbolic dimension of language. This self-reflection in turn promotes what
I have called a 'methodology of active consciousness' (Hecq, 2013a: 181),
which, following Freud, means the process of bringing to consciousness
what previously lay beneath its surface, namely something pre-conscious
or unconscious (Freud, 2001 [1914–16]: 166–167). The term 'methodology
of active consciousness' highlights the active participation in the reflexive
method of inquiry, which is particular to creative writing research, at least
for those of us who describe ourselves as 'explorers' rather than 'planners'.
The 'explorers' overtly use a 'problem finding style' (Lamott, 1994: 22),
which means that they do not know what they are doing until they have
done it. They start a work with only a question mark, an image, a phrase
or even a mere rhythm rather than a plan, and the work emerges from the
improvisational act of writing and revising – or not. I use the term 'overtly',
because the so-called 'planners' often diverge from their plan as they write
and solve problems. What is common to all writers, though, is that 'there
is never a single insight; instead, there are hundreds and thousands of small
mini-insights' (Sawyer, 2009: 176), which happen mostly unconsciously.
However, 'the real work starts when many mini insights are analysed,
reworked, and connected to each other' consciously (Sawyer, 2009: 176).
This happens when we are by choice immersed in, rather than merely
exposed to, theory, and then are encouraged or decide to analyse our own
processes. This is obviously relevant to the way we articulate our own
poetics. I therefore reproduce here questions that may not only enhance
a pedagogy of creative writing, but also enrich the concept of poetics as it
informs practice:

- What are the formative elements of my systems of knowledge and
  belief? What is the impact of such identity on my life and work?
- What are my master signifiers – my ideals and values? Where do these
  come from?
- What is my scenario of ultimate fulfilment?
- What conflicts do I identify in myself? In my work? How is language
  responsible for these? What causes 'writing block'?
- Why do I write?

Othering Theoretical Paradigms

Before we examine further what psychoanalysis of diverse orientations can teach us about subjectivity and writing, taking us deeper into solipsistic terrain, perhaps, let us look briefly at the world and consider the compatibility of 'theories without credentials' with established theories. I would like to select postcolonial theory,[6] a theory drawn from linguistics, psychoanalysis, Marxism and feminism, characterised by resistance, activism and future thinking (Ashcroft, 2001) as a case study: firstly because of its historical and ideological affinities with psychoanalysis, that is, as a counter-discourse; secondly because its conceptual tools can be adapted to other social contexts and methodological frameworks; and thirdly because in postcolonial countries theory can have a practical – and political – impact. In Australia, Marcelle Freiman has advocated an alliance between creative writing and postcolonial theory (Freiman, 2001), including what she calls a 'postcolonial creativity' (Freiman, 2006).

Since the death of Theory announced in the previous chapter, the question of a common cultural literacy for the Anglophone world has joined the list of obituaries in the USA, the UK, Hong Kong, Singapore and Australia. American English has become the language of the advanced capitalist world, and those in this market economy who are involved in teaching, writing, publishing or buying books in English may have wavered between favouring differently accented versions of the language before finally settling on their own spellcheck-imposed brand. Compounding this contraction in culturally diverse influences on literacy is the issue of terminological absolutism found in French-accented 'Theory'. It is in Prague again, but this time at the Joseph Svorecky Academy, that I became painfully aware of yet another theoretical issue. It was uncanny, to say the least, that it should be in 2011, on a freezing Prague morning, that I should be reminded of that which the Indian-born critic Gayatri Spivak had warned us against in 1987, when she denounced Foucault's 'too simple notion of repression', which 'fills the empty place of the agent with the historical sun of theory, the Subject of [Western] Europe' (Spivak, 1999: 254).

As writers, perhaps we ought to become critical composers of texts, selves and worlds. Perhaps we ought, then, to ask again why and when certain cultures are given a universalist status and to what extent we can make room for competing cultures within a particular national context. In other words, perhaps we ought to ask how we can represent otherness without appropriating otherness, by addressing our own anxieties as predicated upon our relationship with language. To a certain extent, this is the common project of both psychoanalysis and postcolonialism. Postcolonial theory developed in response to the flourishing literatures written by colonised peoples in colonial languages and soared by dint of its self-reflexivity. Today, Gantam Basu Thakur suggests that the 'colonial anxiety' felt in postcolonial countries is in fact an 'epiphenomenon of colonial discourse' (Basu Thakur, 2013: 241), itself a product of what Lacan called 'the master's discourse' (Lacan, 2007 [1969–70]: 20). Perhaps it is time to return postcolonialism to its theoretical roots and extend its practice.

Towards a Poetics of Empathy?

The 20th century's emancipatory movements have been characterised by their frequent references to the 'other', whether this be men's relations to men or to women, or blacks to whites, or Hispanic to white, or people of Middle Eastern appearance to whites. Nowhere is this more obvious than in a country like Australia.[7] What is noticeable is that this oft-invoked 'other' usually occupies a subjugated position. Often those intellectual endeavours which purport to analyse and deconstruct such relations are themselves predicated on the maintenance of these patterns of inequality. The impulse to mastery, the nexus between knowledge and power, is a dominant one (Foucault, 1975). It is this particular nexus that writers imaginatively address, despite all the flack they get from critics and historians, and I personally believe that art can be a powerful means to creatively explore history, and in this particular instance Australia's colonial past and reconciliation patterns and possibilities today.

Current emphases on the local, and the politics of location, are in some ways a logical development in the move away from universalism, made all the more pressing by the phenomenon of globalisation, now in its third phase (Wolton, 2009). The constellation of discourses embedded in postcolonial theory has points of contact with 'theories without credentials' through its engagement with Marxism, feminism and, more generally, 'otherness'. Although this is at the core of the idea of political utopia which pervades decolonisation rhetoric in theory (Ashcroft, 2007, 2009a, 2009b) and practice (Wright, 2007, 2013), some writers within Australian universities are engaging with the theory and the practice, devising new ways of relating to otherness from an allegedly dominant position, but with the aim of establishing a dialogue with 'the other'. One such example is Michelle Hamadache's (2011) exploration of otherness in her PhD by artefact and exegesis from the point of view of a white woman in 'Algeria in language and Algiers', which in many ways is a homage to Franz Fanon's *The Wretched of the Earth* (2002). Her discussion of the postcolonial double bind and the solution she finds for it may well have anticipated Yvette Walker's (2013a) concept of 'empathic alterity' in '*Letters to the End of Love* (a novel) and the politics of the modern epistolary novel (an exegesis)', also a PhD by artefact and exegesis. In it, Walker explicitly addresses empathetic alterity in relation to postmodern theories. The fact that her novel (Walker, 2013b) was published to great acclaim testifies to the relevance of theory for creative writing.

Full Circle: The World, the Writer and Theory

The above insights into creative writing research make a case for theories that disrupt our certainties about who we are and thus open up creative possibilities that benefit from being theorised. These theories in turn suggest how the creative process – though mainly addressed here in terms of unconscious material brought about consciously and manipulated in light of its acknowledged ideological underpinnings – needs to be further pursued. I have suggested that a psychoanalytic understanding of subjectivity can indeed shed light on the creative process and that it is not incompatible with other theories, particularly those which problematise alterity. There are deep affinities between creative writing and other kinds of theories which may turn out problematic. For example, many of the methodologies and practices inherent in the work of 20th-century modernists are echoed in postmodern works. This widespread phenomenon is partly due to the dissemination of poststructuralist theories of language. It is nonetheless important to acknowledge, address and redress the ideological bias inherent in such dissemination.

While a psychoanalytic approach to subjectivity enables writers to comprehend and articulate their own creative profiles, an alertness to the ideological positions derived from Marxist and feminist thought which are questioned in postcolonial theories enables writers to become aware of the conditioning implicit in the course of their own socialising. This in turn may allow them to examine the concept of knowledge gathering, processing and critiquing as it relates to their creative practice. Such reflection is particularly relevant to doctoral students who come to creative writing research willing to understand or enhance their creative process in order to define more clearly questions of methodology.

Notes

(1) I am aware that I am taking the risk of alienating some of my readers in countries like the UK and the USA, but the work of authors such as Zadie Smith, Caryl Phillips and Juan Diaz shows that this need not be the case.

(2) Jean-Paul Sartre needs to be credited here for focusing the attention on the 'other', in *Being and Nothingness* (Sartre, 1957 [1943]).

(3) Heartfelt thanks to Elizabeth Colbert for drawing my attention to this issue of a close link between creative and physical states and the possibility of mental illness, conjuring a common view of the creative person as mad. Although this is a prejudice many creative practitioners fight, it is not my intention to imply that there is *necessarily* a link between the two. It is certainly not my aim to stigmatise mental illness – quite the reverse – as will become clear in my discussion of the Lacanian concept of 'suppletion' in the next chapters. In fact, I want to stress that both Freud and Lacan highlight the continuum between so-called 'normality' and 'madness', as did Plato with regard to the nexus between 'creativity' and 'madness'. But we must also remember Foucault's view that madness in its pathological form becomes meaningful only in relation to its immediate outside and complementary dimension: reason (Foucault, 1961). Further, it has been shown that madness is a culturally specific concept (Jaccard, 1979: 32)

(4) This is a reality ignored by most composition courses recently surveyed in the USA (Ninacs, 2011) and in most creative writing workshops conducted in the English-speaking world generally.

(5) It draws on Lacan's famous critique of the discourse of the university as well as on the work of Shoshana Felman and Mark Bracher, while, at the same time, inscribing itself within the discourse of the institution (Lacan, 2007 [1969–70], Felman, 1982; Bracher, 1999, 2006). Inspired by Bracher's work, my own practice mobilises the power of the student–teacher relationship as a pedagogical tool to enhance student self-confidence, performance, social inclusion and peer recognition. As I have written extensively about this (Hecq 2009a, 2013a) I will not rehearse the argument here.

(6) There were precursors to postcolonial theory, of course, and, as with other theories, creative writers paved the way for theoretical rationalisations. Authors such as George Lamming (1953), Chinua Achebe (1958), Wilson Harris (1960) and Oodgeroo Noonuccal (1964) come to mind, but a discussion of their contribution to the field is beyond the scope of this book.

(7) Historically, the Aboriginal people of Australia were perceived as standing in the way of European progress. It is an idea I alighted upon in 1982 when postcolonial studies were still incipient and I wrote my honours dissertation on 'The image of the Aborigine in Australian fiction'. This biographical insert aside, in 1788, when Europeans arrived to establish a penal colony in Australia, they encountered ancient Aboriginal nations that had lived on the land for many thousands of years. The natural world was an integral part of Aboriginal life, and experienced in fundamentally spiritual, cultural, ancestral and physical ways. In 1838, when John Gould arrived in Australia to study its birds, the infamous Myall Creek massacre had just taken place in northern New South Wales, itself later invoked or depicted in fiction by Mary Durack (1959), Randolph Stow (1982) and Kate Grenville (2005), raising much controversy. The colony was in a stir over the issue of this brutal massacre. Some columnists, however, openly expressed their support for the white men who had committed the crime of murdering indigenous people in retaliation for attacks on property. For example, one man wrote to the editor of the *Sydney Gazette and New South Wales Advertiser* describing Aboriginal people as no more than 'monkeys' that should be 'exterminated' (Anonymous, 1838). This complex experience is at the heart of postcolonial discourse, in both acceptance of the term as 'after colonialism' and 'neo-colonialism', concerned as it is with both the 'other' of Western culture and the 'other' of indigenous culture in Australia.

5 Styling the Subject of Creative Writing

When your Daemon is in charge, do not think consciously. Drift, wait and obey.
Rudyard Kipling

Wo Es war, soll Ich werden.
Sigmund Freud

Le style est l'homme même.
Jacques Lacan

These epigraphs in three different languages single out psychoanalysis as 'a theory without credentials', whose language may be international. The phrase 'theory without credentials' signals psychoanalysis' counter-discursive approach and this is one which may be particularly useful to creative writers. This chapter asks a sequence of questions: Why does creative writing need psychoanalysis? What is the value of psychoanalysis for creative writers? What are the *connections* between creative writing and the subject of psychoanalysis? What are the psychoanalytical theories that are useful for writers? The answers draw mainly on the work of Freud and Lacan, who engage with the complexities of the dream work of language. Here I make a case for a theory that does not consolidate our certainties, but rather disrupts these, thereby opening up creative possibilities that can in turn be theorised, for example the notion of style as it pertains to subjectivity. The chapter therefore ends with poetry talking back to psychoanalysis.

The Question of Precedents

In his paper 'In search of the writer's creative process' the psychologist Todd Lubart (2009) employs a third-person narrative utilising the character of a young schoolgirl named Alice as a tool to enter the world of creative practitioners in an attempt to answer the question 'How do writers write?' Alice must 'go through' the tripartite process of writing as described by Hayes and Flower (see Lubart, 2009: 152). This process involves: planning what to write; generating or drafting text; and editing or revising. Lubart then engages in a discussion which compares the description of process through two lenses: English literature; and empirical science, including psychology and neuroscience.

Authors such as Kipling, Lubart argues, explain entry into the writing process in an elusive manner, with an emphasis on the 'muse' (Lubart, 2009: 150). He cites Kipling, who said: 'When your Daemon is in charge, do not think consciously. Drift, wait and obey' (Kipling cited in Lubart, 2009: 150). Lubart's decision is to move away from the ephemeral towards the empirical by posing questions such as 'is one born an author with an innate knowledge of the creative process, or can one learn to be creative and become an author through practice?' (Lubart, 2009: 150). It would appear that he is of the belief that the latter is more applicable and useful, provided an analysis of the creative process were possible. Using the four-stage process of the 1926 evidence-based findings of Wallas, namely preparation, incubation, illumination and verification, Lubart illustrates *how* writers write. His paper seeks to provide examples of a cognitive process at work, thereby demystifying what Ghiselin (cited in Lubart, 2009: 155) rejected as superficial, stage-based descriptions. While this author seems to be intent on providing the reader with a varying number of findings by a varying number of psychologists, including Csikszentmihalyi and Runco, for example, his own confusion – and perhaps frustration – is emphasised by the way he ends the article, returning once again to the narrative of Alice: '[She] thought again about her future career as an author. Perhaps she could explore other career options as well. Maybe she should study psychology and conduct research on creative writers' (Lubart, 2009: 162). I personally think that she should instead re-read Lewis Carroll's, *Through the Looking-Glass* (Carroll, 1992) and, like her namesake, allow herself to dream and get lost in the labyrinth of her own imagination. Or perhaps she should turn to psychoanalysis instead.

While the previous chapter introduced psychoanalysis as a 'theory without credentials', or a set of theories about the nature of the mind which involve a practical technique for analysing psychic phenomena based on the 'talking cure', this chapter takes a closer look at the subject of creative writing, as related to, yet different from, the 'ego'. It is indeed with a little help from his hysterical patients that Freud, at the end of the 19th century, discovered this distinction. By listening to his female patients, he was able to bring out the determining force within utterance. This in turn enabled him to conceptualise the unconscious. What Freud did at first was little more than to point to the role of language as a central aspect of psycho-analytic treatment. His first analysand, Anna O, dubbed the procedure 'the talking cure', for she believed that she had 'talked away' her neurotic symptoms. Throughout his work, Freud draws attention to the effects of desire in language and, in fact, in all forms of symbolic interaction. What he alighted upon is that the language of desire is veiled and does not show itself, except in disguise.

Perhaps we all know this. But Lubart's Alice doesn't. For this Alice, the self, or the ego, and the subject are one and the same. They are predicated upon consciousness and readily explicated by a discourse that occludes the work of dreams and, hence, creativity and its myths, all of which, ironically make us what we are. Alice is relegated to the realm of flat characters.

Dreaming the Subject of Creative Writing

'Wo Es war, soll Ich werden', our second epigraph, comes from Freud's *Gesammelte Werke Bd. 15: Neue Folge der Vorlesungen zur Einführung in die Psychoanalyse* (Freud, 1940 [1932]: 86). The German has been translated into English in various ways and it appears in *The Standard Edition of the Complete Psychological Works of Sigmund Freud, Volume XXII* as 'Where id was, there ego shall be' (Freud, 2001 [1932–36]: 80). This phrase has now become an aphorism concerning the relationship between the conscious and the un-conscious. Lacan himself cites it in the conclusion to his essay 'The instance of the letter in the unconscious, or reason since Freud' (Lacan, 2006 [1957]: 435). Freud insists that all human behaviour can be understood as meaning-ful or significant, but that 'meanings' are often unknown because they are repressed, disavowed or foreclosed. He also claims that the most frequently repressed wishes and desires are sexual ones – these sexual wishes or desires are forbidden in our everyday conventional life, and for a variety of reasons are generally unacceptable to the conscious mind. They are excluded or repressed from consciousness and become 'unconscious'. In other words, because we do not want to acknowledge them and live with them in our conscious life, we attempt to disown them. But they nonetheless continue to exist unbeknownst to us and sometimes they crop up in our fantasy life, and of course, uncomfortable as this may make us feel, in our writing.

For Freud, human beings essentially pose two problems. These can be formulated as two questions. Why is it that, unlike other animals, human beings show such a range of non-reproductive sexual behaviours, and make these behaviours central to the social and political systems in which they live? And why is everything they do governed by the laws of language? Lacan will famously pursue these two questions and produce what have now become aphorisms: for example, 'the unconscious is structured like a language' (Lacan, 1993 [1955–56]: 167), 'there is no such thing as a sexual relationship' (Lacan, 1998 [1972–73]: 68) and 'the unconscious is the Other's discourse' (Lacan, 2006: 10), which can also be translated as 'the discourse of the Other'.

Freud first used the term 'psycho-analyse'/psycho-analysis' in an article on the aetiology of neuroses published in French in 1896 (Freud, 1896: 166). The German *Psychoanalyse* made its first appearance the same year, but in a different article (Freud, 1991 [1896]: 379). This construct marked his abandonment of earlier therapeutic procedures, which included hypnosis, and heralded his exclusive therapeutic use thereafter of 'free association'. This technique involved patients saying whatever came into their minds, no matter how seemingly irrelevant or meaningless. Freud discovered then that he could interpret and make sense of the data so obtained and that the relatively uncensored 'free associations' became meaningful when seen within a larger framework or context.

For Freud, then, 'free associations' are not 'free' at all. They may appear to be haphazard, in the sense of being unrelated to the rest of the talk and wishes of the analysand, but they are determined by unconscious influences. Thus, psychoanalysis concentrates on understanding the derivation of the unconscious dimensions of ourselves as revealed in disguised form through dreams, slips of the tongue, misreadings, slips of the pen, bungled actions, fantasies, myths and so on – all forms of experience which at first may appear to be irrational, random and trivial, but which in reality are full of significance.

Psychoanalysis explores what happens when desire gets directed onto social goals and when bodily needs become subject to the mores of culture. Through language, desire becomes subjected to rules and yet, as we know, language cannot define experience accurately. Can language, for example, adequately define body or mind? Does language perhaps get in the way? What is of particular interest to psychoanalysis is that aspect of experience which has been ignored or prohibited by the rules of language. Words fail to match it but *id* – the German *Es*, which refers to our unconscious self – is there, nonetheless. The energies of this desire become directed outside conscious awareness, attaching themselves to particular ideas and images representing unconscious wishes – which refer to desire associated with particular images, or 'word presentations' as Freud called them. These are distinct from desire itself, which refers to underlying energies not yet bound to specific aims, known as drives. Thus, Freud's conception of the human psyche is a linguistic one. It is one that radically altered how subjectivity and epistemology were to be understood thereafter.

The publication of *The Interpretation of Dreams* at the turn of the century (Freud, 2001 [1900]) was a landmark not only in the history of psychoanalysis but also in the history of the humanities. For Freud, although dreams always have a meaning, their real meaning, or 'latent' meaning, is never the same as their obvious, or 'manifest', meaning (Freud, 2001 [1900]: 324). The dream makes sense only when put into context, and it may then be interpreted in terms of the dreamer's hidden or unconscious motivations. Freud's theory of dreams has many implications for the way in which we understand creative writing and its preliminary 'dream work'. Further, it brings to light the symbolic aspect of human subjectivity. Like our dreams, no aspect of our subjectivity or creative process can be taken at face value. If Freud's papers on the parapraxes (Freud, 2001 [1901]) show human beings as creators of meaning, his writings on dreams show them to be symbolisers, text makers and, by extension, fabulators. What is directly observable about human beings and their dreams – the 'manifest' aspect of psychic life – is not significant. What is significant, though, is its 'latent' aspect. The various material signs, be they verbal, visual or aural, used in language are directly observable, but their importance lies in what they mean or signify. Anyone who thought that a language could be understood by observing its manifest characteristics or properties – the shapes of the letters, the tones of the speech sounds and so on – would of course be doomed to disappointment and incomprehension. It is only, as we now know, after last century's lessons from linguistics, if the marks on the paper or the sounds in the air are taken as signs that they can be understood. Similarly, it is only if we consider human subjectivity, behaviour and creativity as symbolic that we can understand them. Apart from this, Freud's writings on dreams add a further dimension to the notion of the unconscious, in that they show that the unconscious part of the mind has entirely different principles and order of functioning from consciousness. In functioning through mechanisms such as condensation and displacement, what Freud dubbed 'the primary process' is at least as important to us as what we normally would understand by rationalising, as we do in 'the secondary process' (Freud, 2001 [1900]: 324–327). Perhaps what Freud is gesturing at is what Lacan later called 'style' (Lacan, 1966: 9; Lacan, 2006: 9, in translation), a style whose definition necessarily differs from that of rhetoricians like Aristotle or Boileau, to telescope the history of Western poetics as it was no doubt known to Lacan.

Id is Style

Lacan opens the French version of his *Écrits* with the words 'Le style est l'homme même' (Lacan, 1966: 9) – as per the above epigraph – a quote attributed to George-Louis Leclerc Buffon upon his election as a member to the Académie Française in 1753 (Lacan, 2006: 766). Although Buffon's words are translated as 'The style is the man himself' in the most recent English translation of the *Écrits*, it ought to be translated as 'Style is man himself'. In any case, Lacan's point is to set up a critique of the notion of man. Man, he tells us in his preface, is no longer such a certain reference; man is in fact but a magnificent fantasy. As we saw in the previous chapter, such sentiment also features in Michel Foucault's *Les mots et les choses* (*The Order of Things*), published the same year in France. For Foucault, the subject is to be understood not as a fundamental and original form, but rather as one formed by a number of processes, not of the order of subjectivity as such, but of an order that we could call 'archaeological', that is, a subject endowed with a complex genesis. In a sense, Foucault's subject is both ante- and anti-Cartesian. In fact, perhaps Foucault's project was to bracket out the very existence of the Cartesian subject. Conversely, for Lacan, the Cartesian subject was a necessary condition, inasmuch as it was for the emergence of Freud's psychoanalytic subject. In his 'I think, therefore I am', Descartes differentiated mind from body, *res cogitans* (thinking substance) from *res extensa* (matter), subject from object. Descartes proceeded by the method of hyperbolic doubt, putting into question all prior knowledge, before reaching that of which he could be certain: 'I think, therefore I am'.

The Cartesian subject, then, is a subject of certainly, but also a subject of consciousness. It is worth noting that Descartes does not use the term 'subject' in his writings. He does, however, use the word *ego*, or I. In his *Méditations* (*Metaphysical Meditations*), first published in 1641, the *cogito* takes the form 'Ego sum, ego existo' (Descartes, 1974: 38). Descartes's subject is indeed a subject of the ego and this is where we can define the realm of subjectivity. Here we need to make clear that 'subjectivity' refers to the subject of consciousness and hence we need to distinguish this from the psychoanalytical subject of the unconscious.

In separating subject from object, Descartes also provides the basis for the establishment of modern science, including psychology and neuroscience. He separates what is knowable by thought and experience from what is knowable by observation and experimentation. Following Descartes, a suitable object for science is all that is outside the realm of subjectivity, that is, the body and all the objects in the subject's mimetic environment. As Lacan puts it:

> In science, the subject ... is in fact the investigator.... He is the subject
> in so far as he is the reflections, the mirror, the support of the world of
> objects. In contrast, Freud shows us that there is in the human subject
> something which speaks, which speaks in the full sense of the word,
> in other words something that lies, knowing what it is doing, and
> outside the support of consciousness. This reintegrates – in the obvious,
> strict, experimental sense – the dimension of the subject. (Lacan, 1975
> [1953–54]: 218)

Freud's early career was marked by his adherence to the medical
paradigm of his day, as a scientist true to the positivist model. The crucial
turning point was his abandonment of the so-called seduction theory. In the
Aetiology of Hysteria, Freud claimed that sexual experiences in childhood were
traumata which led to the late development of hysterical symptoms (Freud,
2001 [1893–95]). However, in a letter to Wilhelm Fliess of 21 September
1897, Freud repudiated this view:

> The certain insight that there are no indications of reality in the un-
> conscious.... Accordingly, there would remain the solution that the
> sexual fantasy invariably seizes upon the theme of the parents. (Freud
> cited in Masson, 1985: 264–265)

In this movement, Freud can be seen as discarding empirical knowledge
for unconscious knowledge. Or, to put it differently, Freud abandoned
an object of empirical scientific investigation for an object of fantasy. For
psychoanalysis, it is precisely unconscious fantasy which structures the
relationship between subject and object. In Freud's analysis of dreams, the
more the dream makes him doubt, the more it confirms the certainty of a
knowledge, an unconscious knowledge. Hence, in Freud, the Cartesian 'I
think' becomes an 'id thinks'. Here, the Cartesian subject of consciousness
becomes a Freudian subject of the unconscious. It is a subversive move, one
that is, unfortunately, missed in the empirical frameworks of psychology
(Lubart, 2009) and neuroscience (Damasio, 1989), which are not well suited
to an understanding of creativity, for these deny that the id thinks.

Now is the time to ask again what the term 'unconscious' means, for,
as we shall see, it has acquired some differing, if not paradoxical, meanings
over time, even within the writings of particular psychoanalysts such as
Lacan. For Freud, the term 'unconscious' had a precise technical meaning
(Freud, 2001 [1915b]). As an adjective, it simply refers to mental processes
that are not the subject of conscious attention at a given moment. As a
noun, *das Unbewußte* designates one of the psychical systems which Freud

described in his first theory of mental structure, known as the topographical model. According to this model, the realm of the 'unconscious' should be distinguished from the 'pre-conscious', which includes ideas easily accessible to consciousness but not presently in it – for example, a forgotten name or telephone number. Freud deliberately avoids the mistranslation 'subconscious', which covers both the pre-conscious and the unconscious mind. For him, the unconscious consists of ideas, thoughts, feelings, fears, wishes, drives and representations that are permanently excluded from consciousness so that they cannot be directly recalled. For Freud, nonetheless, our conscious selves are partly determined by the unconscious. Thus the most important part of ourselves is the one we do not know.

Freud, it must be stressed, made three distinctions in his work on the unconscious: the unconscious in its descriptive meaning; the unconscious in its dynamic meaning; and the unconscious as a permanently unconscious *system*, namely, the system Ucs (Freud, 2001 [1915b]: 1). The descriptive meaning is the least interesting one, as it merely describes a state of mind. As such, it has been assimilated by most contemporary psychological theories. For creative writers like Alice (Lubart, 2009), the interesting stuff has to do with what she did not want to see, namely the dynamic unconscious and the system Ucs. This unconscious is what emerges in the analytic relationship and, more particularly, in the transference.[1] What baffled Freud was the split between energetic investment and representations of desire, and this led him to conceptualise *Verdrängung* (repression), *Verleugnung* (disavowal) and *Verwerfung* (what Lacan later called foreclosure).[2] It is this dynamic unconscious which is central to what Lacan understands to be a style, something that is of direct relevance for creative writing. In the act of writing, as in psychoanalysis, free association allows the subject to emerge through the formations of the unconscious, that is, through the dream work of language, which takes hold of us in the transference to the text – or to the characters we invent.

Lacan's initial 'return to Freud' attributes to Freud an earlier development in theoretical thinking that highlighted the important role that language plays in the psychic life of human beings. Much has been made of Lacan's 'mirror stage' (2006 [1949]) to argue that it is only when the child acquires language that the unconscious begins to form and therefore that no real or true self exists before the acquisition of language.[3] This view, which presupposes that the imaginary is just a stage in human development, and not an inherent component thereof, is erroneous, for Lacan's tripartite conception of subjectivity only mirrors Freud's earlier model. As such, it is a linguistic model and it emphasises that we, as subjects, are created by language and culture, what Lacan called the Other, a concept I define below.

Lacan articulated Freud's subversive view of the subject in the light of structural linguistics. Hence the subject is represented by a chain of signifiers. Prior to the signifier which represents the subject for another signifier, there is no subject as such. The psychoanalytic subject is not substance nor being but an effect of the psychoanalytic discourse. When the subject appears in its discontinuous manner, it is always disappearing, always fading (Lacan, 2006 [1960]: 678). In the context of writing, the text and the characters become the mechanism of transference – the articulation of unconscious content into the language of consciousness. The unconscious dimension of human thought makes itself known obliquely, through its effects, through the work's internal logic and through its style.

For Lacan 'style' *is* man or woman, but only insofar as it is the man or the woman one addresses oneself (Lacan, 2006: 9). As such, style can only be produced in discourse; style characterises the subject in discourse. We must differentiate style as a symbolic function that marks the relation of the subject to the signifier and defines the particularity of the subject, to what we might call 'personal style' – the idiosyncratic aspects of our imaginary identifications with other human beings.

At this point I want to introduce some key Lacanian concepts. I am well aware that it is impossible – and probably unnecessary – to offer a *précis* of Lacanian theory. Moreover, if I were attempting to do so I might lose my reader. I will therefore ask the poet to guide us. But before we turn to poetry to see if we can 'set the darkness echoing' (Heaney, 1991: 44), we need a few signposts.

The Ego, the Subject and the Question of the Father

Lacan distinguishes between the ego and the subject. Lacan also refutes the idea that our identity can ever be coherent and authentic. For Lacan, the subject comprises the triangulation of three orders: the symbolic; the imaginary; and the real. It is an imperfect structure always 'fading' (Lacan, 2006 [1960]: 678). The symbolic is a universal characteristic of humanity: a group can be said to be human only if it is subordinated to a symbolic structure which is itself articulated in language. In the symbolic, for example, I am the set of facts written in my passport and these facts are inscribed in the Other, or symbolic network. The imaginary invokes a set of similarities, that is, a set of projections, identifications and rivalries which govern intersubjective relationships. In the imaginary, I am the person who gazes in the mirror and hates to see that I look like my mother, the child's specular 'other' *par excellence*. The real is that which is beyond symbolisation: it is the realm of death and madness, which remains hidden from us in the unconscious and is therefore beyond words. In the real, I speak gibberish or not at all. This is an oversimplification, of course, albeit a necessary one, for Lacan's understanding of the workings of these three orders changed over time.

In Lacan's earlier approach, two orders were always opposed to one another, the symbolic being the main point of reflection on human functioning. During the 1950s, Lacan was mainly interested in the relationship between the imaginary and the symbolic, where he assumed that the actual meaning and content of mental representations should not be the focus of our attention. What is important is the interplay between signifiers and the way reality is constructed according to the Law, and more particularly to the Name of the Father – as we will see shortly.

Lacan begins his theorisation of the subject with the infant in an amorphous state, with no boundaries to its experience of sense or need, as a jumble he punningly calls *hommelette*, a portmanteau word evocative of *petit homme* (little man) and *omelette* (Lacan, 1986 [1964]: 197). To mark the initial stages of separation, Lacan returns to Freud's early concept of the ego in the paper 'On narcissism' (Freud, 2001 [1915a]) and to the key metaphor of narcissism, that of the mirror. For Lacan, there is a metaphorical, and sometimes literal, moment of a mirror stage (Lacan, 2006 [1949]: 75–82), in which the infant makes an imaginary identification with its reflection in a mirror. Lacan explores and widens the implications of this metaphor of the encounter with the mirror. The child looks in the mirror and is delighted by several qualities of its own image simultaneously. Whereas before it experienced itself as a shapeless mass, it now gains a sense of wholeness. This gratifying experience of a mirror image is a metaphorical parallel of an unbroken union between inner and outer, a perfect match that guarantees immediate satisfaction of desire. Lacan sees this pre-linguistic, pre-Oedipal event as occurring in what he calls the realm of the imaginary. He takes the infant to be modelling itself upon the mother, since she is the first being with whom it has an interaction. The mirror image is 'a homologue for the Mother/Child symbolic reaction' (Lacan, 1986 [1964]: 196).[4] But this model is an illusion, since the mother is thought, like the mirror stage that follows its every movement, to respond to every impulse. We will return to this in more detail in the next chapter, but my point at this stage is that Lacan initially concerns himself with the *ego* rather than the *subject*.

The importance that Lacan attributed to the paternal function led him to redefine the concept of 'father' and to apply the three orders which he had singled out as necessary for psychic functioning. There are, then, three different fathers in Lacan's work: the symbolic, the imaginary and the real father. From 1957 on, Lacan stressed the importance of the question of the father, specified as being central in the analytic experience, as a questioning which is 'eternally unresolved' (Lacan, 1994 [1956–57]). In Lacan's thesis in his seminar on James Joyce, he identifies the father as being of crucial importance, as writing itself may play the role of paternal function (Lacan, 2005 [1975–76]).

At that time, Lacan was working on the consequences of his ongoing thesis that 'the unconscious is structured like a language' (Lacan, 1998 [1972–73]). He thus tackled the question of the father in the context of those operations which, he argued, were specific to the unconscious: metaphor and metonymy. This led him to define the paternal function as a metaphor; it is what guarantees the metaphorical substitution of one signifier for another signifier. The signifier of the mother's desire, enigmatic, and potentially deadly, for the child, is replaced by the signifier of the Name of the Father, which responds, so to speak, to this enigma with the mediation of phallic signification.

Theorised in this way, the father is not equivalent to the actual person and neither is he an ideal figure, or ideal object. The symbolic father is the agent of castration and therefore has a signifying function – this will enable Lacan to state that the father is a signifier. The presence or the absence of this Name of the Father is of such crucial importance in the establishment of the structure of the subject that it will serve as a criterion to distinguish between three clinical structures, namely neurotic, perverse and psychotic. The key to the father as he who intervenes in the Oedipus complex in a structuring way is situated at this level of metaphor. Thus, the paternal 'deficiencies' that are often invoked to explain psychic suffering, and sometimes invoked to explain art-making, are located at that level.

In the 1960s, the dialectical tension between the real and the symbolic came to hold a prominent place for Lacan, most notably in seminar XVII, through his focus on *jouissance*, an excessive form of enjoyment (Lacan, 2007 [1969–70]). Still starting from the primacy of the symbolic, he is interested in the way in which speech transforms corporeal *jouissance*, and how the *object a*, as object cause of desire, takes shape in the dialectics between the real and the symbolic. The *object a* represents both the impact and the powerlessness of language in relation to the drive, that is, what unconsciously motivates human beings.

In the 1970s, this dialectical view on the relation between the real, the symbolic and the imaginary was replaced by an approach that focuses on the intermingling and connection between the three orders. In this change of focus, Lacan's view on the functioning of language shifts. Before the 1970s Lacan was guided by the Hegelian belief that 'the word is the murder of the thing' (Lacan, 1992 [1957–58]: 260) and that the signifier brings structure to *jouissance* by introducing it to the symbolic. But now he makes a conjunction between both, which brings him to define 'a *jouissance* of the signifier' (Miller, 2007: 141).

To conceptualise the triangular connection between the symbolic, the imaginary and the real, from seminar XX (Lacan, (1998 [1972–73]) onwards, Lacan makes use of knot theory, a branch of topology that studies the spatial composition of knots. And it is in fact with knot theory that Lacan finds a way of conceptualising non-hierarchical links between the three orders. Topology offers configurations of differing evidence, although without discontinuity. Topology allows for Lacan's theses to be reversed without rupture, without the solution of continuity, without letting us perceive what, from another perspective, would be their inconsistency. An example is the simplest of the topological figures, the strip invented by Möbius which allows passage in continuity to its reverse side. From now on, Lacan's teaching is a teaching of psychoanalysis without the Name of the Father – at a time when the Other does not exist. But more of the 'later Lacan' in the latter part of this book.

What needs to be stressed is that the Lacanian subject is discontinuous, always on the brink of silence, always 'fading' (Lacan, 2006 [1960]: 678). Outside the formations of the unconscious, however, the evidence of the subject is style. That is, *style* marks the presence of the subject in its absence, as it were. In the discourse of the subject, as in the reading of a text, style is produced, it is not a given.

We can say that the texts written by Descartes and Freud and Lacan are marked by their style. Both the *Discourse on Method* (1641) and *The Interpretation of Dreams* (1900), to take these examples, are marked by the style of their authors, a style which allows the emergence of something of the subject. It is significant that both Descartes and Freud use the first person singular in these texts rather than the third person of the philosophical and scientific discourses of their day. Both convey a questioning rather than the certainty of a given knowledge. In Lacan's emphasis on style, he puts himself forward in his writings not as an objective narrator but as a subject able to be revealed through style. The last sentence of his preface to *Écrits* reads:

> With this itinerary, of which these writings are the milestones, and this style, which the audience to whom they were addressed required, I want to lead the reader to a consequence in which he must pay the price with a pound of flesh. (Lacan, 2006: 5, translation modified)

Hence, Lacan as subject, who is present through style, invites the reader to engage in a dialectic with his writings, indeed in a transference to the text.

Style is the Poet and the Poet is Style

Let us now follow the poet Seamus Heaney in search of style – within the context of this excursus it will be obvious to the reader that the idea of Heaney's style tracked via Lacanian concepts is necessarily coloured by my own style. I will select for our dialectical reading Heaney's poems 'Alphabets', from *The Haw Lantern* (Heaney, 1987: 1–3) and 'Out of the bag', from *Electric Light* (Heaney, 2001: 1–9). While the first poem could be read as a 'recollection' of the learning of the alphabet and its impact on Heaney's development as poet, it can also be read in terms of the development of a style and idiosyncratic poetics. The second poem tells us something about the function of writing; to be more precise, it gestures towards the therapeutic aspect that writing can have.

The prevalence of the Other of culture[5] as an index of the transformations brought about by the symbolic order may be said to be the theme of 'Alphabets', in which the perspective gradually moves from the imaginary to the symbolic. The 'I' of the poem is seen to develop in direct correlation to the broadening of the Other, as signified by increasingly layered systems of signification. Heaney begins by describing how the unfamiliar is initially seen in terms of the familiar: as the imaginary strives to retain familiarity in terms of identity. Hence, he is able to discuss the steps from reality to writing, as he traces how, initially, the letters of the alphabet were recognised through their similarity to shapes with which his childhood self would have been familiar. Speaking of himself in the third person, he tells of how his initial contact with images was a shadow his father made with joined hands, and goes on to describe his initial contact with letter and number through familiar metaphors: 'the forked stick that they call a Y' and the swan's neck and back that make 'the 2', while two 'rafters and a cross-tie on the slate' represent the letter 'some call *ah*, some call *ay*', and a 'globe in the window tilts like a coloured O'.

In this poem about signs, Heaney traces his stylistic development through different levels of writing and language. He moves on to the different names for the activity, first 'copying out' and then 'English', but he is still in the realm of connecting this activity with the physical givens of his early environment, as his work is marked 'correct with a little leaning hoe' (Heaney, 1987: 1). Here, the scopic drive sought similarity and attempted to impose connections with the familiar in an attempt to forge a form of identity through familial reflection. In this poem, the unfamiliar is initially seen through the reflections of familiar shapes and activities. In this poem, the empty speech of the ego – as it attempts to maintain, in the face of real-life evidence, an imaginary bond with the ego ideals of father and grandfather in terms of shared activity – is replaced by the full speech of a subject who is aware of the growth of the Other, an Other which will progress the development of the subject himself. In this poem, the movement is from ego to subject, from empty to full speech, from imaginary to symbolic, a progress mimetically enacted by the different 'o's in the poem:

> A globe in the window tilts like a coloured O [...]
> The globe has spun. He stands in a wooden O,
> He alludes to Shakespeare. He alludes to Graves [...]
> The astronaut sees all he has sprung from,
> The risen, aqueous, singular, lucent O.

The growth of the Other is paralleled by a growth in understanding of the self of the poem – or, to be precise, its ego. It is through this dynamic interaction with other signs and symbols that growth and understanding of the self is possible.

Heaney's development from the imaginary to the symbolic is charted through different notions of language. In a rhetorical swerve, Latin is seen as a central element in this process; it is another, broader example of the Other. His introduction to, and gradual familiarity with, Book One of *Elementa Latin* is charted and, interestingly, the language, 'marbled and minatory', becomes part of his sense of selfhood as it 'rose up in him'. It is as if the different sign system has made its mark on his sense of self, by changing the focus and direction of that sense of self.

He goes on to explain how another dimension of the symbolic order, another sign system, was to become internalised, as he 'left the Latin forum' for a new 'calligraphy which felt like home' and, again, the letters are compared to the natural world:

> The capitals were orchards in full bloom
> The lines of script like briars coiled in ditches.

Once again, the initially unfamiliar is seen in terms of familiarity and, once again, in a manner redolent of the Irish language, is seen in prosopopeia, a poetic figure in which an inanimate object is given voice:

> Here in her snooded garment and bare feet,
> All ringleted in assonance and woodnotes....

What we see in this poem is that progression from the referent, the thing in the world, to the sign, the linguistic or poetic symbol of that physicality which Lacan deems the progression from the imaginary to the symbolic. Here, as the strangeness of a different language begins to affect the subject of the poem, that strangeness is familiarised by the prosopopeic description of this language as a woman. It is through such linguistic systems, the Lacanian symbolic, that selfhood and identity become socialised and eventually translate the world for the individual.

This development into the symbolic is clear from a later image in the poem, where the perspective of the subject is now mitigated by the structures of language, as the physical world of home, of the familiarity of bales of hay, is now described through the cultural code of the Greek alphabet:

> Balers drop bales like printouts where stooked sheaves
> Made lambdas on the stubble once at harvest
> And the delta face of each potato pit
> Was patted straight and moulded against frost.

Here, language is mediating his vision of reality: the sign or signifier has become dominant over the referent; as Lacan noted, 'it is the world of words that creates the world of things' (Lacan, 2006 [1953]: 229). This is echoed by Heaney's capitalised exclamation: 'IN HOC SIGNO'.

Hence, the self, and the movement from ego to subject, is defined in terms of the development and increasing complexity of the Other, a process which has been a familiar Heaney trope in both poetry and prose. One need only recall the beginning of his *Preoccupations*:

> I would begin with the Greek word, omphalos, meaning the navel, and hence the stone that marked the centre of the world, and repeat it, omphalos, omphalos, omphalos, until its blunt and falling music becomes the music of somebody pumping water at the pump outside our back door. (Heaney, 1980: 17)

Far from repossessing his home place, as the Irish critic Harmon has suggested (see Parker, 1993: 74), or from establishing it as a 'frame of reference from which he can map the Catholic past and present' (Parker, 1993: 95), from the very outset Heaney is opening up his home place to the wideness of the world, and defining his own subjectivity with respect to a broad culturally polyvalent sense of the Other. The seemingly constative sentence that places Mossbawn (his childhood home) at the centre of the world is, in fact, in need of some conceptual unpacking. The homely image of 'our back door' (Heaney, 1980: 17) is contrasted with the mythological force of the Greek notion of 'the centre of the world' and with the phonetic and semantic strangeness of the repeated signifier 'omphalos' (Heaney, 1980: 17).

In fact, the omphalos is not evoked by any process of reification which equates the stone with the pump; rather, it is brought about by the voice, specifically by the voice speaking to itself, repeating the word 'omphalos' like a mantra. The conical stone, located in the temple of Apollo at Delphi, was a physical sign of centrality. However, for Heaney it is the phonetic properties of the signifier as spoken by the voice, properties which dissolve on the moment of translation, which evoke his notion of centrality and home. Instead of grounding his sense of definition in his early home, he begins this discussion by figuring his experience of home in terms of signs of 'absence', or alterity. He is revisioning the simple daily act of pumping drinking water through the sound of the Greek word, as a metaphor (synecdoche) for the Greek origins of Western European culture. Writing many years later, at a distance from the actual experience, he is transforming the simple pieties of home through his use of the foreign signifier of centrality; it is as if he is gesturing towards the point that different cultures have different centres, and it is only through interaction and dialogue that the tribal dirt of which he spoke can be loosened from the roots of his identity. Imaginary empty speech has been replaced with symbolically driven full speech.

In a similar gesture, the poem 'Out of the bag', from *Electric Light* (Heaney, 2001: 1–9), reiterates the same process, specifically in the imagery of birth. In an interview in which Heaney discusses this poem, he examines this trend of a dual perspective on his poetic origins:

> I was saying to somebody the other day that I'm at the cud-chewing stage, or you could put it more stylishly and say that it's a ruminant stage where you begin to get a new perspective. You see what has happened to yourself and you try to put some shape on it. I think I'm going back to the very beginnings of consciousness, almost, in my writing. One of the mysteries in our house, and indeed in any house, was where babies came from. In our house they always came in Dr Kerlin's bag, and I found myself writing a poem recently about Dr Kerlin's bag. (Murphy, 2000: 82)

The opening section of 'Out of the bag' describes the amazement of the children in the Heaney household when Doctor Kerlin arrives with his bag 'the colour of a spaniel's inside lug'. The imagery is homely and colloquial as the past is remembered. However, the more mature perspective, which is revisionist in tenor, is also present in the metonymy: 'a Dutch interior gleam/Of waistcoat satin and highlights on the forceps'. Here, it is the mature Heaney, familiar with aesthetic practices, who is ruminating on his past. In the following sections of the poem, this revisioning of the memory is foregrounded as names of literary figures, Peter Levi and Robert Graves, as well as figures from classical mythology, Asclepius and Hygeia, his daughter, appear in the meditation on birth, death, illness and cure that the poem becomes. Through the mention of the Greek god of health, and through the conduit of 'Poetadoctus [learned poet] Peter Levi' and 'poetadoctus Graves', Heaney compares 'Sanctuaries of Asclepius' to 'hospitals', 'shrines like Lourdes' or to:

> [...] the cure
> By poetry that cannot be coerced,
> Say I, who realized at Epidaurus
> That the whole place was a sanatorium [...]
> When epiphany occurred and you met the god [...].

Here, the temporal duality introduces a complexity to the memory that deepens the layers of meaning of the past, and I would further suggest that the notion of poetry as a cure is connected with this very broadening of selfhood that poetry further expands, with its focus on levels of culture which are not identical to themselves. Interestingly, whereas the initial 'I' of the poem seems to be that of the child, by the end of the poem Heaney places himself as part of the mature world of art and learning: he too is a poetadoctus.

Here, poetry is seen as a vehicle in the making of a style as a discourse which, like that of Lacan, probes the meanings of language and subjectivity, suggesting that the poet's ego literally writes itself into symbolic constellations through an act of reading between perception and consciousness that involves a restaging of the imaginary foundation of the subject. A similar artifice arising from a dialogue between the two orders is employed to suggest the presence of the real of sex and death. This is interesting in itself, as it signals the therapeutic function of writing in response to trauma, an idea we will explore further in our investigation of 'suppletion' in Chapter 8 and beyond.

Notes

(1) Freud coined the term 'transference' in *The Interpretation of Dreams* (Freud, 2001 [1900–01]). It refers to the process through which emotions initially experienced in the past are brought to life in the present. This intense form of relating to an object or subject affects *all* our relationships, that is, with people as well as texts.

(2) These terms are quite technical, but they refer to the three structures that classical

psychoanalysis differentiates to designate material that is repressed, ignored or rejected from consciousness. Thus, while repression is the standard mechanism of defence that pertains to neurosis, disavowal refers to perversion, and foreclosure to psychosis. These mechanisms are significant not only because they provide some ground for establishing particular psychopathologies but also, more importantly, because they allow us to understand how what we do not want to know returns to haunt us and may make us ill.

(3) For Lacan, particularly in light of Kristeva's critique of his early work (Kristeva, 1969, 1974, 1980), there is no pre-verbal subject formed through other sensory interfaces with the 'real' world whereby sensory experiences exist in the unconscious as psychical or physical memory that is not accessible to language. Therefore the 'self' exists before the acquisition of language but cannot be called a subject before it is able to express itself through socially constructed language systems.

(4) What is imagined in particular is a primitive belief typical of this stage, a belief Lacan terms the 'desire of the mother', a double genitive referring to both the mother's desire and the desire for the mother. First, the child imagines itself to be the desire of the mother, in the sense that it is all that the mother desires – desire taken as a metonym for what is desired. The child becomes all that would satisfy the mother's lack, in psychoanalytical terms becoming the phallus for the mother that would complete her desire. Second, the desire of the mother is the child's own desire for the mother, as that part of its experience which has been prompt to satisfy its needs. Hence, it too is drawn into this fantasy of completion. Both these aspects of the 'desire of the mother' combine to keep the child's ego concept in a profoundly illusory state. The absence of a gap for the child between a concept and its application is a proof of the concept's inadequacy; the ego concept has never been tested in use. The gap appears with the initiation of the child into the order of language, what Lacan calls the symbolic order. The structures of language are marked with social imperatives – the father's rules, laws and definitions, among which are those of 'child' and 'mother'. Society's injunction that desire must wait, that it must formulate in the constricting word whatever demand it may speak, is what effects the split between conscious and unconscious, the repression that is the tax exacted and extracted by the use of language.

(5) Lacan's concept of the Other is, arguably, one of the most difficult ones to comprehend, for it refers to radical alterity. As such, it is the index of the symbolic order, assimilated as it is with language and the law. Indeed, the (big) Other is the symbolic insofar as it is particularised for each individual subject. The Other is thus both another subject, in the dimension of radical alterity and unassimilable uniqueness, and also the symbolic order which mediates the relationship with that other subject. However, the meaning of 'the other as another subject' is subordinate to the meaning of 'the Other as symbolic order', for the Other is, first and foremost, 'the locus in which speech is constituted' (Lacan, 1993 [1955–56]: 274). It is therefore possible to speak of the Other as a subject in a secondary turn only in the sense that a subject may occupy this position and thereby 'embody' (Lacan, 1993 [1955–56]: 202) the Other for another subject. To complicate matters, the child's first encounter with the Other is mediated by the mother and there is at times a slippage between the two. We will encounter the Other again in this book, including as 'mOther' to signal this primordial relationship. I hope to make it clear which is at stake in the context of the discussion.

6 The Ego in the Mirror

'MUST a name mean something?' Alice asked doubtfully.
'Of course it must,' Humpty Dumpty said with a short laugh:
'MY name means the shape I am – and a good handsome shape it is,
too. With a name like yours, you might be any shape, almost.'
Lewis Carroll

Creativity does not take place at all; it is a reality that unfolds before the dreamer's eyes.
Bert States

If psychoanalysis is a theory without credentials, its power must lie in the realm of subversive action. But what does this mean for creative writing and poetics in action – in the space where creativity happens? Even though creativity draws from the real, it essentially happens at the intersection of the symbolic and the imaginary, whose prime symbol is the mirror. Whereas the previous chapter looked for the subject, the present one looks at the ego, for it is the mirror which must be negotiated early in infancy if we consider the ego in the light of Lacanian psychoanalysis. This chapter concerns itself with the 'if'. It offers a dialogue across the fields of creative writing and psychoanalysis about practice and theory, including approaches to notions of subjectivity and creativity that precede or, later, counter the Freudian and Lacanian models. Although I introduce the ideas of several psychoanalysts, such as Donald Winnicott and Melanie Klein, I focus on those whose work is explored or referred to later in the book. These include the French feminist trio – Cixous, Kristeva, Irigaray – with special emphasis on Kristeva, because of her extensive study of subjectivity and avant-garde poetics.

But first let us take a closer look at the mirror. The importance of the mirror image to the organisation of subjectivity was highlighted over a century ago by psychologists such as Henri Wallon (1879–1962), Paul

Ferdinand Schilder (1886–1940) and Jean Lhermitte (1877–1959). These psychologists worked from within a positivist tradition and often experimented with animals – in particular our closest cousin the chimpanzee – negotiating their reflection in the mirror to argue that the construction of the self occurs in stages, on the basis of a conscious differentiation between the self and the external world. According to this perspective, the infant gradually becomes capable of objectifying itself and of distinguishing interior sensations from exterior perceptions, thus developing from a consciousness of the body to a consciousness of the self. It is from these ideas and experiments that Lacan arrived at his own version of the mirror stage, the subject of his first official contribution to psychoanalytic theory. The 'mirror test' was first described by the French psychologist and friend of Lacan, Henri Wallon, in 1931. This experiment demonstrated that the response of a six-month-old infant – from the Latin *infans*, indicating a non-speaking being – differs from that of a chimpanzee of the same age, in that the infant becomes fascinated with its reflection in the mirror and assumes it as its own image. However, according to this perspective, the chimpanzee quickly realises that the image is not real and therefore loses interest (Evans, 1996: 115).

Lacan first spoke of his theory at the 14th International Psychoanalytical Congress at Marienbad in 1936, and although the original paper was never published, a rewritten version appeared in 1949 (Lacan, 2006 [1949]: 75–82). In the 1950s and early 1960s the mirror stage was a constant point of reference in Lacan's work, but it became increasingly sophisticated as he reworked it from different angles. In brief, the mirror stage represents the foundation of the structure of subjectivity and it particularly refers to the birth of the ego. Although Lacan at first seems to conceive of it as a *stage* which occurs at a specific point in the child's psychical development – somewhere between 6 and 18 months of age – by the early 1950s he had thought through the concept and shifted emphasis. The developmental stage-of-life theory had progressed into a structural theory of subjectivity, or a conceptual scaffold of the imaginary order. Thus Lacan observes in 1953 that the mirror stage has 'a twofold value' (Lacan, 1953: 14). He explains:

> In the first place, it has historical value as it marks a decisive turning point in the mental development of the child. In the second place, it typifies an essential libidinal relationship with the body image. (Lacan, 1953: 14)

However, he will from then onwards increasingly emphasise the *structural* dimension of the mirror stage – that is, as the point at which the ego and not the subject is permanently captivated by its own specular image. For example, in seminar IV he notes: 'the mirror stage is far from connoting a phenomenon that occurs in the development of the child. It illustrates the conflictual character of the dual relationship' – that is, between mother and infant as well as object and the subject (Lacan, 1994 [1956–57]: 17, my translation).

We could say, then, that, for Lacan, the mirror stage describes the formation of the ego via a process of identification with its specular image. The reason for this phenomenon lies in the prematurity of the human baby. At six months of age, babies still lack the ability to coordinate physical movement; however, the visual system is relatively advanced. This means that they can recognise themselves in the mirror before they have attained control over bodily movements. Babies experience their bodies as fragmented and all over the place, but the mirror sends back a captivating fiction of integration. This contrast or paradox is first experienced as an aggressive tension between the subject and the image (Evans, 1996: 115). In order to resolve this aggressive tension, the infant identifies with the image; this primary identification with the counterpart is what forms the ego. Lacan describes the moment of identification as a moment of jubilation because it triggers an imaginary sense of mastery (Lacan, 1953: 15). Bice Benvenuto puts this more lucidly:

> For the first time the baby perceives himself [sic] as separate from mother, as having another face, as it were. But even more important is the fact that he [sic] perceives himself not as a helpless creature who can hardly sit up if not held by mother, but as a human whole, and he [sic] applies to himself a human Gestalt which, in the previous stage, he had already acknowledged as his own through mother. (Benvenuto, 1999: 29)

However, babies may also experience some feeling of helplessness in the aftermath of this jubilatory moment; that is, when they realise how precarious the sense of mastery is in contrast to the omnipotence of the mother (Lacan, 1994 [1956–57]: 186). In this respect, it is worth noting that Lacan's mirror stage, as a historical milestone in the life of the infant, takes place around the same time as the onset of want that Melanie Klein defined as the depressive position (Benvenuto, 1999: 28–29).

Lacan's mirror stage proposes that the ego is a fiction brought about by misrecognition or misunderstanding, at the site where the subject emerges and becomes alienated from itself. It represents an encounter with the imaginary order. And yet, the mirror stage also has a significant symbolic dimension. In Lacan's scenario, the symbolic order is active in the guise of the mother who is holding the child. The moment after the infant has jubilantly assumed an image as its own, it turns its head around towards its mother, who stands for the Other, as if to request that the image be symbolically validated (Lacan, 2004 [1962–63]: 42).

Thus, the mirror stage is a pivotal experience of identification, in the course of which the infant becomes aware of its own body image. According to Lacan, the infant's primary identification with this image promotes the structuring of the ego and puts an end to that singular aspect of psychical experience that Lacan calls the fantasy of the fragmented body. Indeed, before the mirror stage, the child does not yet experience its body as a unified totality but as something inchoate which, as we saw in the previous chapter, Lacan calls 'hommelette' – the little man made of slackly scrambled eggs (Lacan, 1986 [1964]: 197).[1] The mirror dialectic puts to the test this fantasy experience of the fragmented body, traces of which may reappear in nightmares and psychotic phenomena such as hallucinations or dissociative states, but also in art-making. Its function is to counteract the sense of fragmentation in favour of the illusion of a whole body.

But what is the importance of the illusion of a whole body – the fantasy – in terms of negotiating the crossing into the imaginary in art-making? With Lacan, I would say that the mirror stage is a key structural characteristic of speaking beings and that negotiating the imaginary involves flirting with the real while harnessing symbolic exchanges. As human beings, we put our experiences into words or other symbolic forms. So we could argue that through recourse to the symbolic we negate the multiplicity of what we experience, including the real of the fragmented body. However, as we go about our everyday activities, and perhaps even more so when we are writing, our relationship with the mirror may reveal itself to be problematic. The illusion of wholeness is necessary to our day-to-day functioning, yet also potentially dangerous because it draws its brilliance from the imaginary – some Platonic paradise or unconscious world of perfect harmony that covers over the real. Perhaps the lure of perfect harmony allows us to invent a world behind the pane, where there is some beautiful counterpart to our own daily reality. The dream of crossing through the mirror meets the desire to be reborn on the other side. It creates the fascinating hope of reconciling inside and outside, of living on the side of the imaginary – or fantasy, shimmer in a world devoid of the horrors of the real and the constraints of the symbolic, with its intimations of castration and guilt. Another logic, the logic of dreams and desires, free of mimetic love and rivalry, dictates this crossing to the other side. But the *transition* is also a *transgression*, and as such it can be hazardous.

Lewis Carroll anticipates this for us at the outset of *Alice's Adventures in Wonderland*:

> Alice was beginning to get very tired of sitting by her sister on the bank, and of having nothing to do; once or twice she had peeped into the book her sister was reading, but it had no pictures in it, 'and what is the use of a book,' thought Alice 'without pictures or conversation?'
>
> So she was considering in her own mind (as well as she could, for the hot day made her feel very sleepy and stupid), whether the pleasure of making a daisy-chain would be worth the trouble of getting up and picking the daisies, when suddenly a White Rabbit with pink eyes ran close by her. (Carroll, 1992: 11–12)

So begins Alice's journey to Wonderland, where identity becomes uncertain even before she goes through the mirror. Feeling lonely and annoyed at the blankness of her sister's book, Alice is hovering between boredom and action, waiting and seeking. Alice dreams. She dreams up a rabbit that is running late. Metaphorically speaking, she is *in* the mirror between the reality of everyday life and the place of dreams – where the Law does not apply.

Creative writers cross through this mirror again and again at the risk of getting lost in the labyrinth. If they do not go mad it is because they relate the two sides of the mirror by making up rabbits who do not keep time, for example, which is one way of achieving the first step of symbolic recuperation which writing has the capacity to firm up – as we shall see later on. The French surrealist Jean Cocteau conceived of gloves capable of liquefying mirrors and suggested that mirrors are 'the gates through which death comes and goes', not the death of annihilation, but the promise of an elsewhere, of a luminous light shining from the real which makes it possible to reach the poetic universe. In his film *Orphée* (Cocteau, 1950), derived from his 1926 play, the freedom of the angel Heurtebise, disguised as a glazier, depends on his ability to pass easily from one side of reality to another. This allegory would find its place in a Lacanian scenario whereby the development of the ego, which parallels the consciousness of the mirror image, is integrated in the process of symbolic activity mediated by the Name of the Father – and the Law. But, as we will see in some of the themes explored in the next chapters, those who settle permanently on the other side of the mirror risk madness.

Just as subjectivity and creativity can be achieved by mediation through the mirror, it also happens that the image in the mirror triggers too many affects and, instead of projecting unity, the mirror image liquefies or breaks into pieces. As a powerful vehicle of the imagination, it can also be an agent of dissociation and illusion that threatens the integrity of the self. When not held up lovingly, the mirror may attack or engulf its subject.

The Mother's Mirror

Perhaps the idea of the mother as mirror image is most cogently explained by the British paediatrician and psychoanalyst Donald Winnicott (1896–1971), one of the earliest critics of Freud and Lacan. While Lacan's concept of the mirror stage may be more useful in detailing subjectivity, Winnicott's theoretical framework may be more useful in understanding and fostering creativity. Whereas Lacan's mirror stage is the site of necessary alienation, Winnicott's version incorporates an expanded perspective which reflects an exchange between two people:

> In this stage, commonly called symbiotic, when the baby tries to find its completeness in the offerings and in the body of mother, Winnicott introduces the idea that among the mother's objects that link the baby to her there is also a special one, mother's gaze. (Benvenuto, 1999: 28)

Moreover, the infant's 'true self' is called into being in the mirroring gaze of the 'good-enough mother' (Winnicott, 1971: 11). But, interestingly enough, should such a mother fail us, for Winnicott, we have a second chance, through creative play, art-making or analysis (Winnicott, 1971: 83). Winnicott also maintains that creativity may be enhanced through internalisation of the 'good-enough mother' and, by extrapolation, the 'good-enough internal critic'.

For Winnicott, the child's first mirror is the mother's gaze. But it is a relational mirror. If, for example, it reflects the mother's blank gaze of a troubled inner world, the mirror becomes a threatening object that we do not dare to look at, just like 'the baby afraid of his mother's face, putting aside his own needs' (Winnicott, 1971: 156). This deficiency or primordial frustration obscures all mirrors and distorts all face-to-face encounters. The mirror image becomes a source of fear and anxiety. Winnicott must have been an optimist, for he believed that, through defensive reaction, the image could be repaired, thereby nurturing a narcissistic impulse. This impulse is potentially creative, just as we witness in *Alice's Adventures in Wonderland* and *Through the Looking-Glass*, as well as in countless works of literature, particularly novels about the writer (notionally at least), including Joyce's famous modernist text *A Portrait of the Artist as a Young Man* (Joyce, 1986 [1916]). Sometimes this narcissistic impulse will feed grandiose dreams and the subject may fear and avoid the gaze of others. It may even be that the image becomes terrifying and aggressive, and loses its symbolic status to such an extent that it takes on a life of its own and becomes persecutory. If it is resistant to all fantastical projection, it may also disintegrate or disappear. The elusive mirror of dream and of doubt, the terrifying mirror of lunacy, and the petrifying mirror of insignificance all shine on the fragile bridge between inner and outer worlds. This is something of which writers and psychoanalysts are only too aware.

A paediatrician by training, Winnicott underwent several analyses: first with James Strachey, the translator of the standard edition of Freud's work and intimate member of the Bloomsbury group; then with Melanie Klein; and finally with Joan Riviere, a pioneering thinker about feminine sexuality as 'masquerade' (Riviere, 1929). Disappointed by his experiences of analysis, Winnicott became critical of the dogmatic potential of psychoanalysis. In an oft-quoted line, he takes one Kleinian analyst to task for not understanding the processes unique to each analysand:

> One felt that if he were growing a daffodil, he would think he was making the daffodil out of a bulb, instead of enabling the bulb to develop into a daffodil by good enough nurture. (Winnicott cited in Rodman, 1987: 34)

This comment anticipates Winnicott's famous concept of the good-enough mother, a concept developed further by Bruno Bettelheim in *A Good Enough Parent* (1987). Winnicott's concept refers to the mother–child dyad, of which Winnicott states that the mother's task is not to meet every need and demand of her baby but rather 'to gradually disillusion' the child of his or her own omnipotence (Winnicott, 1971: 13) while providing a holding environment,[2] an idea conspicuously lacking in Lacan's work.

In contradistinction to Lacan, Winnicott's view of subjectivity revolves around the mother–child dyad, a relationship predicated upon 'primary creativity' (Winnicott, 1971: 2). In fact, Winnicott believed that primary creativity immediately follows birth, when the infant's identity evolves from a state of total dependence and symbiosis to one of increasing autonomy. However, for Winnicott, there is an intermediate period of transition, involving 'transitional objects' and 'transitional phenomena', before individuation is achieved.

> When symbolism is employed the infant is already clearly distinguishing between fantasy and fact, between inner objects and external objects, between primary creativity and perception. (Winnicott, 1971: 7)

Winnicott himself admitted that 'there is a wide variation to be found in the sequence of events' from attachment to objectivity (Winnicott, 1971: 2). The infant is born to the mother and the mother, or the mother's breast more specifically, is felt to be an extension of the infant. It could be said that the baby is 'feeding on the self, since the breast and the baby have not yet become – for the infant – separate phenomena' (Winnicott, 1971: 104). The infant thus begins a relationship with its physical self that reflects the relationship between the breast and the baby, usually involving the fingers and mouth (Benvenuto, 1999: 27–28). At this stage, a first mother-as-not-me awareness arises in the infant. As we will see shortly, this process is akin to the relationship between infant and mother described by Melanie Klein (Klein, 1988a), but I agree with Benvenuto when she says:

> With Klein one has the impression that the baby relates to the world through and in spite of mother rather than communicating to her. The baby in the Kleinian fantasy world lives inside the empire of the mother's body. (Benvenuto, 1999: 28)

For Winnicott, 'Sooner or later in an infant's development there comes a tendency on the part of the infant to weave other-than-me objects into the personal pattern' (Winnicott, 1971: 3). He calls such an object a 'transitional object' (Winnicott, 1971: xi). This is what many would understand from their own experience of childhood to be the treasured object, for example a toy or a comforter, whose special status is often endowed with a special name. In Winnicott's developmental view, the transitional phenomena – objects which comfort the child in the absence of the mother or the mother's breast – would be replaced by the infant's ability to internalise that sense of comfort and thus develop self-soothing capabilities.

The transitional phenomena occur in a space between the time when the identity of the infant involves objects-as-me, that is, primal attachment, and objects-as-others, that is, objectivity. Winnicott calls this the 'potential space' and it is through playing and experimentation within this potential space that creativity as play is exercised. Crucially, this potential space 'varies a very great deal according to the life experience of the baby in relation to the mother or mother figure' and Winnicott contrasts 'this potential space (a) with the inner world (which is related to the psychosomatic partnership) and (b) with actual, or external reality (which has its own dimensions, and which can be studied objectively)' (Winnicott, 1971: 48).

The creativity of the developing infant and the creativity that gives rise to art are inextricably linked for Winnicott: the potential space the play world in which children can live out the paradox of separation and union with the mother is retained throughout life in cultural and creative activities. In this, he follows in the footsteps of Freud, who somewhat scandalously suggested that there was a correlation between the creativity of the child and the creativity of the adult. 'A piece of creative writing', says Freud, 'like a daydream, is a continuation of, and substitutes for, what was once the play of childhood' (Freud, 2001 [1906–08]: 152). However, where Freud says that the artist at work is in fact entering a world of fantasy similar to the world a child enters in play – one divorced from reality – Winnicott sees the potential space in which such creativity takes place as a far more complex activity, at the intersection of fantasy and reality, which involves all kinds of activities, including religious and scientific activities. In the adult's case, the transitional space enables the ego to overcome the threat of separation from the other – the mother. The potential space can thus be defined as the ground where the imaginary can find an outlet and resolve conflicts symbolically.

Paul Pruyser has developed a concept of the transitional sphere incorporating the intermediate area of experience and creativity (Pruyser, 1983). In his view, our needs for pleasure, play, emotional recognition and satisfaction are first of all rooted in a space that nourishes the imagination and then transposed onto the cultural plane through cultural conventions and symbols. He develops the concept of what he calls 'the illusionistic world', the realm of 'tutored fantasy', adventurous thinking, orderly imagination, verbalisable images, cultural needs, symbols and creativity (Pruyser, 1983: 103). The 'illusionistic world' is thus a broader and more sanitised version of Winnicott's transitional sphere or potential space. It finds its place between what Pruyser sees as the traditionally opposed 'autistic' and 'realistic worlds', an opposition that has dominated literature since Plato and psychoanalytic discourse since Freud. Pruyser discusses how imagination has been expressed in the fields of religion, arts and sciences. Speaking of creative writing, he justifies the existence of the transitional sphere as follows:

> The illusionistic world of fiction not only transcends but transposes material from both the autistic and the realistic worlds into new entities that can afford a modicum of pleasure even when the original material is gruesome.... The kind of enjoyment resulting from these transpositions is of course an *aesthetic* enjoyment that cannot be reduced to crude drive satisfaction. (Pruyser, 1983: 106)

This intermediate area, akin as it is to Winnicott's potential space, may be the space of creativity, but it is a peculiarly sublimatory one, as the use of the verb 'transcend' implies.

Thus, whereas Freud and Lacan are interested in the unconscious processes at work in the making of art, Winnicott is more interested in the psychical processes which mediate the relationship between self and world, and ultimately the consequences this has for the formal aspects of art. He explains in *Human Nature*:

If there is true creative potential then we must expect to find it, along with projection of integrated detail, in all productive effort, and we shall distinguish the creative potential not so much by the originality of the production as by the individual's sense of the reality of the experience and of the object. (Winnicott, 1988: 110)

This widens out into an investigation of what psychoanalysis might have to contribute to understanding what goes on between the artist and the medium, the writer and the characters, the critic and the text. The focus thus moves from what happens within the psyche to what happens between one psyche and another or, indeed, other spheres.

Positions In-Between

The work of Melanie Klein (1882–1960) needs to be credited, for in many ways she challenged the ideas of Freud and Lacan. Moreover, she also had a huge impact on some of Lacan's most vocal critics, in particular those who objected to Lacan's phallocentrism from within the institution of psychoanalysis itself, namely Hélène Cixous, Julia Kristeva and Luce Irigaray. For Klein, the instincts of the body and the tensions and conflicts these give rise to are of critical importance to the development of the ego (Klein, 1988a). In a sense, Klein is faithful to Freud and sympathetic to Lacan. For example, she defended against the dogmatic approach of ego psychology until the end of her life. She also allowed the unconscious its due place in the interaction between inner and outer worlds, which infants have at first no means of distinguishing. It is this interaction that distinguishes the psychoanalytical orientation of 'object relations', of which Winnicott was a proponent as well, with the dialectic between 'projected' outwards and 'introjected' inwards that establishes the pattern of a self in its dealings with the external world.[3] Darian Leader sums up Klein's unique position:

> Winnicott wrote a book called *Playing and Reality*, Charles Rycroft, *Imagination and Reality*, but Melanie Klein avoided this sort of conjunction. She shared with Lacan a basic suspicion of any attempt to contrast reality with phantasy, remaining true to Freud, who had stressed in his *Introductory Lectures on Psychoanalysis* that the two terms should be equated rather than opposed. (Leader, 1999: 93)

At the heart of Klein's theory is an awareness that good and bad coexist in the child's psyche – an insight that has wide-ranging implications: for Klein, ambivalence taints all our interactions with the world and people

(Wright, 1984: 72). The relevance of this insight is of course pertinent to creative writing, for the creative process is embedded in this ambivalence – the oscillation between acceptance and rejection, satisfaction and denial, love and hate. This is something that Julia Kristeva will follow up, and at times contest, in her own work.

Klein holds that the infant's ego 'becomes exposed to the destructiveness of instinctual aggressive urges' (Wright, 1984: 81) and that this produces anxiety, which in turn 'causes the primitive ego to split' (Wright, 1984: 81). The infant defends itself by means of projection – rejecting the bad– and introjection – taking in the good. Klein believed that it all starts at the breast, the infant's primary object. She explains:

> it is because the baby projects its own aggression on to these objects that it feels them to be 'bad' and not only in that they frustrate its desires: the child conceives of them as actually dangerous – persecutors who it fears will devour it, scoop out the insides of its body, cut it to pieces, poison it – in short, compassing its destruction by all the means which sadism can devise. These imagos, which are a phantastically distorted picture of the real objects upon which they are based, become installed not only in the outside world but, by the process of incorporation, also within the ego. (Klein, 1988a: 262)

It is a rather alarming picture of an infant's psyche that Klein portrays here. It is as though the multiple images in the mirror turn against the ego in indiscriminate fashion. The bad feelings projected by the child onto the mother are then re-experienced as if the mother were herself persecutory. The child then has to re-defend against the unintended consequences of its own defences. It must be said, though, that the intensity of the infant's response may be mediated by the mother's good-enough response that satisfies the need and appeases the ambivalence and therefore the aggression.

For Klein, there are two fundamental positions of psychical organisation. While these are to some extent largely developmental, they are named 'positions', to stress the fact that 'the infant can move from one to the other and back again, a possibility that remains throughout life' (Wright, 1984: 81); these are the 'paranoid-schizoid position' and the 'depressive position' (see Klein et al., 1952). The first of these positions, the paranoid-schizoid position, is traced to the first three months of life. During this period, the infant's characteristic defences are those of splitting and projection, defending sadistically against the objects or part objects that assault it. As the child develops, its reality-testing capacities become more nuanced, and concurrently it starts recomposing the part objects with which it has been engaging into a whole object, for example the mother. And yet, it is precisely when it has acquired such an object that the child realises that it is threatened with the loss of this object. Like *le petit prince* (the little prince) immortalised in Saint Exupéry's eponymous tale (Saint Exupéry, 1946), it then recognises that it is responsible for that object, even though the anguish about further persecution persists. Hinshelwood summarises this turning point for the child:

> The confluence of hatred and love towards the object gives rise to a particularly poignant sadness that Klein called depressive anxiety (or 'pining'). This expresses the earliest and most anguished form of guilt due to ambivalent feelings towards an object. (Hinshelwood, 1991: 138)

Thus, it is not quite right to say that 'the infant can adopt one of two "positions"' (Wright, 1984: 81), as, for Klein, these are marked historically in the development of the psyche. Yet, structurally speaking, where the paranoid-schizoid position relies on mechanisms of splitting and projection, the depressive position relies on fantasies of omnipotence and on denial of its own psychical reality. These positions need noting here because they are relevant to art-making. In the paranoid-schizoid position, the infant lives in fear of the 'bad' object, whose prototype is the breast, as imaginary persecutor out to get the infanct for its aggressive impulses. As Wright remarks:

> This is accompanied by an idealisation of the 'good' breast in which the infant mentally abolishes the 'bad' breast and sees the 'good' one as never failing to satisfy her. (Wright, 1984: 81)

Thus, if anxieties about the ego define the paranoid-schizoid position, fears about the object regulate the depressive position. For Klein, then, both positions play a crucial part in different stages of the creative process.[4] The shift from one position to another revolves around the subject's 'ability to invest fantasy with symbol' (Wright, 1984: 82). In the grip of harmful fantasies, the subject has the option to resort to some form of symbolic control. This is articulated by Klein in the paper 'The importance of symbol-formation in the development of the ego' (Klein, 1988b), which shows how she views the beginning of symbol formation and illustrates the central place of fantasy in the course of psychical development. Lacan discusses this article for its relevance to his expansion on 'the mirror stage' (Lacan, 1975 [1953–54]) and it may even have contributed to his conceiving of *suppléance* (suppletion).

Cherchez la Femme: Cixous, Kristeva, Irigaray

It would seem that no matter how hard we may try, we cannot escape the mirror and its specular illusions. And not surprisingly, we always seem to come back to Lacan. It must be said that his 'return to Freud' has elicited serious interest, not least in France, from the 1960s onwards. As is well known, a number of French feminists, particularly Julia Kristeva (1941–), Hélène Cixous (1937–) and Luce Irigaray (1930–), were profoundly influenced by his thinking, especially his emphasis on the role of language in the organisation of the psyche. However, more importantly, they found aspects of Lacan's thought outmoded and unreasonable, especially due to what they perceived as its phallocentric bias, and therefore worked to subvert some of his concepts and theories. But who are these three women, and what do they make objection to?

Julia Kristeva, a Bulgarian linguist, critic, philosopher, novelist and psychoanalyst who has been living in France since she moved there to write her *doctorat d'état*, a massive work far surpassing what we understand as PhD thesis, under the guidance of Roland Barthes in the 1960s, was one of Lacan's first critics. Her dissertation is replete with criticisms and it is obvious that early on she tried to undermine what she perceived to be Lacan's supremacy of the symbolic order. In her early work in particular, she celebrates the feminine, which, for her, is not sexually specific but simply a position of marginality to the symbolic. The linguist, philosopher and psychoanalyst, Belgian-born Luce Irigaray, and the writer, poet, playwright and critic Hélène Cixous, an Algerian born to a German Ashkenazi Jewish mother, also counter Lacan's phallocentrism.

Despite wide differences between them, what Kristeva, Cixous and Irigaray object to in Lacan's work, an indeed in the whole project of psychoanalysis, is that the (absent) Ideal Woman as object of male discourse replaces real women. Consider, for example, Lacan's assertion that '*woman* does not exist' (Lacan, 1998 [1972–73]: 7), whereby he means that Woman (with a capital W), that is Woman as singular essence or idea, does not exist. For Kristeva, Cixous and Irigaray, such a statement demands the lack of the Woman (as well as women) as a visible emptiness, which is contradictory, since Lacan also ascribes Woman a privileged position with regard the Other. But, say Irigaray and Cixous, in giving woman a privileged relation to the Other, that *no place* of the Law which generates the signifying order, Lacanian psychoanalysis places her in the position of being 'absent as a subject' (Irigaray, 1985b: 94) from that relation (see also Cixous, 1981). The discourse about feminine *jouissance*, as deployed in Lacan's seminar XX, 'On feminine sexuality: The limits of love and knowledge' (Lacan, 1998

[1972–73]), is a discourse of men and, according to Irigaray: 'to speak *of* or *about* woman may always boil down to, or be understood as, a recuperation of the feminine within a logic that maintains it in repression, censorship, nonrecognition' (Irigaray, 1985b: 78). Because of her interest in 19th-century romantic authors and avant-garde 20th-century writers, Kristeva has been less critical of psychoanalysis' complicity with the logic it exposes. No theory can better account for the desire that structures 19th-century romantic narrative or the revolutionary thrust of avant-garde writing than Lacanian psychoanalysis, with its concept of the desiring subject as a metonymic displacement towards an impossible self-completion and self-presence, represented within the symbolic order by woman *as* mother.[5] She functions as the absent object on which desire depends, the fantasy which the desiring subject substitutes for the Other.

Phallocentric desire is instituted through what Kristeva calls the 'triangulating function of the paternal prohibition' (Kristeva, 1982: 59). The Name of the Father, forming the apex of the triangle, intervenes in the immediately erotic dual union between mother and son. From present body, the mother becomes the absent object, which the son can now approach only through the mediation of language or symbolic activity. The Oedipal triangle organises his drives into a desire to regain immediate union with the lost object, but every move towards the desired object consists of trying to name that ineffable union with her, producing yet more signifiers to substitute for her. The mother must remain absent and desired for the subject to remain a subject of language.

The Law of the Father, which decrees that the son abandon the mother and take his place in the triangular structure of the symbolic order, is also the law of sexual difference. The symbolic order codes the subject as masculine, the object as feminine. In addition, many feminist revisions of Freudian psychoanalysis, like those of Nancy Chodorow and Luce Irigaray, find that women's separation from the mother and their entry into the symbolic order remain incomplete and unstable (e.g. Chodorow, 1978; Irigaray, 1979). To the extent that women have not lost the early union with the mother, they would not desire to seek it. Given those two ways in which women are excluded from the subjective structures of the symbolic order, what form can feminine subjectivity take?

Cixous, Kristeva and Irigaray offer different answers to this question. Yet, despite their differences, they share two theoretical elements. First, in their attempt to reclaim the feminine space of an oscillating undecidability between presence and absence, they seek a language that refuses the symbolic castration which established the subject by separating her from the mother, repressing her immediate relation to the mother's body and to the subject's unconscious drives (Cixous, 1976: 880). Secondly, this writing plays at, and attempts to displace, the border between the symbolic order and the a-symbolic excluded feminine – which Kristeva calls the semiotic – that supports it. What they seek is to inscribe within their texts a 'dislocation' (Cixous, 1976: 885) of the phallic symbolic system.

Cixous's critique of psychoanalysis and objection to Lacan in particular – by far the most strident at first – profoundly influenced the feminist movement in France and elsewhere. Cixous's objection to, and subsequent rejection of, Lacanian psychoanalysis is motivated by her interpretation of 'the mirror stage': for Cixous, the Lacanian ego is created not through 'the murder of the thing' (Lacan, 2006 [1953]: 262) but through 'the murder of the other' (Cixous & Clement, 1986 [1975]: 70). An early influential claim for the relevance of binary oppositions for feminism was made in 'Sorties: Out and out: Attacks/ways out/forays' – an essay published in French the same year as 'The laugh of the Medusa' (1975). 'Sorties' begins with a dramatic question: 'Where is she?', and then presents the following list:

Activity/passivity
Sun/Moon
Culture/Nature
Day/Night

Father/Mother
Head/Heart
Intelligible/Palpable
Logos / Pathos...

Thought [Cixous continues] has always worked through opposition ... dual, hierarchical oppositions. Superior/Inferior. Myths, legends, books. Philosophical systems. Everywhere (where) ordering intervenes, where a law organizes what is thinkable by oppositions (dual, irreconcilable; or sublatable, dialectical). And all the pairs of oppositions are *couples*. Does this mean something? Is the fact that Logocentrism subjects thought – all concepts, codes and values – to a binary system, related to 'the' couple, man/woman?
(Cixous & Clement, 1986 [1975]: 63–64)

For Cixous, the answer is that everything is related to the man–woman opposition. So, not only does she, like Derrida, attack Western philosophy on the grounds of logocentrism, she also attacks it on the grounds of phallo-centrism:

In philosophy woman is always on the side of passivity. Every time the question comes up; when we examine kinship structures; whenever a family model is brought into play; in fact as soon ... as you ask yourself what is meant by the question 'What is it'; as soon as there is a will to say something. A will: desire, authority, you examine that, and you are led right back – to the father.... And if you examine literary history, it's the same story. It all refers back to man, to *his* torment, his desire to be (at) the origin. Back to the father. There is an intrinsic bond between the philosophical and the literary ... and phallocentrism. (Cixous & Clement, 1986 [1975]: 65)

We can see here the influence of structuralism, especially that exemplified by Ferdinand de Saussure and Claude Lévi-Strauss, and deconstruction. Cixous integrates these sources in the important argument that the male–female opposition is central to Western culture (if not all cultures) and is pervasively present in all sorts of oppositions that, at first sight, have nothing to do with either sexuality or gender. The inferior term is always associated with the feminine, while the term that occupies the privileged position is always associated with masculinity. For Cixous, this privileging of the masculine consists in the 'murder of the other' (Cixous, 1986: 70). It results from what she calls the 'solidarity of logocentrism and phallocentrism' (Cixous, 1986: 65) and it damages women and men alike, for it restricts the imagination. 'There is no *invention* possible', Cixous argues, 'whether it be philosophical or poetic, without the presence in the inventing subject of an abundance of the other, of the diverse' (Cixous, 1986: 65, my italics). In 'The laugh of the Medusa,' Cixous (1976) suggests that laughter, sex (if not policed by patriarchal heterosexuality) and writing may have some liberating effects. Aware that writing usually consolidates patriarchal structures, Cixous proposes what she calls *écriture féminine*, that is, a feminine writing practice or female writing that would escape the restrictions imposed by the historically inscribed 'phallocratic system' of Western civilisation:

It is impossible to define a feminine practice of writing [*écriture féminine*], and this is an impossibility that will remain, for this practice can never be theorized, enclosed, encoded – which doesn't mean that it doesn't exist. But it will always surpass the discourse that regulates the phallocentric system; it does and will take place in areas other than those subordinated to philosophico-theoretical domination. It will be conceived of only by subjects who are breakers of automatisms, by peripheral figures that no authority can ever subjugate. (Cixous, 1976: 83)

Although Cixous does not invoke Lacan, it is tempting to see *écriture féminine* in terms of his concept of the imaginary. Cixous's position, though, is radically opposed to that of Lacan. In Lacan's universe, the conscious intentionality that is suggested by the phrase 'figures that no authority can ever subjugate' is, in Lacan's own terms, a 'mirage' (Lacan, 2006 [1949]: 76). Yet, in line with Lacan's conception of the formulas of 'sexuation' (Lacan, 1998 [1972–73]: 73–81), for Cixous, *écriture féminine* is not the exclusive domain of women. It is a sort of writing practice that transgresses what Lacan calls the symbolic and that might be associated, but not identified, with the imaginary. However, for the post-Freudian subject, repression is gender-blind and is as much at work with male subjects as with female subjects, even though Lacan's formulas of sexuation might intimate a different perspective (Lacan, 1998 [1972–73]: 79–80). At that time in her thinking, Cixous chooses to call the subversive writing that she has in mind 'feminine' because, in her view, the forces of repression are so clearly on the male side. If Cixous's ideas have evolved since the mid-1970s, her writing continues to perform the transgressive function of *écriture féminine*, defying as it does the laws of genre and gender.

Luce Irigaray, on the other hand, attempts to undercut the mastery of 'phallocentric' discourse by asserting women's specificity. She argues, for instance, that women's multiple erogenous zones – their plurality – explains the difficulty they have with masculine logic. Even if she is using female physiology as an elaborate metaphor, as some claim, she is nonetheless trying to subvert phallocentric oppression by emphasising biological *difference* in a similar gesture to Hélène Cixous.

In the opening of *Speculum of the Other Woman*, Irigaray (1985a) quotes an infamous passage where Freud declares femininity to be a 'riddle'. 'Through history', Freud says in his 1933 lecture on the topic, 'people have knocked their heads against the riddle of femininity'. Pursuing its Sphinx-like status, he adds: 'Nor will you have escaped worrying over this problem – those of you who are men; to those of you who are women this will not apply – you are yourselves the problem' (Freud, 2001 [1932–36]: 113).

Answering Freud's apparently accusatory remark, Irigaray retorts:

> So it would be a case of you men speaking among yourselves about woman, who cannot be involved in hearing or producing a discourse that concerns the *riddle*… she represents for you. (Irigaray, 1985a: 13)

Much of Irigaray's early work focuses on Freud's contrary gesture – both summoning women and warding them off. Addressing this contradiction, she says that psychoanalysis has the inestimable value of making explicit, and thus accessible to analysis, the hidden repression of the feminine (Irigaray, 1985b: 67). The problem, according to her, is that psychoanalysis does not distance itself from this 'truth' and 'logic' of scientific and philosophical discourse. Even while unveiling the repressed feminine and the operation of repressive structures, psychoanalysis continues to perpetuate what it unveils.

Irigaray's polemic examines the psychical and somatic dimensions to women's desires that Freud's work excludes. In quite provocative ways, after studying of the language of madness (Irigaray, 1973), Irigaray turns towards the realm of auto-eroticism and homosexuality, where a whole world of pleasures can be sustained without being subordinated to the Freudian penis or Lacanian phallus. Her argument begs many questions and, as is well known, Irigaray has been attacked for her essentialism (see for example an early critique of her work in Jones, 1981: 255). Nevertheless, her work opens up questions that are pertinent to discussions of subjectivity, embodiment and creativity.

Julia Kristeva, who has written extensively on language, poetics and psychoanalysis, stays somewhat closer to Lacan with her concepts of the semiotic *chora* – which is a version of Lacan's imaginary. For Kristeva, what has been repressed and consigned to the semiotic finds its way into the not yet fully regulated language of children, into poetry, into the language of mental illness – into all uses of language that, for whatever reason, are not fully under the control of the speaker or writer – or cultural conventions. Symbolic and semiotic codes are never to be found in their pure state, as all language is a mixture of the two:

> These two modalities are inseparable within the *signifying process* that constitutes language, and the dialectic between them determines the type of discourse (narrative, metalanguage, theory, poetry, etc.) involved; in other words, so-called 'natural' language allows for different modes of articulation of the semiotic and the symbolic. (Kristeva, 1984: 24)

Purely semiotic representation is possible only in non-verbal signifying systems, such as music. Through our use of language, both our consciousness, which partakes of the symbolic, and our unconscious, which bears traces of the semiotic, code it with their presence. As with Lacan, Kristeva's subject is irrevocably split. Kristeva details her version of Lacan's three orders in *Revolution in Poetic Language*, first published in France in 1974 (Kristeva, 1984). Here she explains how the semiotic refers to its Greek etymology, where the word means 'distinctive mark, trace, index, precursory sign, proof, engraved or written sign, imprint, trace, figuration' (Kristeva, 1984:

25). Since the word implies 'distinctiveness', it helps to identify 'a precise modality of the signifying process' (Kristeva, 1984: 25): that is, the process that sustains the subject. Like Freud and Lacan, Kristeva wants to define how the infant's multiple drives are influenced by its encounters with both its body and its cultural environment:

> Discrete quantities of energy move through the body of the subject who is not yet constituted as such and, in the course of his development, they are arranged according to the various constraints imposed on this body – always already in a semiotic process – by family and social structures. In this way the drives, which are 'energy' charges as well as 'psychical' marks, articulate what we call a *chora*: a nonexpressive totality formed by the drives and their stases in a motility that is as full of movement as it is regulated. (Kristeva, 1984: 25)

Adapted from the cosmology detailed in Plato's *Timaeus*, the *chora* denotes 'an essentially mobile and extremely provisional articulation constituted by movement and their [the drives'] ephemeral stases' (Kristeva, 1984: 25). Not yet fully woven into the signifying chain, the *chora* is a presymbolic realm that provides the dual rhythms of freedom and constraint from which a relation to signification will gradually emerge, as it is already in contact with the symbolic. Above all, then, the *chora* refers to the prelinguistic space where the child remains unable to differentiate itself from the maternal body, yet in which perceptions and sensations are taking on some semblance of organisation (Kristeva, 1984: 25). At this point in her reasoning, Kristeva is perhaps closer to Klein and Winnicott in the way that she conceptualises the object and its future trajectory in creative play and cultural production.

Following the semiotic comes the rupture marked by the thetic, also a liminal zone constituted by its very ambiguity: 'a break in the signifying process, establishing the *identification* of the subject and its object as preconditions of propositionality' (Kristeva, 1984: 43, original emphasis). 'All enunciation', Kristeva adds, 'is thetic'. So the creation of a word or sentence is based on 'propositionality': that is, a proposing of meaning. Placed on the 'threshold of language' (Kristeva, 1984: 44), the thetic is where symbolisation can begin. The thetic stage combines both the Lacanian mirror stage and Freud's Oedipal model of castration. It marks the moment where subjectivity necessarily emerges through imaginary misrecognition and through a relation to the primary, yet veiled, signifier: the phallus.

Kristeva's third order is called the symbolic, and it bears some resemblance to the field of signification to which Lacan gave the same name.

Here, Kristeva echoes Lacan: 'Dependence on the mother is severed, and transformed into a symbolic relation to an other; the constitution of the Other is indispensable for communicating with an other' (Kristeva, 1984: 48). Entry into the symbolic marks 'the first social censorship' because the subject, as it propels its image of itself into the world, meets with symbolic castration (Kristeva, 1984: 48). But for Kristeva, the symbolic is enmeshed with the semiotic. For this reason, she favours avant-garde literary writing in her work, such as the French symbolists, as different as these might be as Lautréamont and Mallarmé, for example, for their 'distortions of the signifying chain' (Kristeva, 1984: 48).

Kristeva's later work, *Powers of Horror: An Essay on Abjection* (Kristeva, 1982), first published in French in 1980, makes it clear that her concern with the semiotic *chora* means, in concord with Klein, that sexual desire refers as much to the maternal body as it does to the phallic signifier that constitutes the subject's lack. What she calls 'the abject' marks 'our earliest attempts to release the hold of the maternal entity even before existing outside of her'. This 'abject-ing', argues Kristeva, constitutes a 'violent, clumsy breaking away' that carries the 'risk of falling back under the sway of a power as securing as it is stifling' (Kristeva, 1982: 13). This focus on the significance of the maternal to the inchoate human subject provides a counterpart to the phallocentrism of Freud and Lacan's paradigms.

The sort of writing that Cixous and Kristeva have in mind, whether we call it revolutionary or feminine, is not rare in the history of literature. James Joyce's *Finnegans Wake* (Joyce, 1992 [1939]) may be a prime example. Or, to stay in modernist territory, we could mention Virginia Woolf's *The Waves* (Woolf, 1931). We could cross the Channel and find works by Maupassant, Gérard de Nerval, Jean Genet, Marguerite Duras or even Roland Barthes. In Australia we would have to consider the works of Patrick White. My point is that the attitude that *écriture féminine* presupposes is quite common and not determined by the gender of the writer; this is if we understand it as not only being both thematically and stylistically transgressive and exploratory, but also honouring the other – *pace* Terry Eagleton. In *Surfacing* (1972), by the Canadian writer Margaret Atwood, for example, we find a young woman caught in a rational, patriarchal and often exploitative world exemplified by her lover, her father and other male characters. During a trip to the wilderness, ostensibly in search of her missing father, she gradually strips herself of the perspective and the accoutrements of the rational modern world. Not accidentally, a dive deep into a pristine lake with a shimmering surface – into what hides under the surface – constitutes the novel's turning point. When the protagonist metaphorically resurfaces at the end of the novel from a brief period of almost complete surrender to instinctual drives and unconscious desires on what is, metaphorically speaking, the other side of the mirror, she is shown to assimilate her experience and the resulting knowledge.

The Father's Mirror

It may seem outrageous for a theorist so often assimilated to feminism, but for Kristeva the mirror is not the imaginary mother but the imaginary father. Kristeva's early works – in translation *Revolution in Poetic Language* (Kristeva, 1984) and the Bakhtinian essays in *Desire in Language* (Kristeva, 1980) – were deeply influenced by her rigorous training as a linguist, philosopher and critic. In these she notoriously attacked Lacan's phallocentrism and privileging of the symbolic. Some critics and feminists therefore found some of her later work, such as *Powers of Horror* (1982), disconcerting. The latter located the roots of borderline psychosis in the failure to separate from an engulfing pre-Oedipal mother as 'abject', a not-yet-object for a not-yet-subject, 'magnet of desire and hatred, fascination and disgust, … an infection' (Kristeva, 1987a: 374). *Tales of Love* (Kristeva, 1987a) and a shorter, summary version, *In the Beginning Was Love* (Kristeva, 1987b) locate the foundation of the subject's loving relation to the Other in a pre-Oedipal father, an 'imaginary father' (Kristeva, 1987a: 311). It is not the pre-Oedipal mother, but a loving father, distinguished from the stern, tyrannical Lacanian father of the Law, who acts as object of primary identification. Kristeva thus revises both the Freudian and Lacanian narratives by having the father rescue the subject from the stifling maternal body even before entry into the symbolic order. *Tales of Love* (Kristeva, 1987a), *In the Beginning Was Love* (Kristeva, 1987b) and, later, *The Feminine and the Sacred* (Clément & Kristeva, 2001) take the 20-year odyssey of Kristeva's increasingly complex and problematic relation to psychoanalysis and feminist theory one step further. An increasing conservatism in these books, however, makes Kristeva's later work far less interesting for what is at stake in creative writing.

The analyses of philosophical and literary texts from the Western canon in *Tales of Love*, and the comparison between Catholic faith and the psychoanalytic transference from *In the Beginning Was Love*, for example, grow out of the concept of this loving imaginary father as providing the earliest structuring condition, not for desire, but for relations in which the speaking being identifies with an idealised Other. The varieties of intersubjective structure resulting from this identification are traced in religious thought, imaginative myth and literature, metaphoricity as the 'linguistic correlative' of 'amatory experience' (Kristeva, 1987a: 275). If 'amatory discourse' combines narcissism and idealisation of the Other, then Kristeva's discourse allows her to idealise this position and open it to narcissistic investments which Cixous never allows herself to do because of her self-awareness and the cultural self-reflexivity of her discourse. Kristeva's position may in itself be dangerous as it fosters identifications with what amounts to the master's discourse – and its canon, no matter how *alternative* this might be.

RB's Mirror – After Lacan

This chapter would be incomplete without mention of Roland Barthes (1915–80), whose work, like the writings of Kristeva, Cixous and Irigaray, was profoundly influenced by Lacan. Many consider his autobiography, of sorts, *Roland Barthes by Roland Barthes* (Barthes, 1977a), first published in French in 1975, to be this versatile theorist's masterpiece. Perhaps this is because Barthes had, through attending Lacan's seminars and immersing himself in the French version of *Écrits* (Lacan, 1966), reached a point where he could speak with authority on Lacanian theory while at the same time contest it. In this autobiography which is not one, Barthes deconstructs notions of reality, truth, representation, subjectivity and genre. The title of this work at once highlights that it is a text, not a life. Barthes's text is not a cohesive life story; instead, it is made up of fragments, thereby replacing story – the *histoire* or *récit* we are familiar with from Russian formalism onwards, with its roots in the work of Benveniste and Saussure – with discourse arranged not chronologically, but alphabetically, arguably a gesture towards linguistics' conception of the arbitrariness of the sign and Lacan's argument against it (Lacan, 1998 [1972–73]: 14–25). Thus *Barthes by Barthes* may be seen as an act of defiance towards the conventions of both literature and psychoanalysis.

Barthes begins his putative autobiography in mock existentialist mode, asking 'Am I?' Although he does not doubt his existence *per se*, he flags it as an illusory construct, nodding in the direction of Lacan, and actually quotes Lacan with added emphasis: 'the subject is *merely* an effect of language' (Barthes, 1977a: 79). Since, for Lacan, the subject and the ego – the ego and its image – never coincide, it seems that Barthes's project is to explore the hiatus in-between, indeed, to explore it in an attempt to halt it, as if espousing Lacan's middle period:

> It is actually the imaginary I am resisting, which is to say, the coalescence of the sign, the similitude of signifier and signified, the homeomorphism of images, the mirror, the captivating bait. (Barthes, 1977a: 44)

Barthes goes on, disputing ideas of verisimilitude, authenticity and truth traditionally associated with the genre of autobiography, only to scoff at such an enterprise:

> I abandon the exhausting pursuit of an old piece of myself; I do not try to restore myself (as we may say of a monument). I do not say: 'I am going to describe myself' but 'I am writing a text, and I call it R.B.' I shift from imitation (from description) and entrust myself to nomination. Do I not know that, in the field of the subject, there is no referent? (Barthes, 1977a: 56)

Symbolic codes are no longer guaranteed by the Name of the Father at the time Barthes is writing. This may be why, like a good hysteric, Barthes seems to be openly enjoying transgressing established codes. Put another way, it is clear that he is testing, resisting and subverting the not-so-solid solidity of the symbolic order after May 1968 and the publication of Lacan's seminar XVII, 'The other side of psychoanalysis' (Lacan, 2007 [1969–70]). In any case, the fact that Barthes should entrust himself to 'nomination' may betray that he paid attention to the symposium on Joyce held in Dublin on 16 June 1967 that was to spur Lacan's seminar XXIII, 'Le sinthome', on Joyce and the phenomenon of writing as prop, or support system for the ego, what he called *suppléance* (suppletion), a concept we will approach from different perspectives in what follows.

Barthes's text is faithful to Lacan and to his own famous essay 'The death of the author' (in Barthes, 1977b), as it constantly denies its own authority:

> What I write about myself is never the last word: the more 'sincere' I am, the more interpretable I am ... my texts are disjointed, no one of them caps any other; the latter is nothing but a further text, the last of the series, not the ultimate in meaning: text upon text, which never illuminates anything. (Barthes, 1977a: 120)

The challenge that Barthes sets himself is to write about himself in such a way as never to lapse into the kind of description that would solidify him into an image, be it the one he sees in the mirror at the start of the book (Barthes, 1977a: 9) or in the ones he may conjure up for his audience. To achieve his goal, he avoids adjectives and adverbs – for they fix the imaginary; he also avoids description, lyricism, sentimentality, emotion and, less successfully, the use of metaphor. His aim, it seems, is to achieve the neutrality of the *Nouveau Roman*, yet through sheer generic transgression.

This is interesting in itself, for unlike Cixous, Kristeva and Irigaray, who manipulate and disrupt the symbolic system, it is rhetoric, and in particular its potential to appeal to emotions, that Barthes attacks.

Barthes's idea of subjectivity and creativity is slippery. He has read his Freud and Lacan and Klein and Kristeva, no doubt to the letter, and so he can give way to play: sometimes referring to himself as R.B., sometimes as I, sometimes as he, you or we. Nevertheless, one of his personas remains 'troubled by an image of himself ... when he is named' (Barthes, 1977a: 43). Here is the spectre of the Other or the real that always catches up with us, a theme we encounter in the next chapter, where we reconsider what philosophy can offer creative writing, and in Chapter 8, where we ask what shapes the writing self.

Roland Barthes conveys that the act of writing is heavily charged with meaning, yet a meaning that is elusive. In his self-styled autobiography, this is most obvious in the way he distinguishes between writing and authorship. Lacan's work shows how an unconscious and decentred discourse parallels conscious narration and imbues it with the voice of the Other, a concept variously reconceptualised by Cixous, Kristeva and Irigaray. What the work of Lacan's critics highlights is the sheer complexity of discourse of the Other and the countless ways in which it can be dismantled and reconfigured.

Notes

(1) The French and the English differ in their approach to cooking as to love-making. This is why I am reluctant to equate *omelette* with 'scrambled eggs' – while the former is beaten for quite some time in laid back fashion, the latter is stirred swiftly and vigorously.

(2) This section is indebted to two former students, Kylie Stevenson and Christine Hill. In varying ways and to varying degrees, both have significantly altered my understanding of Winnicott's work and directly contributed to some of my insights.

(3) Projection is a process whereby states of feelings and unconscious wishes are expelled from the self and attributed to another person or thing. Introjection is a process whereby qualities that belong to an external object are absorbed and unconsciously considered to belong to the self. For Klein, the infant thus creates an ideal object for itself by getting rid of bad impulses and taking in what is 'good' from the object.

(4) The prototype for art-making in relation to the interaction between artist and medium, on the one hand, and audience and art-object, on the other, is, as for Winnicott, the relationship between infant and mother. But for Klein, this relationship harks back to a more primitive encounter of bodies, not gazes. While the medium represents the mother's body, the separating out of the bodily self from the primal object becomes the experiential mode. In other words, the creative act repeats the experience of separating from the mother. According to Elizabeth Wright, it can take place in the context of either of the two Kleinian positions, the schizoid-paranoid or

the depressive, depending on whether the art-maker is experiencing her or his object as fragmented or integrated (Wright, 1984: 81). However, if I read Adrian Stokes correctly, Kleinians regard the depressive position as providing the 'mise-en-scène for aesthetic creation', and therefore artists invest their medium with the fantasy appropriate to the sustenance of desire (Stokes, 1978: 222).

(5) For Lacan, as for Freud, woman and mother are not dissociated (Lacan, 1998 [1972–73]: 35). Kristeva takes this idea to the letter.

7 Between Thought and the Real in Creative Writing and Philosophy

Let's say that between thought and the real there is a hole, an abyss, a void.
Alain Badiou

Despite the waning of a 20th-century 'linguistic turn', which, according to France's leading philosopher, Alain Badiou, never existed (see Clemens, 2002: 201), perhaps we should look at philosophy again before we get lost in the labyrinthine topos of theorists who nevertheless keep asking: 'What does language mean and to what does it refer?' This question relies upon another abiding question which has in fact been the subject of philosophy since the dawn of Western metaphysics: 'What is the meaning of life?' Traditionally, theorists have tried to describe human experience by abstracting it from their own experience, generalising and articulating the critical components of that experience. As theory has become more aware of itself and of the self-reflexivity of language, itself complicated by sexual and cultural politics, it has become increasingly concerned with the relation between experience and its articulation, hence the multiplicity of theories about subjectivity at our disposal. The question is now of defining what may get lost in the translation from experience in its lived forms to our articulation of it. In the context of a poetics of creative writing, this raises questions about truth and knowledge, two concepts dear to philosophy and creative writing. I will therefore select two philosophers who are also creative writers to approach answering this question.

I will begin with Jean-Paul Sartre (1905–80), whose work addresses the question of knowledge and in some ways anticipates where philosophy is at now. For example, his emphasis on individual agency and responsibility antedate Alain Badiou's philosophical position, particularly with regard to the concepts of fidelity and event, that is, if I read Badiou rightly, for his work is, to say the least, complex. Further, some of the seeds of poststructuralism can be traced back to Sartre's work, particularly his conceptualisation of subjectivity. I will then turn to Badiou to explore his work on aesthetics in order to test its relevance to some hypothetical poetics of creative writing.

The Problem of Consciousness and Its Relation to Knowledge

Himself a prolific writer of novels, plays, essays and biographies, Sartre's ideas are useful for creative writers. It is clear from his autobiography, *Les mots* (Sartre, 1964), that literature occupied a huge place in his life from his earliest years, and his evolution as a philosopher developed in parallel with his literary preoccupations. His *L'imaginaire* of 1940, for example, a phenomenological psychology of the imagination, is a study of the imaginary in its relation to the work of art, and can be seen as a philosophical working out of the main themes of his novel *Nausea* (Sartre, 1965), first published in 1938. What is interesting here from the point of view of creative writing is that the novel was written before the scholarly work, thereby suggesting that, for Sartre, there was a strong relationship between these two aspects of his work. Sometimes this created conflicts. He worried that his novel *The Age of Reason*, the first part of the trilogy *The Roads to Freedom*, would appear abstract and artificial, whereas he had set out to write with an existential grasp of the real. In a letter to his lifelong lover Simone de Beauvoir, herself a prolific writer and thinker, he writes of the novel: 'It's a Husserlian work and that's a bit sickening when one has become a Heidegger fanatic' (Sartre, 1983: 180, my translation).

Though contentious, his conception of subjectivity itself is useful in that it considers the problem of consciousness and intentionality. His critique of philosophical models of knowledge is also valuable, particularly in the context of defining knowledge production. Sartre's first novel, *Nausea* (Sartre, 1965 [1938]), approaches the notion of the 'subject in process' and proposes that the meaning of a person's life is not something obscure and in need of interpretation. Rather, it is something that is creatively produced through self-reflection and through the act of writing. In it, the fictional narrator, Antoine Roquentin, suggests that however much he searches the past, he can retrieve only fragments of images, and he is not sure whether they are remembered or invented. 'Nothing is left but words: I could still tell the stories, tell them only too well ... but they are only skeletons' (Sartre, 1965: 52). Ten pages or so later, Roquentin remarks:

When you are living, nothing happens. The settings change, people come in and go out, that's all. There are never any beginnings. Days are tacked on to days without rhyme or reason, it is an endless, monotonous addition…. But when you tell about life, everything changes; only it's a change nobody notices: the proof of that is that people talk about true stories. As if there could possibly be such things as true stories; events take place one way and we recount them the opposite way. (Sartre, 1965: 61–62)

Sartre calls memory 'the crossroads of the real and the imaginary' (Sartre, 1973: 1526), by which he means that we remake the past from the perspective of our present values and objectives. Our motive for doing this, he suggests, hinting at an unconscious desire whose existence he rebuts, is that 'we continually preserve the possibility of changing the meaning of the past' (Sartre, 1965: 116). Thus, the same event may be remembered with quite different details at different times or in different circumstances: it will be rearranged in our minds according to our needs of the moment and we will have different intellectual and emotional responses to it accordingly. The past has no definite meaning of its own. Quite the opposite: it exists in a 'relation of interpretation with the present consciousness' (Sartre, 1969: 28). Sartre clearly gestures here at his indebtedness to Freud. And yet, Sartre disputed Freud's very idea of the unconscious in one of his first lengthy essays, *The Psychology of the Imagination* (Sartre, 2004 [1940]), where he drew the distinction between imagination and metaphorical processes. Was it bad faith on his part? If it was, it was well repressed, for when he argues in *Being and Nothingness* that we choose our lives, it is equally clear that he is not being literal. What he means is that we choose to give meaning to contingent facts, and this choice is not necessarily a fully conscious or deliberate one. According to Sartre, our choices can be discovered only by means of existential psychology, a method by which we look back upon our life and reconstruct the choices that were made as illustrated in our actions.

In contrast to these monumental works, Sartre's discussion of the idea of intentionality in a 1939 article covers only two pages (Sartre, 1970 [1939]). It might not be an exaggeration to say that the foundation for the 800 pages of *Being and Nothingness* (1957 [1943]) can be found in those two pages. While Sartre claims to be describing Husserl's theory of mind, he actually gives it a bit of a twist. He starts with the idea that to know something is to assimilate or digest the object within consciousness. Both realism and idealism, he says, have assumed that 'to know is to eat' (Sartre, 1970 [1939]: 4). He then rebukes this claim:

Husserl persistently affirmed that one cannot dissolve things in consciousness. You see this tree, to be sure. But you see it just where it is:

at the side of the road, in the midst of the dust, eight miles from the Mediterranean coast. It could not enter into your consciousness, for it is not of the same nature as consciousness. (Sartre, 1970 [1939]: 4)

The relation of a mental act to its object is not containing, but intending. The tree is beyond the person who sees it, not only because it is at some distance from the observer, but insofar as it transcends any impression that we might have of it. The reality of the object is not something concealed within, but rather the unlimited series of appearances which are determined by it. Thus the object must always remain beyond consciousness.

As for consciousness, Sartre stresses its lack of content. In *Being and Nothingness*, he writes: 'The first procedure of a philosophy ought to be to expel things from consciousness' (Sartre, 1957 [1943]: li). Consciousness is wholly transparent, empty, insubstantial. Sartre goes on to argue that this amounts to a refutation of determinism, because something which has no content of its own cannot enter into a causal relation. This means that for Sartre, dear reader, you may be aware of what motivates your actions, but this implies that it is the object of intentionality. Sartre concludes: 'I am condemned to exist forever beyond my essence, beyond the causes and motives of my act. I am condemned to be free' (Sartre, 1957 [1943]: 439). None of this is explicit in the short article on Husserl, but Sartre's conclusion encompasses the preoccupations of his existentialist psychology:

Imagine us thus rejected and abandoned by our own nature in an indifferent, hostile and restive world – you will then grasp the profound meaning of the discovery which Husserl expresses in his famous phrase, 'All consciousness is consciousness of something'. (Sartre, 1970 [1939]: 5)

Sartre uses the concept of intentionality to show that we are abandoned in an indifferent world and condemned to freedom. There are some nuances between the various motives that lead to an insistence that knowledge is not a process of assimilation. It is in fact a novel, not a philosophical essay, which explains the general tone of Sartre's remarks on the 'digestive' philosophy of mind. Returning to *Nausea*, Roquentin's experiences show that it arises out of a direct encounter with assimilation:

The thing which was waiting has sounded the alarm, it has pounced upon me, it is slipping into me, I am full of it. It's nothing: I am the Thing. Existence, liberated, released, surges over me. I exist. (Sartre, 1965 [1938]: 143)

The experience of being occupied by existence itself is the central theme of the novel, returned to again and again. It is hard not to read this passage in Freudian terms or to assimilate it with Lacan's theory of anxiety as a signal located at the intersection between the imaginary and the real (Harari, 2001: li). In any case, this certainly anticipates Badiou's take on Lacanian psychoanalysis. But I digress. The experience of being occupied by existence itself, like some mythical thing, is reflected upon when Roquentin says:

> Existence is not something which allows itself to be thought of from a distance; it has to invade you suddenly, pounce upon you, weigh heavily on your heart like a huge motionless animal – or else there is nothing left at all. (Sartre, 1965: 143)

While this may be the only way of realising the meaning of existence, it is also presented as an overwhelming and even horrifying experience, undergone not without some ambivalence: 'I should so like to let myself go, to forget, to sleep. But I can't, I'm suffocating: existence is penetrating me all over, through the eyes, through the nose, through the mouth' (Sartre, 1965 [1938]: 181). We certainly get an idea why Sartre insists that the first task of philosophy is 'to expel things from consciousness'. His motive, it appears, is not so much theoretical as therapeutic. His use of the concept of intentionality is intended not to correct a mistake, Husserl's presumed mistake, but to avoid a danger. Again, it is tempting to interpret this in terms of a defence against the Freudian Thing.

Towards the end of *Being and Nothingness*, Sartre returns to a similar theme when he discusses the idea of possession. He argues that the success of possession brings about an unexpected result. The most complete form of possession is assimilation, where the object gives up its independence. However, this is an ambiguous, if not ambivalent, process. Sartre writes: 'There is underneath this docility a surreptitious appropriation of the possessor by the possessed' (Sartre, 1957 [1943]: 609). It seems that the object has its revenge. The old saying that we are what we eat turns out to be true. Yet in *Being and Nothingness* there is also a complication to this rule. In discussing relations with other people, Sartre suggests that a fundamental element in any such situation is the attempt to absorb the freedom of the other. 'The lover does not desire to possess the beloved as one possesses a thing: he demands a special kind of appropriation. He wants to possess a freedom as freedom' (Sartre, 1957 [1943]: 367). But this freedom lacks any substantial content; it would seem that this project is a very different case from other kinds of possession. Its advantage is obvious enough: if this freedom is a nothingness, its assimilation would seem to present no serious problem. It can be absorbed painlessly and digested with the greatest ease. As a mode of consumption, this may have advantages, for it is not hard to see that one would be hungry again soon. This is not exactly a joke: Sartre himself points out the need for a relentless renewal of the process. But more important, perhaps, is his argument for the ultimate futility of the project itself: it would seem that one freedom cannot stand in a direct relation to another freedom. The need for mediation leads to a dialectical development in which newer forms of relationship can arise. But this, as far as I know, is not the case in Sartre's work. These more complex attempts to reconcile freedom with facticity are no more successful than the one they replace. In the end, Sartre's account does not provide an exception to his general view of possession. Badiou, on the other hand, will provide an alternative, by returning to Lacanian psychoanalysis and turning to mathematics.

Some further insight into Sartre's rejection of a 'digestive' philosophy of mind and his use of the concept of intentionality arise in other places in *Nausea*. I have suggested that his 1939 article on Husserl corresponds to the starting point of *Being and Nothingness* (1938). In point of fact, it also corresponds to the ending of *Nausea* (1943), which begs the question of knowledge production and the relevance of artworks in the scheme of research – indeed, as research, or knowledge production. Towards the close of the novel *Nausea*, Roquentin's ordeal ends with the achievement of a consciousness which has managed to overcome the threat of invasion by existence: 'Lucid, motionless, empty, the consciousness is situated between the walls; it perpetuates itself. Nobody inhabits it anymore' (Sartre, 1965 [1938]: 241). The expulsion of things from consciousness includes even the self: this is just another object towards which intentionality might be directed. All that remains is 'a small living and impersonal transparency' (Sartre, 1965 [1938]: 241). The relation between this and the analysis of consciousness Sartre gives elsewhere is evident enough, yet deeply puzzling.

Another feature of the account given in *Nausea* is worth mentioning. Just as the predicament of Roquentin is due not to philosophical reflection but rather to a direct encounter with existence, so is his liberation brought about through a transformation of experience itself. One particular experience seems to throw light on the reason for this. When Roquentin listens to a recording of a jazz tune, his nausea disappears. Finally, he reflects that the explanation lies in the fact that the music is not something that exists. It is beyond the world of real things. A scratch on the record does not alter the tune itself; even smashing the record would not make a difference. 'It does not exist, since it has nothing superfluous: it is all the rest which is superfluous in relation to it. It is' (Sartre, 1965 [1938]: 248). For Sartre, music has this in common with other forms of art, such as literature: it offers a way of escaping from the contingency of existence. Although Sartre does not say so, the same point might be made concerning logic or mathematics and this is a theme that Badiou will explore at length in his work. As far as *Nausea* is concerned, though, the point is not so much that we cannot affect the transcendent object as that it cannot affect us. A work of art is like an Epicurean god who makes no demands on human beings and threatens no intervention in their pursuits. And like those beings, it provides an ideal at which we can aim in our own lives. This, at least, is the sentiment with which the novel ends.

Sartre insists that the ultimate aim of consumption is 'the dream of a non-destructive assimilation' (Sartre, 1957 [1943]: 579). He explains why in terms of his ontological account of human reality. But can we really have our cake and eat it? We have it from Hegel that desire always destroys its object. His dialectic of consciousness points out the necessity of that aim; and Lacan picks up this point, specifically in 'The subversion of the subject and the dialectic of desire in the Freudian unconscious' (Lacan, 2006 [1960]: 671–703), where he shows, among other things, how desire and the death drive are irrevocably enmeshed. Sartre, however, believes that the goal of knowledge is again an assimilation in which the object nonetheless maintains it integrity. 'That is why the desire to know is one of the forms which can be assumed by to have' (Sartre, 1957 [1943]: 580). It is unclear to what form of knowledge Sartre refers to here, but I take it to be knowledge in general, for what he is doing here is surveying the whole range of human activity in which doing, having and being all come down to the same thing. On this account we would have to conclude that the 'digestive' model of consciousness, against which Sartre argued earlier, is not simply a mistaken view taken by some philosophers, but also what he himself has taken to be the immediate structure of consciousness.

Sartre identifies consciousness with a pure spontaneity and therefore must reject any causal account of knowledge. He criticises Husserl for admitting a certain element of passivity into consciousness. But mental acts are so called because they are actual rather than potential, not because they are active or passive. Mental acts involve something happening in the mind, but they do not imply that any agency is in question. Thus, the uses of the concept of intentionality as a replacement for the 'digestive' model of mind do not represent a move from thinking of knowledge as consumption to thinking of it as production. In order to understand what knowledge production is with reference to creative writing, we cannot negate the unconscious; we also need to make the distinction between knowledge and knowing. More of this in Chapter 9, 'On experiential knowing as creative research mode'

Psychoanalysis, of course, further complicates these matters, a fact that Sartre did not seem to want to see, but that Badiou clearly saw and simplified to advocate a purer form of philosophy and aesthetics. Psychoanalysis has long been involved with other disciplines, including aesthetics and philosophy, in the pursuit of a theory of human creativity. For example, prompted by Heinz Kohut's theory of subjectivity, George Hagman, in 'Art and self' (2009), ponders the relevance of aesthetics for human affairs and argues that creative artists are concerned not only with expressing emotional states but also with 'refining and perfecting an internal vision' (Hagman, 2009: 164). In this respect, Hagman talks at length about Freud's interest in aesthetics, and concludes with neo-humanistic flourish:

> Perhaps one of the reasons that Freud claimed reverence for beauty as a required trait of civilization was because beauty elevates human subjectivity and human values to a transcendent level. The sense of beauty in its reparative and preservative function asserts love over aggression, life over death, and harmony over disintegration. It may even be one of the ways that we reconcile our relationship with the world. Our sense of beauty may not always be certain or consistent with high aesthetic standards. We may challenge cultural assumptions about the beautiful or we may even rebel against beauty. But beauty, like sex and aggression, has been a reality of human life in all cultures, throughout history. Beauty is not illusory nor does it stand in or cover up for something else. Beauty may be one of the most exquisite forms of human meaning that exists. As we view the sense of beauty through the psychoanalytic lenses, we see in it man's search for perfection, transcendence, and hope. (Hagman, 2009: 171)[1]

However, as we have seen, psychoanalysis essentially concerns itself with misunderstandings of language as these are expressed in symptoms. For psychoanalysis, the question is not whether or not language can adequately capture, reflect or convey experience, but how we can either *interpret* or simply *read* the meaning of this language as it points to that which necessarily is lost in translation. What concerns both philosophy and psychoanalysis in the 21st century are the occluded meanings of our language use – that is, precisely that which language does *not* represent.

Interestingly, in the aftermath of the death of Theory, if one pits philosophy against psychoanalysis, one encounters poetry in the final event. This may not come as a surprise in the scheme of Freud's return of the repressed, given that it is Plato who excluded poetry from his Republic, but it is odd that both philosophy and psychoanalysis at the end of the last century, and indeed in the 21st century, end up reconceptualising subjectivity via incursions into the realm of poetry, a phenomenon I have partly attributed to the influence of Julia Kristeva and called the 'poetic turn' (Hecq, 2012c). Lacan, who proclaimed his psychoanalytical approach to be an 'antiphilosophy' (Lacan, 1980: 17; Lacan, 2001: 314), rethought the human subject through studying in depth the work of James Joyce and, later, Chinese poetry. Alain Badiou, now France's leading philosopher, also took poetry to task for rethinking being, event, subject and truth at both individual and collective levels. In his book *The Century* (2008), it is in fact the discourse of poetry which dominates the argument. Isn't this odd? Isn't it odd that the two major advocates of formal language since the 1970s, through their fascination with what Lacan famously called the real – that is, that which is beyond representation – end up arguing in favour not of *interpreting*, but of *reading* poetry. This, it must be stressed, might perhaps only be made possible by their rigorous engagement with mathematics – in particular logic, topology and set theory. Still, it is even more ironic that such engagement with mathematics and poetry now seem to promote, if not proclaim, the return of ontology as well as humanist values.

Why Poetry?

Perhaps this return to poetry was, and remains, *necessary* for philosophy, if only to articulate anew the old problem of the meaning of life after Sartre, among others, heralded the death of metaphysics. For philosophy, this entails rethinking ontology and metaphysics, whose obituaries nourished the work of Derrida, a philosopher who notoriously owes a lot to literature. To a certain extent, this is Badiou's project. According to Slavoj Zizek, cited on the back cover of *Infinite Thought* (Badiou, 2005), it would seem that we must credit Badiou with enacting 'a return to full-blown philosophy striking a thunder into the morass of postmodernist sophisms and plati-tudes'. As the following suggests, we may indeed be witnessing the return of the repressed, as may have been already the case at the dawn of Western thought:

> Plato in his rendition of the hierarchy of pleasures relegated poetry (and by implication the arts) to an inferior status due to its distance from truth. It has nevertheless always been a curiosity that Plato in his philosophical writings in which Socratic thought was privileged draws unashamedly from the language of poetry to argue his case. The black and white steeds that represent oppositional forces in the soul come to mind. Plato, along with Aristotle, laid the ground for metaphysics. In

being concerned with the ultimate nature of reality they found that answers were not forthcoming and that no certain knowledge of metaphysical questions was possible. (McCulloch, 2008)

As this excerpt implies, Plato, who himself induced the repression of poetry by philosophy, could not help its insidious return in his own work. More than two millennia later, it is Peter Hallward (2003), who, among others, signals the return of the repressed, with pointed reference to Badiou:

[Badiou] confirms the Platonic move as essential to a generalized desacralization of thought: poetry must not be placed above philosophy. But unlike Plato, he recognizes that a poetry that has escaped its mimetic function is very precisely a condition of philosophy, rather than its antithesis or rival. To the degree that the poem asserts a subject without an object, or a City without community, or a being without Nature, it deserves to escape its Platonic proscription. (Hallward, 2003: 200)

The interesting question, however, is how this return of the repressed is being effected. Perhaps it has to do with metaphor as event. Taking its cue from the relationship between philosophy and psychoanalysis at the point of their encounter with poetry in some kind of Badiou–Lacan dialogue, this section argues that the knowledge produced by truth in both discourses is fostered by that which was repressed, or foreclosed, namely, that which may be dynamised at the core of the irreducible kernel of the real through metaphor. This will lead us to re-examine the concept of knowledge as it applies to creative writing research and pedagogy.

Plato's problem with poetry and its makers was the problem of representation, that is, mimesis. He blamed it on metaphor, on poets' predilection to use it and to mar the mirror of representation. He therefore sanctioned poetry's disruptive or transgressive impulse and its failure to hold society together. Now that we have had nearly 100 years to acknowledge that 'the centre does not hold' (Yeats, 1982: 99), we seem to be drawn back to the power of metaphor, which, at its core, resides in the ability to understand one thing in terms of another – as a process of translation.

Badiou, as we shall see, provides us with a new approach to being and subjectivity, one that is not 'abstractive' but rather 'subtractive' and thus seemingly antimetaphorical. However, it is precisely through his engagement with the purely formal aspect of mathematics, one that 'isolates the pure gesture of presentation as such' (Hallward, 2003: 57), that he, like Lacan before him, hits upon the materiality of the signifier, and more specifically on metaphor's very kernel, one which may not be representable as such because it is of the order of the real, but one that is nonetheless at the intersection of truth and knowledge. This real kernel, or kernel of the real, is in fact a *thing* which intrudes into a situation or state while confronting this situation or state with its repressed, foreclosed or disavowed ground. It is an anomaly which produces an *event*.

Badiou's philosophy primarily relies upon a distinction between *savoir* (knowledge) and *vérité* (truth), which echoes psychoanalysis' distinction between these two terms as formulated in Lacan's famous 'return to Freud' (Lacan, 2006: 334–364). Moreover, as Adrian Johnston specifies, Badiou's philosophy is founded on 'truths generated by aleatory events in the four "generic procedures" of truth-production (art, love, politics, and science) as "conditions" for philosophy' while appearing to be 'an heir of Lacan, inheriting some of his defining features' (Johnston, 2010: 156). It seems to me that Badiou is closer to Sartre for his privileging of agency over the vagaries of the unconscious. The 'aleatory events' that Johnston is referring to here are incursions, if not intrusions, from the real into the symbolic. The manifestation of such 'aleatory events' also conjures up the 'body–mind' conundrum, one that may just be solved by neuroscience (Damasio, 1989) via pointed detours in the realms of philosophy and linguistics only to assert that the mind is but an extended metaphor (Hopkins, 2000, 2004) and that, perhaps, our thinking processes may not be linear, but work by allusion.

Indeed, forays into the origins of psychoanalysis, especially into Freud's conceptualisation of the primary process, reveal that networks and webs of associations which are meaningless from the perspective of (self-)consciousness – such as associations made on the acoustic and graphic resemblances between signifiers as material rather than meaningful entities (*Vorstellungen*) – encompass the unconscious grounds of psychical life itself. If philosophy scrutinises the presumed depths of the soul in order to discover profound *a priori* meanings anchoring the unified self in its relations with the world as a coherent global whole, psychoanalysis, as intimated by both Lacan and Kristeva, examines the surfaces of the subject to detect traces of the real. This means taking into account what philosophy does not, namely a strange thoughtless thinking out of sync with sensible worldly reality – a thinking in which currents of *jouissance* retrospectively aggregate fragments of phonemes, words, images, affects and memories in movements whose susceptibility to formal articulation and analytic interpretation makes them no less meaningless, at least relative to common-sense.

This is precisely what prompts a philosopher versed in neuroscience and psychoanalysis such as James Hopkins (2000, 2004) to posit how Freud's work on desire, belief and fantasy helps to extend current thinking involving symbolism and metaphor. Hopkins draws useful links between psychoanalysis and recent work on conceptual metaphor, and suggests that such thinking is an important part of our concept of mind; he shows, via Wittgenstein, how it can provide an approach to the mind–body problem. He suggests that the metaphorical or symbolic mapping studied in psychoanalysis, or the conceptual metaphor in cognitive linguistics, could structure our mind in the way Wittgenstein envisaged, and that there may therefore be more to it than various disciplines which emphasise linear and discursive thought, including neuroscience.

For Badiou, what poetry forbids is indeed linear, discursive thought. Structurally speaking, a poem is in direct opposition to a matheme, for poetry relies on images rather than syntax, and this is why poetry, as Julia Kristeva has shown, can be so 'revolutionary' – that is, not only exhilaratingly and dangerously liberating. Contrast, for example, her advocating the destabilisation of the text in *Revolution in Poetic Language* (1984) with her cautioning against it in *The Sense and Non-Sense of Revolt* (2002a: 54–57). Poetry breaks the confines of thought:

> when what is at stake is the opening of thought to the principle of the thinkable, when thought must be absorbed in the grasp of what establishes it as thought, we witness Plato himself submitting language to the power of poetic speech. (Badiou, 2003: 19–20)

The relationship between poetry and philosophy also hinges on the distinction between knowledge and truth – or Truth and truths. However, as Justin Clemens points out, for Badiou, 'philosophy is concerned with Truth (capitalized, singular): it produces no truths (small t, plural) of its own', whereas poetry is one of four discourses capable of producing 'truths (small t, plural)' (Clemens, 2002: 205) – the other three discourses being love, mathematics and politics. A poem is always finite, and as such may be antithetical to philosophy. Nevertheless, the problem of the relationship between the two is not philosophy, which does not hold truth, but rather the singularity of the artistic schema. In his *Handbook of Inaesthetics* (2003), for example, Badiou argues that art ought to be specifically positioned with regard to the event of truth.

Poetry, Truth(s) and the Real

How can an artistic production, which is always finite and singular, Badiou asks, be related to a philosophical schema that transcends the dominant paradigms of the 20th century? Badiou's answer leads us to a definition of the artistic by way of the event as chance encounter with 'the thing' (*das Ding*), perhaps, or at least with its shadow. An event is an encounter with the real as Badiou, not Lacan, understands it: for Badiou's order of the real is a Platonic one – one which is stripped of desire and, more pressingly, *jouissance*. Yet this event occurs in the field of the symbolic. Thus, the artistic production that ruptures an event is the only possible way to think of an art form as singular. Every art form is indeed a thinking of the thought that it itself is, which is why the artwork is always a finite singularity: 'Philosophy does not produce any effective truth. It seizes truths, shows them, exposes them, announces they exist' (Badiou, 2003: 14). The origins of this idea are worth noting, and it is ironic that it is Karl Popper who should provide the link here. Badiou seems to refer first and foremost to Plato, who, in his doctrine of forms, spoke of an objective autonomous third world which existed in addition to the physical world and the world of the mind (Popper, 1972: 154). Karl Popper himself developed this idea, taking his cue from Frege: 'Thoughts are neither things in the external world nor ideas. A third realm must be recognised' (Frege, 1977: 17). Just as Plato took his forms to be timeless and unchangeable, Frege insists that his 'thoughts' could never be altered by any mental activity, and said: 'In thinking we do not produce thoughts, we grasp them' (Frege, 1977: 25).

One could say that Badiou's thesis therefore focuses on how we might think of a new artistic schema that can link the truth of the event to an old schema of artistic production which is not contingent on Sartre's acceptance of the term or even on Lacan's own definition, with its subjection to the discourse of the Other. From his *Handbook of Inaesthetics* (2003) to *The Century* (2008), Badiou's thesis is that the 20th century contained its own aporias: that its three dominant modes of artistic schema (German hermeneutics, Marxism and psychoanalysis) failed to create a satisfactory relationship between art and philosophy. It is from within these aporias that he invites us to approach new modalities and ways of revitalising thought. The main challenge of contemporary thought thus becomes to ascertain a thinking of choice which is not reliant on the master's discourse in any way, one that neither invokes nor sacrifices the master (Badiou, 2003: 54). To sum up Badiou's premise regarding 'Inaesthetics', of which poetry partakes:

(1) Truth (with a capital letter T) does not exist – only truths (with lower-case t).
(2) Each truth is a process and as such it is infinite.
(3) One will call the subject of a truth every finite moment within the infinite part of each truth.
(4) Every truth begins with an event and as such it is unpredictable.

(5) The event shows the void of the situation, because it shows that what there is now was previously devoid of truth.

(6) The choice that binds the subject to the truth is either fidelity (loyalty) to the void, or fidelity to the event.

In order to show how the event emerges into truth, Badiou brings Mallarmé into dialogue with the Arabic poet Labîdben Rabi'a, whose bodies of work link truth, the master and place: 'truth results from the fact that the place – the ordeal of absence and void – first nostalgically and then actively arouses the fiction of a master that would be capable of truth' (Badiou, 2003: 50). Truth thus results from the disappearance of the master into the anonymity of the empty place. This is an event, albeit forced, whereby the master has to disappear in order to make space for truth.

On Badiou's account, the main problem for the modern subject is not being able to choose between mastery and truth, because it is only when truth does not rely on the master that democracy is possible. Similarly, thought must arise *ex nihilo*. It would seem, then, that the modern poem identifies itself as a form of thought, or as a matheme in the Platonic sense. However, it does not yield a sensible expression of the Idea, in the Platonic sense but, rather, relies on a displacement whereby the idea is of the poetic as finite. The sensible presents itself in the modern poem as the enduring nostalgia for the Idea. Thus, poetic truth leaves at its core what it does not have the ability to present or represent. Every truth dwells at the limit that validates it as singular truth, which is to say independent from the whole, or, as Lacan would say, 'extimate' to it. At the core of the modern poem is the unnameable, that is, the *thing* whose naming cannot, and must not, be forced by a truth – the thing whose entry into truth, truth itself, as an event, cannot anticipate. Every regime of truth is grounded in the real by virtue of its own unnameable kernel of truth – in Lacanian terms, its own irreducible *letter* (Lacan, 1998 [1972–73]: 28). Admittedly, Badiou is a long way from a truth established by Aristotelian logic here.

For Badiou, every poem brings power into language, the power of eternally ensuring the disappearance of what presents itself through the poetic retention of its own disappearance: the power of producing presence itself as Idea. We can therefore say that language as the infinite power devoted to presence is the unnameable in poetry. Like a matheme, a poem is an operation, not an artistic extension of the world. The world is that which is designated as more essential than objectivity. For Badiou, for example, the Mallarméan poem *par excellence* depends on the dissolution of the object from its own purity (Badiou, 2003: 57). Accordingly, the task of the modern poet is thus to nominate him- or herself as spiritual performer.

Paul Celan, Badiou suggests, shows us the way for thinking about modern poetry through dealing – rather tragically – with his recognition that the whole, or the Other, is actually void: it is nothing (Badiou, 2003: 63; Badiou, 2008: 87).

In order to escape the opacity of the letters that the poem is made of, Badiou seems to suggest that the reader ought to be dedicated to the operation of the poem itself. In other words, the reader must literally will his or her own transliteration in the act of reading. Following Badiou's logic further, such reading proscribes interpretation. This is, oddly enough, also Lacan's thesis from seminar XVIII onwards, where, in 'D'un discours qui ne serait pas du semblant' (2006 [1971–72]), reading takes precedence over interpretation – with theoretical and clinical consequences which are currently the object of international research in the area of subjectivity studies and psychoanalysis. While Lacan firmed his thoughts on the subject via selective incursions into the writings of Joyce and Chinese poetry, Badiou firmed his via no less selective incursions into world literature. He favoured the works of Arthur Rimbaud, Stéphane Mallarmé, Paul Celan, Samuel Beckett, Friedrich Hölderlin, Georg Trakl, Osip Mandelstam and Fernando Pessoa. Although Badiou dwells on Mandelstam's poem 'The age' (reproduced in Badiou, 2008: 12–13), whose central figure, the beast, provides an allegory for the 20th century, it is the work of the Portuguese poet Fernando Pessoa which seems to be emblematic of the century in light of the Badiouan logic of the poem broached above.

Over the span of his relatively short career, Pessoa created over 80 heteronyms in writings devoid of either reference to self or interpretation of autobiographical surroundings. His poems in fact may embody some mathematical code which has yet to be cracked. Moreover, each of Fernando Pessoa's heteronyms have distinct philosophical, poetic and political positions. It is in fact Pessoa's failure to stick to any one identity or subject position, as well as his refusal to be subjected to any knowledge system, which inflects his poetic selves with enigmas. Badiou contends in both the *Handbook of Inaesthetics* and *The Century* that any attempt at identifying any singularity in Pessoa's work is meant to elude our grasp, that his poems are like cubist paintings: they stare into the light, in an anti-Platonic sense, and are opposed to any absolute Idea. Thus, each text becomes a sort of game, a mathematical code that makes its way throughout a body of work which is eventful, indeed, 'evental' *par excellence*: an encounter with the utter aloneness of the one, its own negativity and its constant displacement in a non-representational realm – the real as Badiou understands it. If am I not misrepresenting Badiou's ideas, this does not seem at all helpful for creative writers. Moreover, I cannot help but associate these last sentences with the words 'being as nothingness', which, of course, resonates with Sartre's *Being and Nothingness* (Sartre, 1957).

This is an opportune resolution, for my aim in this chapter was to offer the reader a reading experience that offered alternatives to the dominant Lacanian one of this book, as one might with the reading of a poem. In a similar vein, but starting from a different perspective and very much in poetic mode, the next chapter investigates the creative process in its intimate relationship with subjectivity.

Note

(1) I am grateful to Joan Howard for pointing out, albeit tongue in cheek, this passage in Hagman's paper.

8 Inking the *In-Between*

To write –
The inkwell, crystal as a consciousness, with its drop,
At the bottom, of shadows ... casts the lamp aside.
Stéphane Mallarmé

This notion of the death instinct must be broached through its
resonances in what I will call the poetics of Freud's work.
Jacques Lacan

Writing is bound by two silences: the one from which it emerges, and the one towards which it tends. Thus the writing process entails a dialectic between the self and non-self that, before death arrives, can only be translated as self and other – its twins, doubles, mirrors, ghosts, daemons, antagonists or secret-sharers. From a psychoanalytic viewpoint, this process constantly re-stages a dialectic between the love object and its imaginative recuperation, the Other bearer of the Law and its imaginative creation, the ego and its alter ego or, indeed, the defective ego and its symbolic avatars.

But what is writing? This chapter seeks answers to this Mallarméan question in personal experience and in the teachings of psychoanalysis. In order to approach this question, it tackles two subsidiary themes, namely the *why* and the *where from* of creative writing. It begins with a mediation on writing as a mode of being *in-between* – life and death, sanity and insanity, self and other – in order to focus on Lacan's seminar on Joyce, which addresses these questions from a theoretical point of view (Lacan, 2005 [1975–76]). I suggest that writing may have two functions. In most cases, it fulfils a lack, and as such it is an uninterrupted work of mourning, a continuous linking and inking of the 'in-between'. In some cases, it may also be a structural necessity, as Lacan argues was the case for Joyce, who avoided psychosis by deploying his art. By way of introduction, let us see what insights my other, the creative writer, may have gleaned on this topic.

The *In-Between*

> One morning before the dawn I stood on a cliff-top above Beehive Falls in the Grampians, mountains that roll west of Melbourne, Victoria, Australia. In despair I spread out my arms and uttered a primal cry. The waterfall kept running. The darkness before dawn remained dark.
>
> And then, that glorious sunlight.
>
> In the darkness, there came a turning. It was as though the dark itself offered a *leitmotif*. At that point I saw just two qualities: an ability to *be*, and to be *attentive*. Contemplating that space, I was aware of some presence, aware of souls inhabiting the apparent void, aware of the long and newly dead. There, in that *in-between* space, everything seemed to come together. In the light of this inward sun, it all made sense again.
>
> The turning happened. I surrendered to some invisible force. An inner world opened up in me. I began to walk and as I walked I began to speak again. I was being walked along, spoken in, thought through and feeling for. (Hecq, 2013b)

It is this magical turning that I seek when I write, especially poetry. The turning comes when I am not paying attention. It comes when I am distracted by my imaginative body, an extension of my bodily self into some imaginative space. I learn to surrender to the wise or crazy forces in this imaginative body, a body that knows what I don't know. Thus it seems to me that the creative process cannot be forced to happen. A poem will not come through the use of reason and intention alone. In the first instance at least, a poem just happens. As I write these words, I am reminded of Keats's notion of 'negative capability', a state in which the poet 'is capable of being in uncertainty, mysteries, doubts, without any irritable reaching after fact and reason' (Keats, 1947).

As is well known, many creative writers have experimented with ways of attaining 'negative capability' in the creative process. Some, like the 19th-century essayist Thomas De Quincey, advocated drugs as a means of bypassing the critical faculty and giving rise to spontaneous mental imagery; and writers such as Rimbaud, Huxley and Burroughs continued this line of experimentation into more recent times. A less hazardous approach would be exploiting Winnicott's concept of 'transitional space' (Winnicott, 1971) or Jung's method of 'active imagination' (Jung, (1997 [1916]), devised for the therapeutic purpose of achieving a healthy balance between the conscious and the unconscious, but which has an obvious application to developing artistic creativity.

'Active imagination' is the method Jung applied from 1913 till 1930 for what he described as 'his confrontation with the unconscious' (Hoerni, 2009: viii).[1] Jung believed that it was possible to train ourselves to produce 'free fantasies' through 'systematic exercises for eliminating critical attention, thus producing a vacuum in consciousness', an inner space not intruded upon by the 'inner critic or judge who immediately comments on everything' we say or do (Jung, 1997 [1916]). Active imagination can be practised through any of the arts; it involves turning the attention inwards and focusing on a feeling, however vague, and allowing it to emerge into a visual image, idea or shape, which is then given form. For the writer, this might be done through automatic writing, and it is also well known that writers from André Breton and the Dadaists to Allen Ginsberg and the Beat poets have used automatic writing as the basis of their creative process.

Through this by-way of 'negative capability', let us return to poetic *attentiveness*, a term I use here simply because it conveys the active involvement of the imaginative body in the creative process. What I mean by poetic attentiveness is not a *state*, but rather a *gesture* enhanced by a state of hyperawareness. It is an inner gesture whereby the 'I' relinquishes its usual control and takes, as it were, a step back, allowing an inner space to open up, so that it can simultaneously be inside and outside, both the observer and the observed. This gesture involves an alteration of the senses. It therefore alters the way 'I' relates to things: 'I' attends to the world not so much in thinking mode, the sharp-pointed focusing with the mind, but in feeling mode, the broad, hovering attention with the body.

What emerges spontaneously at this turning point is always surprising, and therefore exciting. However, it is not always benign. In the act of relinquishing control of the rational mind, angels may emerge. But so may ghosts and daemons. Giving free rein to unconscious forces is an unpredictable and dangerous business. Time to pay attention, again.

My point is that creative writing and the kind of attentiveness it presupposes *is* or *becomes* a way of being. The creative writer is Janus-like at one and sometimes two removes: looking both ways into the past and the future, but also inside and out, triangulating two ways of looking at the world into what I have called 'reading in Braille' (Hecq, 2012b: 34). This triangulation denotes how creative writers reconcile two essentially different modes of knowing. For me, the 'turning' happens when I hover and pick up traces – affects, rhythms, images, meanings.

But how does a poem, for instance, come into being? I used to think that the very first stage in writing a poem was the conceiving of an image: a couple of words or lines gathered into some linguistic haiku-like artefact that is instantaneously grasped. In actual fact, often an image is the conclusion of the poem; the hard work is to blaze a trail through the ink of language towards the flickering light which reveals shadows of what the poem is and who I am, or might become. On reflection, I write or, rather, the poem writes itself, in Mallarmé's words, 'black on white' (Mallarmé, 1973b: 230), that is to say, darkening with the very inkwell of my unconscious, producing a light only by projecting shadows. The image is the point of arrival initiating another journey through linguistic blindness towards other shadows, which, paradoxically, will inform flashes of insight or moments of clarity. This suggests that what is at stake when I write is a reversal, a shaking up of subjective knowledge (of that knowledge which thinks it knows itself), a reversal and a shaking up of 'my self' and its self-knowledge. Each poem is a drop of ink which contains knowledge that escapes me, but through which I become 'some one other' (insisting on some elusive singularity and alterity) who knows how to escape in order to be.

The true beginnings of a poem lie somewhere way back of beyond, as we say in Australia, that is, in trackless territory. The conception of the image may well be the last stage of the process, before the very last drop of ink – the perception of the image. The earlier stages are almost imperceptible, because they occur prior to consciousness in language; and as I am, after all, looking for words, these pre-verbal, or proto-verbal, events may not be noticed. I first become aware of them through their effects on my mood and conduct, and then only gradually do I recognise the pattern that confirms their connection with the creative process.

A poem begins as an inner disturbance – the loss of equilibrium that impels rhythm. In this proprioceptive moment, I seemingly become restless, unable to settle or to focus. 'My self' is a caged animal and it begins to pace inside its cage. The best thing would be to go for a walk or a swim to escape from this inner disturbance. Yet often I don't go out at all, and this loss of equilibrium can become disturbing both for myself and for others around me. If I don't recognise it, I may become fractious and reactive. But if I walk, or pace, I find the rhythm – or perhaps it finds me. A formative structuring emerges out of the inkwell of my unconscious.

Initially, while moving about, I am aware of the world around me, but gradually I become absorbed in my own inward processes: thoughts, feelings, memories, anxieties, fears.... Whatever rhythm I adopt, or whatever rhythm adopts me, the event of pausing is crucial, for it initiates the next stage. Then I will notice my mood – or, rather, I will notice that I inhabit a mood. It has particular qualities, which are best characterised as tonal: there is some resonant affect or undefined feeling as if awaking from a dream. I live intensely in this mood. And then the image comes.

This is a thrilling moment, and I settle down with any blank page or scrap of paper at hand. I write the image down. I write the other words which will have accrued already as well. I pace again, re-awakening the rhythm of the poem. As I balance equilibrium and movement, the disturbance wanes and the poem grows. Then all motion is suspended, and I live wholly in an inward mood, stilled and reflective. I now have to press myself into this inwardness, into something which is really a state of 'nothing there'.

This experience of the 'nothing there' occurs at a distinct threshold in-between two states – a combination of sensory limits, memory limits and everyday consciousness operating within those limits. I have to work my mind past the inner resistance of two obstacles: my mind's own subjective habits, and the 'already known'. I have to guide my mind towards a vitalised state of consciousness where something else might be fully realised and not just reformulated by my intellect. I have to strive each time to stand in that experience of uncertain shadows. Often I want to avoid doing this: it is demanding work; it is dream work, except that I'm awake. At times it is frightening, and the desire to escape is strong.

I finish the poem in the 'nothing there', subsequently testing each word, each line, each stanza or section against the pacing and the stillness, with the mood and the absence. Sometimes I have to choose whether to admit or deny phrases or thoughts which are part of the 'already known'. Occasionally, they remain with the body of words as a trace of 'my self' or some cultural Other whose words I have incorporated – the phantom hand that pushes the poem to its resting place: the inhabited silence beyond its own limits.

It is a strange place, the 'nothing there'. It is that place of language where writing is located for me: where I think 'my self' is being played with. But this may be a delusion. And it is a strange thing, this business of wanting to discard the 'already known', for upon re-reading my own body of work I am only too aware of its repetitions, replications, reiterations. Perhaps I only write crab-like what I already know, but don't know that I know. I took as an example the act of writing a poem, but I believe that, as far as I am concerned, all writing happens in that way, including research, an idea I develop in the next chapter.

Before turning to more theoretical matters I would like to invite Mallarmé to speak again from the shadows of time as the privileged Other of my poetic self and its many others. Here is an excerpt from 'Le mystère dans les lettres' ('The mystery in letters'), which brilliantly captures the task of the poet as relinquishment of self, and accidental, yet necessary, labour of love:

To bear down, according to the page, on the white, which inaugurates it, its simplicity, in itself, forgetful even of the title which would speak too loudly; and when there is aligned in a break, the least, disseminated break, chance vanquished word by word, indefectibly the white returns, gratuitous before, certain now, to conclude that nothing is beyond, and to authenticate silence. (Mallarmé, 1973b: 233)

Doubling the Other, Ever Absent

Writing bears the mark of symbolic castration – the cut which produces the letter in the aftermath of the Oedipus complex. It signifies a loss and expresses a desire to retrieve the primary love object, namely, the mother, or its substitutes (Hecq, 2005). In the handling of this loss, writing presupposes an encounter with the unconscious and a doubling of the other. Marguerite Duras knew this well. Writing, she says, comes from the 'inner shadow', or the 'black block', where one supposes the archives of the ego are, 'some region which hasn't been explored yet' (Duras, 1993: 72). When writing, she wants to show the 'blank in the chain', the 'hole' (Duras, 1993: 18); in other words, she wants to pen down the hole in the real, the very faltering of language, even though, like Joyce, she also wants the enduring fame inscribed in the name she chose for herself (her real name is Donnadieu). Thus, if writing is, as Freud (Anzieu, 1981) and Derrida (2001) have shown in their own ways, an uninterrupted work of mourning, it may also produce, through its own artifice, a kind of prop for the writing subject. In this sense, writing is indeed 'stronger than the mother' (Duras, 1984: 12).

> *all* writing of the narrative kind, and perhaps all writing, is motivated, deep down, by a fear of and a fascination with mortality – by a desire to make the risky trip to the Underworld, and to bring something or someone back from the dead. (Atwood, 2002: 156)

Undeniably, the requirements of the ego meet the aims of the unconscious in the compulsion to write. These, Freud argued, are founded on a third party which takes into account the imperatives of both superego and ego ideal. Freud, however, did not develop this thesis further: because he believed in the desexualisation of the drives, he did not take into account the unconscious significance of sublimation (Freud, 2001 [1923–25]: 45). Melanie Klein (1988a) saw writing as a desire for reparation in the wake of the destructive drive – if only because of the negation of the real world that writing entails. Winnicott (1971) placed writing in a potential space where it has the status of transitional object, the space of play and illusion between ego and object. Worth considering though these views are, they do not enlighten us about the structural function of writing – how it may, for example, assist in the remaking of the ego.

In his famous essay 'The death of the author', Roland Barthes points out that to write is both a transitive and an intransitive verb, the intransitive form being performative, 'in which the enunciation has no other content ... than the act by which it is uttered' (Barthes, 1977b: 145–146). Like the early Lacan (2006 [1953]) – and unlike Derrida (1976 [1967]) – Barthes takes into account the precedence of speech over writing. What Lacan teaches us is that if an enunciation produces an utterance, it also veils the fact that it is the void that supports it. Some *unutterance* is included in the act of uttering – included, but hidden. The task of the poet is to utter that which cannot be enunciated. Writing in the intransitive sense testifies to this movement, this game of hide and seek with the real – the unnamable. Writing is 'both keeping silent and speaking' (Duras & Gauthier, 1974: 19). If it tends towards silence, it is in the sense that Flaubert expressed it, he, who aspired to write a book about nothing – a book where some unknown substance would appear in a pure state with no characters for support (Brown, 2006: 289). This is the silence of the Other *jouissance*: the silence of the drive at work in the 'ciphering' of 'literary writing' (Attié, 2005: 192); the silence at stake in Gerald Murnane's 'The breathing author' (Murnane, 2005); not the silence of exhaustion of the phallic *jouissance* that Maurice Blanchot hints at in *L'espace littéraire* (Blanchot, 1974) but the silence of the finishing line, whereby the farther along in the process of creation, the closer the work draws to that point of inescapable silence, the vanishing point where the desire to become silent lies.

Of Necessary Artifices: Writing the Father

'Only writing is stronger than the mother', insists Marguerite Duras (1984: 12). Would writing then play the role of paternal function? For Lacan, writing is a knotting, not a tracing. In this sense it is radically different from Derrida's 'arche-writing' as the transcendental backdrop of linguistic systems (Derrida, 1976 [1967]). Yet for Lacan, the written is inherent in the act of speaking (Miller, 2003b: 6) and so writing is ingrained in the act of speaking. It has 'the effect of a pure signifier' (the signifier of the Father as author of the Law and death) because there is a law which is 'revealed ... as identical to a language order' (Lacan, 2006 [1953]: 229), a law whose 'subjective pivot' (Lacan, 2006 [1953]: 229) is the prohibition of incest, a law which is dialectically opposed to the desire of the mother as Other. It is the function of the father to impose this law on the subject in the Oedipus complex. Indeed:

> It is in the *name of the father* that we must recognize the basis of the symbolic function which, since the dawn of historical time, has identified his person with the figure of the law. (Lacan, 2006 [1953]: 230, original emphasis)

In other words, to speak is nothing else but to consent to the prohibition of incest. Nowhere is this made clearer than in Lacan's paper 'On a question prior to any possible treatment of psychosis' (Lacan, 2006 [1959a]: 445–488), where he presents the Oedipus complex as a metaphor, namely, the paternal metaphor, in which the signifier of the Name of the Father substitutes for that of the desire of the mother. The importance of the Name of the Father as structuring agent is developed in the seminar on the psychoses (Lacan, 1993 [1955–56]), where he shows that if this signifier is foreclosed or, arguably, *de facto* foreclosed (Harari, 2002), psychosis results. Thus, the function of The Name of the Father is to confer identity on the subject by naming and positioning him or her in the symbolic order as well as to signify the prohibition of incest.

For Lacan, psychosis results when the key signifier of the Name of the Father is not admitted to the symbolic system and thus leaves a hole where this signifier should be, inscribed in the unconscious. Though foreclosure occurs at the moment of the Oedipus complex, the onset of psychosis is triggered years later by a particular type of encounter that Lacan calls an encounter with 'One-father' (Lacan, 2006 [1959a]: 481). For Lacan, this implies that the psychotic structure will have existed long before a psychotic episode, when the illness suddenly and dramatically appears, as is obvious in the case of Paul Daniel Schreber, who had led a relatively normal personal, social and professional life until the age of 51 (Freud, 2001 [1911–13]; Lacan, 1993 [1955–56]). The encounter with One-father, which is a call for symbolic recognition, is brought about in situations that arise under two circumstances: when the subject is in a particularly intense relation with a narcissistic component; and when, in this situation, the question of the father arises from a third position, one that is external to the erotic situation. This would mean that once the psychosis is triggered, everything will have changed for good. But what about before the onset? It is in pursuing this question that Lacan proposes that, in some cases, there is something that plays the role of *suppléance* (suppletion) – a substitute, a stand-in, or artifice.

It is indeed intriguing that some psychotic individuals have been capable of making important scientific or artistic contributions. The German mathematician Georg Cantor and the French writer Antonin Artaud are famous examples because the psychotic episodes they went through are well documented. Lacan also speculates that there may be cases where the psychosis never declares itself. In these cases the pre-psychotic subject seems to find a substitute for the foreclosed signifier that enables him or her to maintain the symbolic links necessary for relatively normal, or even stunningly creative, functioning. Lacan argues that James Joyce was such a case (Lacan, 2005 [1975–76]) and this line of thought has more recently been taken up by a number of analysts (Brousse, 1988; Miller, 1993; Skriabine, 2005; Soler, 1993).

But let us return to the Oedipus complex, whose outcome is a symbolic castration that signifies a renunciation, a loss, but is also 'as such a symptom. It is because the Name of the Father is also the father of the name that everything holds together, which doesn't make the symptom less necessary' (Lacan, 2005 [1975–76]: 22, my translation). Speech needs to be anchored in an enunciation, anchored by way of inking, perhaps, with writing as the trace of the anchoring process. In that sense, writing would be the archiving of speech. By signing the subject's inscription, writing would testify to its own enunciation – writing as a recognition of the place where speaking originates from. Thus, writing brings into being the subject's renunciation of the mother, a cut usually performed by the father. Writing inscribes the void – the hole with no support but itself. It is in this sense that writing has a paternal function. To write oneself into the symbolic order is an act of self-creation. One might say that the process entails symbolic matricide and patricide, or, as Barthes puts it, 'a staging of the (other, hidden, or hyposta-tized) father' (Barthes, 1977b: 10).

The American Paul Auster wrote his first literary novel, *The Invention of Solitude* (Auster, 2012 [1982]), 'in response to [his] father's death' (Auster, 1998: 275). Here is what he says about his experience of the writing process:

> The astonishing thing ... is that at the moment when you are most truly alone, when you truly enter a state of solitude, that is the moment when you are not alone anymore, when you start to feel your con-nection with others. I believe I even quote Rimbaud in that book, 'Je est un autre' – I is another – and I take that sentence quite literally. In the process of writing or thinking about yourself, you actually become someone else. (Auster, 1998: 276)

If there is such a thing as the pleasure of the text, it is because the text is a substitute for a lost satisfaction. There is a kind of victory over this loss, which manifests itself in the work of mourning – as fury, ecstasy, denial, anxiety, negation, for what inhabits the text is, like couch grass, silently pushing its way forward. Between the loss and its symbolic recuperation, there is something else: the trace of desire in the transgression, which is no other than a symbolic killing of the father as symptom. In the case of James Joyce, as in the case of his fictitious alter ego Stephen Dedalus, this symbolic murder is necessary to ensure redemption in the construction of the ego, what Lacan calls *sinthome*.

Joyce's Ego as Work in Progress

Sinthome is an archaic spelling of the French *symptôme*, from which the English 'symptom' derives. Lacan (re-)introduces the term in 1975 as the title for his seminar on James Joyce for its punning possibilities. Through an elaboration of his topology of the subject as underpinned by the concept of the Borromean knot (so-called because the figure of the three interconnected rings is found on the coat of arms of the Borromeo family) and a reading of Joyce's writings, Lacan redefines the symptom not as a formation of the unconscious underpinned by linguistic concepts – a definition he upholds consistently until seminar V – but as that which ensures the subject's survival by providing a unique organisation of *jouissance*. The conceptual shift from linguistics to topology which is typical of Lacan's later work proposes the *sinthome* as a kernel of *jouissance* immune to the efficacy of the symbolic – as the indelible trace of a subject's unique mode of enjoyment.

Lacan's seminar on Joyce elaborates upon his theory of the Borromean knot. The knot we are dealing with, regarding Joyce and the function of his art, is the Borromean knot as Lacan envisages it in *Encore*, namely, as a group of three rings which are linked in such a way that if any one of them is severed, all three become undone (Lacan, 1998 [1972–73]: 124). It is worth remembering that Lacan at this stage conceives of the subject's structure as a Borromean knot that ties the real, the symbolic and the imaginary orders together so that if one is cut loose all three are set free. The three orders, it must be stressed, operate on the same plane, which also means that there is no beginning and no end, no first word and no last word – as in *Finnegans Wake* (Joyce, 1992 [1939]). With regard to Joyce, Lacan claims that there is an extra ring to the knot, a fourth ring that he calls *sinthome*, an umbrella term for symptom, father, ego, *suppléance* (suppletion), for it is Lacan's thesis that Joyce's writing is symptom brought about by the deficiency of his father (Lacan, 2005 [1975–76]: 19).

Lacan reads Joyce's writing as an extended *sinthome*, a fourth term whose addition to the Borromean knot enables Joyce's ego to cohere. In other words, Joyce, who, as a child, faced the deficiency of the Name of the

Father, managed to fend off the onset of psychosis through his art. Writing acted as a suppletion, a supplementary link in the subjective knot.

For Lacan, the art of the writer who made his name famous was a way of compensating for the fact that in his case the knot had come undone (Lacan, 2005 [1975–76]: 87). Joyce's desire to become an artist would hence have been a way of compensating for the fact that his own father never was a Father. Joyce's symptom consists in substituting his own ego for the other, faulty, *de facto*, foreclosed, Name of the Father. Joyce's father had indeed neglected his son's education, leaving him instead in the hands of the Jesuits. For Joyce, Lacan says, 'the fact of being a writer compensates for the fundamental deficiency of the father, for the abdication of his paternal responsibility' (Lacan, 2005 [1975–76]: 89, my translation). To give one's name value is one way of compensating for the father's resignation of his part. And so Joyce's name and self-made ego, Lacan argues, is the mythically inflected Stephen Dedalus.

Studying Joyce prompts Lacan to speak of the failure of the knot, namely, the slip of the knot – as in slip of the tongue. Joyce's valuing of his ego compensates for the slipping and untying of the knot. The knot is faulty, not properly tied with respect to the three dimensions of the real, imaginary and symbolic. This faultiness is due to the fact that the father becomes other as signifier, namely, from the symbolic dimension. In the chapter titled 'The writing of the ego', Lacan dwells on Joyce's relationship with his own body. Joyce's ego, he suggests, has the specific function of an object that can be discarded. It is abject. Writing is that which props it up, indeed, is necessary to its (re)structuring (Lacan, 2005 [1975–76]: 147).

Let us see how fiction stages Joyce's family romance with writing as a work of mourning and as a structural prop that appears in the place of the paternal function.

In *A Portrait of the Artist as a Young Man* (Joyce, 1986 [1916]) Stephen Dedalus is only six when he joins Conglowes Wood College. On his first day at school he is flanked by a teary mother and a father who urges him never to 'dob in' a friend. At school, Stephen feels different. He lacks the physical abilities and worldly knowledge which is part of his schoolmates' social grammar. He longs 'to be at home and lay his head on his mother's lap' (Joyce, 1986 [1916]): 12).

Stephen is 11 when the family moves to Dublin due to his father's bankruptcy. At one point, walking at his father's side, listening to the same old stories, 'hearing again the names of the scattered and dead revellers who had been the companions of his father's youth', Stephen listens with no compassion but 'a faint sickness sighed in his heart' (Joyce, 1986 [1916]: 84). Stephen remembers his father's voice:

I'm talking to you as a friend, Stephen. I don't believe a son should be afraid of his father. No. I treat you as your grandfather treated me when I was a young chap. We were more like brothers than father and son. I'll never forget the first day he caught me smoking.... He didn't say a word.... (Joyce, 1986 [1916]): 84)

From these confidences from Simon Dedalus to his son, two statements strike the reader: 'I don't believe a son should be afraid of his father' and 'We were more like brothers than father and son'. It seems that Simon Dedalus does not make much of what Lacan calls 'the authority of the father's speech' (Lacan, 2006 [1959a]: 481). This 'letting down' is a 'falling down' for Stephen and it glaringly and noisily enhances his feelings of alienation, indeed, dissociation:

nothing moved him or spoke to him from the real world unless he heard in it an echo of the infuriated cries within him. He could respond to no human appeal, dumb and insensible to the call of summer and gladness and companionship, wearied and dejected by his father's voice. (Joyce, 1986 [1916]: 85)

It is at this point that Joyce evokes the feeling of estrangement that Stephen experiences towards his own thoughts:

I am Stephen Dedalus. I am walking beside my father whose name is Simon Dedalus. We are in Cork, in Ireland. Cork is a city. Our room is in the Victoria Hotel. Victoria and Stephen and Simon. Simon and Stephen and Victoria. Names. (Joyce, 1986 [1916]: 85)

For Stephen, there is nothing to hold on to but names. Names without referents. The order of language collapses. Stephen is even unable to read the signboards of the shops he passes, for he can 'scarcely interpret the letters' (Joyce, 1986 [1916]: 85).

Later, on the night of the day the family home is sold, Stephen follows his father around the city from bar to bar, with Simon Dedalus telling the same old tale:

that he was an old Corkonian, that he had been trying for thirty years to get rid of his Cork accent and that Peter Pickackfax beside him was his eldest son but that he was only a Dublin jackeen. (Joyce, 1986 [1916]: 86)

One humiliation succeeds another, and when the question of Simon's paternity arises in a tease, a further experience of dissociation befalls Stephen:

An abyss of fortune or of temperament sundered him from them. His mind seemed older than theirs…. No life or youth stirred in him as it had stirred in them. He had known neither the pleasure of companionship with others nor the vigour of rude male health nor filial piety. Nothing stirred within his soul but a cold and cruel and loveless lust. His childhood was dead or lost and with it his soul capable of simple joys, and he was drifting amid life like the barren shell of the moon. (Joyce, 1986 [1916]: 88)

This passage marks Stephen's final rejection of everything his impostor of a father stands for. It also suggests how Stephen's imagination functions. To the chaos and ugliness he associates with the world of the father, he opposes a new order. Presently he invokes Shelley's unfinished poem 'To the moon' (1824), the lost object – both mother and ego – of the above passage. At other times he builds his own new order, drawing upon linguistic inventiveness, literary lore and mythological references. But when the illusion of resisting the sordid fails him, he re-finds and makes use of that which he loathes in a gesture of *père-version* – a pun on 'father version' and 'perversion'.

In this *Bildungsroman*, Joyce famously evokes the torments of puberty and tells of Stephen's first encounter with woman – this does not necessarily take us away from the Name of the Father and the Last Judgment, only closer to perversion. Stephen is 13 and ablaze with desire: he turns to woman as fantasy 'to appease the fierce longings of his heart before which everything else was idle and alien' (Joyce, 1986 [1916]: 89). Joyce makes it clear that, despite all attempts at sublimation, there is no barrier between within and without. The real of *jouissance* constantly threatens to erupt:

From without as from within the waters had flowed over his barriers: their tides began once more to jostle fiercely above the crumbled mole. (Joyce, 1986 [1916]: 89)

Moreover, desire is a guilty desire: 'beside the savage desire within him to realize the enormities which he brooded on nothing was sacred' (Joyce, 1986 [1916]: 90). Stephen's transgressive fantasies are presented thus:

He bore cynically with the shameful details of his secret riots in which he exulted to defile with patience whatever image had attracted his eyes…. A figure that had seemed to him by day demure and innocent came towards him by night through the winding darkness of sleep, her face transfigured by a lecherous cunning, her eyes bright with brutish joy. Only the morning pained him with its dim memory of dark orgiastic riots, its keen and humiliating sense of transgression. (Joyce, 1986 [1916]: 91)

Stephen's desire is an infernal desire for transgression, a desire to sully his language and his faith: 'verses passed from his lips and the inarticulate cries and the unspoken brutal words rushed forth from his brain to force a passage' (Joyce, 1986 [1916]: 91). Thus, Joyce speaks of a breaking in, out and through, namely, a forcing. Stephen is drawn to sin as though he were animated by some daemonic, sardonic, infernal force. This *push-to-sin* proves to be a *push-to-jouissance*. 'He wanted to sin with another of his kind', writes Joyce, 'to *force* another being to sin with him and to exult with her in sin' (Joyce, 1986 [1916]: 91, original emphasis). The *jouissance* adumbrated here is equivalent to some mental invasion brought about by a slow and painful infiltration of the drive:

> He felt some dark presence moving irresistibly upon him from the darkness, a presence subtle and murmurous as a flood filling him wholly with itself. Its murmur besieged his ears like the murmur of some multitude in sleep; its subtle steams penetrated his being. (Joyce, 1986 [1916]: 91)

The being at stake here is a sinning one, and so one obscene word imposes itself on Stephen's mind:

> the cry that he had strangled for so long in his throat issued from his lips. It broke from him like a wail of despair from a hell of sufferers and died in a wail of furious entreaty, a cry for an iniquitous abandonment, a cry which was but the echo of an obscene scrawl which he had read on the oozing wall of a urinal. (Joyce, 1986 [1916]: 92)

Stephen is now 16. In his first encounter with a prostitute: 'A young woman ... laid her hand on his arm to detain him and gazed into his face' (Joyce, 1986 [1916]: 92). Joyce describes Stephen's first embrace as a fall, an abandonment to sin – utter symbolic castration:

> Give me a kiss, she said.
>   His lips would not bend to kiss her...
>   With a sudden movement she bowed his head and joined her lips to his and he read the meaning of her movements in her frank uplifted eyes. It was too much for him. He closed his eyes, surrendering himself to her, body and mind, conscious of nothing in the world but the dark

pressure of her softly parting lips. They pressed upon his brain as they pressed upon his lips ... and between them he felt an unknown and timid pressure, darker than the swoon of sin....
(Joyce, 1986 [1916]: 92–94)

In *A Portrait*, the fear of God both exists and doesn't exist, just as the father is and then disappears, yet Joyce insists on the impossible redemption of sins. The *jouissance* portrayed above as a flowing of substance out of the body has neither brought about the wrath of God nor the much-feared castration: 'At his first violent sin he had felt a wave of vitality pass out of him and had feared to find his body or soul maimed by the excess' (Joyce, 1986 [1916]: 96).

What exultation.

There are two other crucial passages in *A Portrait* which Lacan dwells on, where Joyce presents Stephen's relation to his body. Interestingly, both passages revolve around a beating episode: first, when aged six, Stephen has undergone some corporal punishment, which is qualified as being *unjust* and *cruel;* and second, following a fist-fight in his early teens.

In the first instance, soon after starting school, Stephen breaks his glasses, which prevents him from carrying on with tasks such as writing. When Father Dolan, the prefect of studies, barges into the classroom in search of 'little loafers that want flogging' (Joyce, 1986 [1916]: 44) he catches Stephen idle. When questioned about this idleness, Stephen cannot speak, out of fear. Father Arnall, the class teacher, explains why Stephen can't write, but Father Dolan does not want to hear. He calls Stephen a little schemer and crashes the cane again and again on each of Stephen's hands. Despite the terror and the pain, Stephen manages to withhold his tears and 'the cry that scalded his throat' (Joyce, 1986 [1916]: 46) until Father Dolan is done. Then, 'the scalding water burst forth from his eyes and, burning with shame and agony and fear, he drew back his shaking arm in terror and burst out into a whine of pain' (Joyce, 1986 [1916]: 47), his body shaking 'in shame and rage' (Joyce, 1986 [1916]: 47). When ordered to kneel down, he does so, quickly pressing his hands to his sides. 'To think of them beaten and swollen with pain', Joyce comments, 'made him feel so sorry for them as if they were not his own but someone else's that he felt sorry for' (Joyce, 1986 [1916]: 47), suggesting that it is because of the pain that the child willed his hands metaphorically cut off from his body.

The second episode sees Stephen, aged about 12, discussing with his schoolmates the literary canon. Stephen ends up being beaten up by Heron, the leader of the mob. They are discussing Byron, whom Stephen ranks as the finest poet. Heron disagrees and demands that Stephen retract his judgement. Stephen refuses to comply and is sent crashing 'against a barbed wire fence' (Joyce, 1986 [1916]: 75). The rage and hatred Stephen feels as he stumbles on after this episode dissipates in no time and Joyce has Stephen wonder 'why he bore no malice now to those who had tormented him' (Joyce, 1986 [1916]: 75). Lacan ponders the metaphor in Joyce's sentence 'Even that night as he stumbled homewards along Jone's road he had felt that some power was divesting him of that sudden woven anger as easily as a fruit is divested of its soft ripe peel' (Joyce, 1986 [1916]: 77). Lacan sees in this metaphor a reference to Stephen's relation to his own body, the sign of a reaction of disgust, of a feeling of detachment. Stephen's rage dissipates, falls away, and this is imposed on Stephen in the same involuntary way as speech is imposed. Stephen's experience is an event in the body, a certain manner of not feeling it, of letting it down, letting it fall like superfluous peel. For Stephen, the knotting of thought, soul and body depends on the relation between the abdication of the father, an acute awareness of sin and the corporeal sensation of a letting fall.

Two situations determined by the Borromean knotting arise in Joyce with regard to the three orders. First, from his early epiphanies to *Finnegans Wake* (Joyce, 1992 [1939]), his writing poses enigmas. An enigma, namely, a statement that cannot find its enunciation, presents us with a fault in the imaginary and its eventual patching up (Lacan, 2005 [1975–76]: 67). Thus, Joyce cares little for whether he is understood or not; this is why his enigmas give way to a writing of the letter (Lacan, 1998 [1972–73]: 26–29) and eventually to deciphering rather than the interpreting we are all familiar with from practical criticism.

For Lacan, the epiphany may be 'the result of this error, namely that the unconscious is tied to the real' (Lacan, 2005 [1975–76]: 73). The unconscious tied to the real: the enigma as epiphany bound up with Joyce's ego, or rather, bound up with the slip – through excess or absence, which occurs in the writing of the Borromean knot, namely, in this instance, a trefoil, with a slip that calls for the reparation to be crafted by the ego.

This is poetically adumbrated in two epiphanies of the artistic vocation in *A Portrait*. The first, cryptically, epiphanises Stephen's name and presents a moment of near imaginary collapse occurring at the climax of Stephen's exilic positioning in Ireland, namely, when he has rejected father, Church and country. As a visionary insight, the epiphany is also a creative event but, as a slip of the imaginary, it bears the mark of manic omnipotence. Either way, it is possible to read into it the traces of three registers of foreclosure. Similarly, this complex correlation of the three registers can be traced in Stephen's first epiphany of the artistic vocation: in this instance, what he calls 'the soul' (Joyce, 1986 [1916]: 152) is born after he has rejected a possible career in the religious orders. Teased by his schoolmates who disfigure his name, he suddenly understands how his name contains the potentialities of his vocation. Thus, realising the prophetic meaning of his own name, Stephen's imagination takes wing. He sees a Daedelian figure 'flying above the waves and slowly climbing the air' (Joyce, 1986 [1916]: 153). This causes him to wonder whether this 'hawklike man' (Joyce, 1986 [1916]: 154) stands for 'a prophecy of the end he had been born to serve … a symbol of the artist forging anew in his workshop out of the sluggish matter of the earth a new soaring impalpable imperishable being?' (Joyce, 1986 [1916]: 154). As Stephen identifies with this birdlike figure he struggles to articulate a cry:

> His throat ached with a desire to cry aloud, the cry of a hawk or eagle on high, to cry piercingly of his deliverance to the winds. This was the call of life to his soul, not the dull gross voice of the world of duties and despair, not the inhuman voice that had called him to the pale service of the altar. (Joyce, 1986 [1916]: 154)

For Lacan, then, Joyce's ego is a writing and Joyce's writing is one that inscribes something that never 'stops not being written' (Lacan, 1998 [1972–73]: 145), for, indeed, writing is *essential* to Joyce's ego because it bears witness to the failure of an inscription, that of the Name of the Father. This is highlighted in the conclusion to seminar XXIII, *Le sinthome* (Lacan, 2005 [1975–76]), when Lacan sums up his views about the structure of Joyce's ego, namely, what he calls 'the writing of the knot', with the emphasis on *writing*. The emphasis on writing as essential for the ego reveals itself to be derived from Joyce's thrust to attain the position of 'egoarch' with regard to pleasure and hence with regard to the Name of the Father, namely, what Lacan calls *père-version*. Interestingly, page 188 of *Work in Progress*, to become *Finnegans Wake* (Joyce, 1992 [1939]), anticipates Lacan's thesis:

> Condemned fool, anarch, egoarch, hiresiarch, you have reared your disunited kingdom on the vacuum of your own most intensely doubtful soul. (Joyce, 1992 [1939]: 188)

The ego evoked here is one concisely linking heresy with the law in relation to subjectivity, as it does with writing and the knot, namely, the idea that 'a fourfold structure can be always demanded from the unconscious in the construction of a subjective ordering' (Lacan, 2006 [1959]: 657). In order to approach this question, the next chapter tackles two subsidiary themes, namely the *why* and the *where from* of creative writing.

Note

(1) Hoerni writes: 'During the experiment, [Jung] developed a technique to "get to the bottom of [his] inner processes ... to translate the emotions into images", and "to grasp the fantasies which were stirring ... underground"' (Hoerni, 2009: viii).

9 On Experiential Knowing as Creative Writing Research Mode

We are all haunted houses.
H.D.

The house of fiction does not readily admit the self.... Your relationship
with it, as its creator, is tenuous, complex, subtle, utterly demanding.
Sue Roe

Mirror Conversions

In this chapter I want to further develop the notion of triangulation introduced in previous chapters with reference to the creative process, in order to theorise the research process as may be pertinent to the 'domain specificity' (Baer, 2012) of creative writing studies. My premise remains that creative writing is a way of apprehending, knowing and being in the world; and, more specifically, that it functions simultaneously as a perspective, an epistemology and an ontology specific to *writing*. I rekindle the argument put forth in the first chapter that our conceptual tools need to be made over in order to fit creative practice in writing and that these should enable us to deal specifically with writing in relation to the experiential and to subjectivity – that is, from the inside out. Reading Kristeva's central argument in *Revolution in Poetic Language*, first published in French in 1974, against the grain, I reassess the relevance of the term 'practice-led research' for creative writing, asking how the poetic text can challenge the dominant paradigm and how it can be considered research.

Because creative writing is an experiential form of practice involving an intertextuality which is first and foremost intratextual, that is, played out from within, I argue here that we need conceptual tools tailored to the domain specificity of writing rather than taken off the rack of a germane domain such as the visual arts, or even the wider field of the creative arts. Drawing on the work of metaphor (Lakoff & Johnson, 1980), the practice of *methexis* (Carter, 1996: 80) and more specifically on Kristeva's concept of the *chora* (Kristeva, 1974: 25–26), I refute that practice-led research is a mere dialectic practice which could be theorised in terms of Deleuze's concept of 'disjunctive synthesis' (Deleuze & Guattari, 2004: 14) and suggest instead that creative writing research is a triangulation of two seemingly mutually exclusive discourses, one recognising the reality of the unconscious, and the other the importance of rational and critical process. To put it differently, this triangulation would encompass tacit *knowing* and explicit *knowledge*. This is because creative writing practice and research *are* reciprocal, thereby *creating* a third element which covers the spectrum from *knowing* to *knowledge*.

Chapter 1 sketched the nature of this reciprocity with reference to 'experiential knowing' (Lakoff & Johnson, 1980: 19), whereby affects and emotions interact with rational processes, thereby linking subjectivity to reciprocal process (Mullin, 2012: 185) via metaphor, because 'human *thought processes* are largely metaphorical' (Lakoff & Johnson, 1980: 6, original emphasis). Although this might at first seem problematic, I briefly draw on Lakoff and Johnson's *Metaphors We Live By* (Lakoff & Johnson, 1980) to assist in the transition from the arts to creative writing and then turn to Julia Kristeva's concept of the chora in order to suggest how creative writing research might work as a dialectical practice that is both subversive and inclusive of the social order, suggesting a triangulation of two modes of apprehending the world rather than a mere dialectic between two mutually exclusive paradigms, or discourses as Deleuze would have it (Deleuze & Guattari, 2004: 14). The triangulation at stake here concerns the interplay between *knowing* and *knowledge*. Knowing would denote grasping a situation or event using prior (unconscious) knowledge and synthesising as well as integrating new information, affects or stimuli into a personal knowledge base. Knowledge, on the other hand, would include identifying and evaluating new (rational) knowledge and making decisions about what the next steps or possible course of action might be.

Going Through the Mirror: The Funhouse of Language

The funhouse metaphor comes from the American writer John Barth; refers to language and literature and, further, to the world itself as a variable funhouse of pleasure, anxiety and terror. A study of the artist and the art, Barth's collection of short stories *Lost in the Funhouse*, published in the now considered mythical year of 1968, invites considerations as a postmodern text writing back to its arch modernist predecessor, Joyce's *A Portrait of the*

Artist as a Young Man, itself first published only some 50 years earlier (Joyce, 1986 [1916]). The parallel draws attention to allusions, decentrings and the possibilities of play with words, ideas, selves and texts which is only compounded and expounded by David Foster Wallace's homage to it in *Girl With Curious Hair* (Wallace, 1989).

Barths's collection is a useful point of reference as it offers a provocative metaphor for creative writing research (Barth, 1988 [1968]). It evokes the sense of an intriguing structure composed of entrances, multiplicities of choice, deceptions and diversions. Barth proffers an explicit invitation to the reader to enter the funhouse as an explorer and essential part of the purpose of the enterprise; and the promise along the way of gamesome experience that may be simultaneously real and unreal – or surreal. Barth's prototype hero, Ambrose Mensch, sadly gendered despite the attempt to obliterate him in the annals of philosophy, is present by name in three stories. His progress from birth and childhood to early adolescence is brilliantly inter-rupted in post-theory fashion by pieces about art and art-making, with some references to classical origins – see 'Menelaiad' and 'Anonymiad', for example – and emblematically, therefore, to the origins of creative writing, especially fiction-making. Although Ambrose is named and given a context in time and relationships, interests and hopes, he is only a fleeting metaphor for the latent postmodern maker amid elemental markers of the arts.

From the experientialist perspective, to repeat Lakoff and Johnson's words, 'metaphor is a matter of *imaginative rationality*' (Lakoff & Johnson, 1980: 235, original emphasis). Because metaphor is a figure of speech in which one thing is described in terms of another, it enables 'an understand-ing of one kind of experience in terms of another, creating coherences by virtue of imposing gestalts that are structured by natural dimensions of experience' (Lakoff & Johnson, 1980: 235). This is why new metaphors are capable of creating new understandings and, therefore, new realities, as is 'obvious in the case of poetic metaphor, where language is the medium through which new conceptual metaphors are created' (Lakoff & Johnson, 1980: 235). As we shall see, although seemingly confined to the realm of the symbolic, Lakoff and Johnson's point about metaphor does not necessarily exclude Kristeva's concept of the metaphorical object, which concerns the very splitting that establishes the psyche and 'bends the drive toward the symbolic of an other' (Kristeva, 1987a: 31). Indeed, as was pointed out, for Lakoff and Johnson, metaphor is not merely a matter of language, but also of 'conceptual structure' (Lakoff & Johnson, 1980: 235).

In order to examine the relationship between 'mundane experience' and 'aesthetic experience', or 'language' and 'conceptual structure' (Lakoff & Johnson, 1980: 235), we need to pay attention to the nature of subjectivity, and more particularly to the intersection between the symbolic and the imaginary, including the body and pre-linguistic or proto-linguistic states.

'Since Plato, Western philosophy and culture have had an ocular bias', says the narrator, a psychiatrist and psychotherapist in one of Siri Hustvedt's novels, adding that 'vision is our dominant sense' (Hustvedt, 2009: 36). This may be the case. As stated earlier, Freud himself has shown that the eyes carry an unusually high affective charge (Freud, 2001 [1915b]) and Lacan's concept of the mirror stage would suggest that sight is crucial to the child's accessing the symbolic order of language (Lacan, 2006 [1949]). The eyes are close to the brain and as such may be critical to the secondary process. However, it is important to note that humans hear before they can see – indeed, humans can hear *in utero*. Besides, 'the world', writes Morwenna Griffiths, 'is understood through the body and perceptions of our bodies constrain our relationships with others and our relationships with others and ourselves' (Griffiths, 2012: 169). Arguably, this observation was made by the British painter, psychologist and psychoanalyst Mary Milner (1952, 1971) long before her writing was published and long before it entered the realm of theory in different guises. Nevertheless, our perception of the body is also at the heart of the imaginary as Jacques Lacan first conceptualised it (Lacan, 2006 [1949]: 75–82) and as Julia Kristeva (1974, 1980) later reconceptualised it, according to her own psychoanalytic orientation. Yet, as Lacan and Kristeva show in their differing ways, if art-making is a way of making sense of ourselves, including 'our relationships with others' (Griffith, 2012: 169), this process is and ought to be mediated through language.

Lacan's initial 'return to Freud' demonstrates that Freud was, as we saw earlier, the first to identify the important role that language played in the psychic life of human beings. Much has been made of Lacan's 'mirror stage' (2006 [1949]) to argue that it is only when the child acquires language that the unconscious begins to form and therefore that no real or true self exists before the acquisition of language. As we also saw earlier, this view, which presupposes that the imaginary is just a stage in human development, and not an inherent component thereof, is erroneous, for Lacan's tripartite conception of subjectivity only mirrors Freud's earlier model. As such, it is a linguistic model and it emphasises that we, as subjects, are created by language and culture.

Kristeva, strongly influenced by Lacan, also believes that the subject is an effect of language, and that we do not become fully conscious of ourselves until language acquisition. However, unlike Lacan, she posits a role for pre-linguistic affectivity and perception in our sense of self. Thus, in her *doctorat d'état* thesis, published as *La révolution du language poétique* (1974), she flies in the face of Lacan's imago in the mirror, as it were. Drawing on

Plato's *Timaeus*, Kristeva famously revised the notion of *chora* to evoke an imaginary space where subjectivity begins through awareness of sounds, rhythms and bodily sensations (Kristeva, 1984: 25–26). This pre-linguistic 'semiotic' realm of experience is, it should be stressed, not lost when the subject moves into the realm of language, and it remains as an essential part of signification or meaning-making. It is particularly prominent in poetic language, which, Kristeva maintains, has the power to disrupt our tendency to take on fixed identities in language by enhancing our capacity as 'subjects-in-process' (Kristeva, 1984: 28).

Kristeva's departure from Lacan, influenced as it was by the work of Melanie Klein, is her own 'return to Freud'. In *Revolution in Poetic Language* (1984), she argues that Freud's theory of the drives is the key to the 'semiotic', and therefore to the negativity of poetic language repressed by the bourgeois symbolic system, of which, in her view, Lacan's writings partake. *Revolution in Poetic Language* refers to the capacity of poetic language to bring symbolic performance to interact intimately with its own process of production, namely what Kristeva calls *signifiance*, for it involves a performance that is not simply symbolic. Semiotic performance, though paired with the symbolic function, is distinct. However, as we shall see, these two functions meet at the heart of the Freudian drive.

The central argument of *Revolution in Poetic Language*, however, is that poetic language of the non-mimetic or experimental kind is the means by which the ideological notions of subject, structure and meaning can most readily be challenged:

> Within this saturated if not already closed socio-symbolic order, poetry – more precisely, poetic language – reminds us of its eternal function: to introduce through the symbolic that which works on, moves through and threatens it. The theory of the unconscious seeks the very thing that poetic language practices within and against the social order: the ultimate means of transformation or subversion, the precondition for its survival and revolution.... Literature has always been the most explicit realization of the signifying subject's condition. Indeed it was in literature starting in the second half of the nineteenth century, that the dialectical condition of the subject was made explicit, beginning in France with the work of Nerval, but particularly with Lautréamont and Mallarmé. (Kristeva, 1984: 81–82)

In viewing the text as a revolutionary practice whose operations cannot be recuperated by the linguistic sign (Kristeva, 1984), Kristeva's concept of the semiotic sees the literary work 'as irreducible to the level of an object for normative linguistics' (Kristeva, 1986: 86). Thus, Kristeva establishes the specificity of the literary work by viewing it as different from other modes of discourse, thereby reinstating the distinction between the literary and the non-literary concept of the text. This distinction is reinforced by Kristeva's assertion that literature, and more particularly poetry, may work against the social order. Claiming that poetry's rhythmical patterns, rhyme schemes and intonations have already performed an opening in the linguistic sign, Kristeva suggests that poetic language is the means by which the ideological notions of subject, structure and meaning can most readily be undermined. In a similar vein, although Kristeva insists that 'literature does not exist for semiotics' (Kristeva, 1986: 86), that it is merely one productive practice among many, with no particularly privileged status, she argues that the poetic text has the 'advantage' of 'making more accessible than others the production of meaning' (Kristeva, 1986: 86). At first, the modern text, written after the 'epistemological break' in the late 19th century, is in her view most effective in this regard. In Lautréamont's *Poésies II*, for example, she finds that the accumulation of short, choppy sentences produces an 'accelerated rhythm that engages the reader in a way that makes their meaning fade into the background' (Kristeva, 1984: 354), while Sollers' *Nombres* performs a similar function, by disrupting syntax and privileging the auditory register over the visual register of language (Kristeva, 1984: 356). In a lecture delivered at the Collège de France in 1975, Kristeva acknowledges that her thesis may be applied to all poetic texts (Kristeva, 2000: 77–79).

As suggested above, the practice of writing is an experiential activity which mobilises both unconscious and conscious processes. As such, it presupposes an intertextuality which is intratextual, that is, played out from within. From reading Kristeva's (1984) *Revolution in Poetic Language* – and earlier work such as Σημειωτική: *Recherches pour une sémanalyse* (Kristeva, 1969) – the privileging of these textual aspects would seem to go against the grain of Kristeva's argument. The *semiotic chora* makes its impact through *negativity* – the negativity at work in the Hegelian dialectic as the play of contradiction and which Kristeva conceptualises via Freud as material process – through which the rhythm of drives and their ephemeral stases impact at the level of the *thetic* or the threshold of the symbolic – stabilising syntax, maintaining hierarchical order, logical procedure, grammaticality, stability of register, tendency to the monological and so on. As this chapter recognises, Kristeva's argument is not so much about the *sign* as entity, but what radically *destabilises*, disrupts and dissolves the sign – *into the metonymic relay of signifiers* – and thus what destabilises the 'unitary' subject before the symbolic as Law of the Father. The *semiotic chora* is the space where the subject's originary split is *reiterated* – rather than smoothed over as in the Lacanian mirror stage. Negativity is a play of contradictions, a movement of destabilising and heterogeneous drives which, when at work in an avant-garde text – taken as working through the materiality of the signifier – leads to the potential infinitisation of signifiers and, in extreme cases, the pulverisation of subjectivity. However, in later works Kristeva increasingly conceives of the poetic text as destabilising and even warns against this movement of negativity and calls for the containment of the semiotic by the symbolic, for the text – and the writer – not to break into the realm of the psychotic (see for example her radical advocating of sublimation in the context of *The Sense and Non-Sense of Revolt* (2002a: 54–57).

As intimated allegorically, or parodically, throughout some of the previous chapters with reference to the mirror of representation, he or she who settles permanently on the other side of the mirror risks madness. The Belgian writer Georges Rodenbach speaks about such an experience: 'the friend of mirrors' leans tirelessly over 'their fluid mystery' (Rodenbach, 1997 [1914]: 32). But then one day, out of the blue, mirrors reject reciprocity and become greedy and voracious. Mirror images, which connect like roads and form a labyrinth, through which seductive women constantly pass back and forth, invite the poet to enter: 'It must be really pleasant in the mirror' (Rodenbach, 1997 [1914]: 38). The dreamer projects himself into the only too real world of his hallucinations. At dawn he is found, delirious and covered in blood, at the foot of the mirror, *presentifying* the mortifying effect of the loss of the symbolic and invasion by the imaginary and the real.

In other words, if, as creative writers, we are tempted by mirrors and labyrinths, we need to ensure that the reflections and creatures they release don't replicate *ad libitum*.

For enjoyment and distraction from the density of theory, here is 'Fabulations', an allegory of the creative process gesturing in this direction:

Sometimes I dream I undress her –
the cross-dressed muse that smothers
time. She is Janus-like and she spreads
the circumference of words in wide arcs
that run smoothly down the throat
all the way through to the chambers of the heart.

And I look at this bizarre body with the gaze
that cannot see its own image
even less the peculiar navel –
the scar where truths gather unscathed

from poems that are but fictions
before I throttle the dream.
(Hecq, 2014b)

The impulse to throttle the dream is, of course, the key to sanity, the key to the symbolic that unlocks the semiotic only to lock it again.

While the Kristevan semiotic is at first understood as the engine of creative work in avant-garde poetic language, it must also be taken *in its dynamic relation* with the symbolic. One of the two key writers Kristeva focuses on in the first half of *Revolution in Poetic Language* (1984) is Mallarmé, who wrote of his own experimentation that there needs to be a guarantee against the dissolution of all meaning: that is, syntax. In her analyses of Mallarmé, Kristeva examines negativity working in terms of sound – paranomastic play, or the sound chains which she, after Saussure's 'anagrams', termed 'paragrams'. The paragram, running through an avant-garde text such as Mallarmé's, tends to dissolve the boundaries of lexemes, or signifiers, and thus 'pulverise' the subject implied in the text, in what Lacan called *jouissance*, which, as the term denotes in French, is a form of enjoyment to excess, and therefore bordering on suffering. For Kristeva, the gaps in the poetic text, as in the work of Céline or Barthes, it should be stressed, fulfil a similar function to syntax (Kristeva, 2002a), that is, as stop gaps against subjective dissolution (see also Hecq, 2011a).

Nevertheless, despite ambiguities and shifts of an ideological nature, for Kristeva, the early life of the drive consists essentially of instinctual activity. As such, it is a primordial registering of the infant's encounter with the symbolic through the mother and Other, upon whom she entirely relies for survival. Kristeva conceives of the semiotic *chora* on the principle that:

> corporeal life before the appearance of linguistic capacities, which, since it is a life dependent on and thereby exposed to the symbolic being of another, is never 'mere' corporeal life. (Beardsworth, 2004: 44)

Thus, the *chora* denotes 'an essentially mobile and extremely provisional articulation constituted by movements and their ephemeral stases' (Kristeva, 1984: 25–26). This is of critical importance for creative writing, as, in this light, all discourse, that is, everything within the field supported by the distinction between the symbolic and the real, depends on and refuses this realm of the not-yet-symbolised, in which the inside versus outside – and consequently subject versus object positions – are not yet established.

Revolution in Poetic Language (1984) conceives of the drives as partaking of an economy founded on the primordial impact of the symbolic encounter during the emergence of the sign itself and the ensuing configuration of the death drive. Interestingly, the most archaic moment in Kristeva's logic of the drives can be captured in a metaphor, thus showing how conceptual work is performed by metaphor. The logic of this movement is likened to the formation, breaking off and moving of wave patterns on a shoreline, conveying that drives and their vicissitudes are *both* corporeal and psychic inscriptions. Kristeva therefore stresses the meaning of the drive as an articulation, more particularly in terms of 'rhythmic totality' (Kristeva, 1984: 68) which orients and connects the infant's body to the mother's body.

Although this 'rhythmic totality' of the *chora* is conceived of as a preliminary space, it manifests itself only at the symbolic level, presupposing the 'break' which posits the signifier/signified articulation, as well as the positions of object – outside – and subject – absent from the signifier. Semiotic functioning in the symbolic field is 'an activation … of the heterogeneous contradiction of semiotic and symbolic' (Kristeva, 1984: 171), which is precisely Kristeva's *signifiance* or signifying process. The affirmation of art, and more specifically a modern non-mimetic kind of literature, in *Revolution in Poetic Language* (1984) rests on the claim that the heterogeneous contradiction of the semiotic and symbolic is recovered when significations, by which Kristeva means the meanings that compose prevailing discourses, are taken apart and thereby returned to their non-signifying, drive-invested elements, which are then amenable to a reconfiguration.

This thought makes up Kristeva's psychoanalytic version of the project in which modern literature departs from its role as representation (of an outside object) and seeks out the conditions of its own appearance as work. In this version, what is vital is the thesis that certain material supports – voice, tone, inflection, gesture, colour, for example – are susceptible to the imprint of semiotic motility and hence drive rejection. The semiotic network is 'more or less integrated as a *signifier*' (Kristeva, 1984: 47) and this is what enables the semiotic combinatorial system to obtain 'the complex articulation we associate with it in musical and poetic practices' (Kristeva, 1984: 68). Poetic language brings semiotic motility to bear on symbolic functioning that is literally powerless in the face of a referent-less though mastering signification. In Beardsworth's words, 'dismantling the meaningful object (representation, idea, thing) deprives the object of the unity which it obtains in the specular captivation (optical, as in the mirror stage, and/or conceptual), substituting signifying elements for the meaningful object' (Beardsworth, 2004: 47). This crystallises Kristevan thought regarding the semiotic impact on the symbolic in the radical modernist text and, by extension, on all poetic texts of the non-mimetic or experimental kind. Although this seems to concern a narrow view of writing, it is to some extent relevant to all literary texts.

The signifying elements – signifiers – are drive-invested fragments informed by rhythm, tone, inflection, colour or words, which tend to return to non-symbolic negativity, which is to say, semiotic functioning. Although the return to the signifying elements brings the subject and meaning to the threshold of drive rejection, in poetic language the fragments are equally subject to a combinatory moment – 'fitting together, detaching, including, and building up "parts" into some kind of "totality"' – which prevents symbolic dissolution (Kristeva, 1984: 102). It would, thus, seem that for Kristeva:

> the poetic text is rhythm made intelligible by a symbolic barrier. Moreover, given that the semiotic network is more or less integrated in the signifier, non-symbolic functioning is always in excess of intelligible translation, an excess that represents the possibility of the return and renewal of poetic subversion. (Beardsworth, 2004: 47)

That the poetic text is made intelligible by a symbolic barrier is not lost to this reader/writer, as it has major repercussions for the way Lacan's concept of suppletion, as both device and process, may be both articulated and understood, as will become clear in the next two chapters. It may also shed light on the very mechanism which prevents subjective dissolution. To come back to Kristeva's seeming paradox, though – whereby, on the one hand, the heterogeneous contradiction of the semiotic and symbolic never goes so far as the complete loss of symbolic functioning, and, on the other hand, symbolic functioning can never fulfil the abstraction from semiotic functioning – it should be stressed that symbolic functioning as such involves a refusal of the semiotic and a social symbolic order may be especially inflexible with respect to that refusal. This is Kristeva's thought when she characterises the bourgeois social symbolic system as what brings everything back within the field of unity. That is to say, the bourgeois symbolic system suppresses the recognition that symbolic functioning involves a refusal of the semiotic. In these conditions, poetic language recovers the dynamic relationship between the semiotic and symbolic dimensions of language (Beardsworth, 2004: 48), as opposed to academic language, for example.

(A)Mazing Encounters

Thinking 'agnostically' (see Webb & Brien, 2008), this conception fractures the nexus between, on the one hand, lack and desire, and, on the other, form, knowledge and subjectivity. It enables a reconfiguration of the relationship between art-making and subjectivity in terms of a sustained dynamic dialectic that is necessarily transformative. This reconfiguration can be further theorised in terms of the performative principle of methexis (μέθεξις), a term denoting the relation between a particular and a form in philosophy (Plato), group sharing in Greek theatre, or a 'non-representational principle that involves an act of concurrent actual production' (Carter, 1996: 84) in practice-led research. As such, methexis is transformative and not merely representational. It engenders a material transformation that is not of a representational mode. Translated in Kristevan terms, this material transformation is enacted in the *chora* or, more particularly, at the intersection of the symbolic and imaginary, and thereby constitutes a form of knowing, or 'fore-knowledge', if one wanted to shift epistemological paradigms – the root of mathematics is *mathesis*, itself meaning fore-knowledge.[1]

What is critical here is that, as an experiential practice viewed through the lens of methexis, creative writing is an 'act of concurrent actual production', through which embodied knowledge is produced (Carter, 1996: 80), and therefore an act of research in its own right. Meanings emerge by accretion, oscillating between intuitive and reflective modes of knowledge creation. Rather than meaning being revealed or clarified, it is also through experiential practice that social meanings are produced. But this is unsettling and paradoxical in itself. In his putative autobiography, for example, Barthes worries that he is caught between two discourses and that the fixed quality of language makes him appear more certain than he is. Referring to himself in the third person, he writes of his dilemma:

His (sometimes acute) discomfort – mounting some evenings, after writing the whole day, to a kind of fear – was generated by his sense of producing a double discourse, whose mode overreached its aim, somehow: for the aim of this discourse is not truth, and yet this discourse is assertive.

This kind of embarrassment started, for him, very early; he strives to master it – for otherwise he would have to stop writing – by reminding himself that it is language which is assertive, not he. An absurd remedy, everyone would surely agree, to add to each sentence some little phrase of uncertainty, as if anything that came out of language could make language tremble. (Barthes, 1977a: 48)

This is methexis in operation and not representation. It generates discomfort and uncertainty because language is inextricably associated with who we are, with our lack and desire.

In this scheme, the terms of the economy of representation shift and accrue, for meaning is necessarily unstable. Images or words no longer stand in for concepts, ideas or things, nor are they mere signs that ceaselessly circulate; rather, meaning is produced as an embodied, situated event structurally akin to metaphor, whereby rhythm, voice, tone, inflection, colour, image and word are reconfigured into patterns. This reconfiguration, indeed, *works like a metaphor*: it has an internal logic and it produces material effects. To put it differently, in methexis a pattern begins to emerge from among the swirling shapes of relational analogies. Methexis digs desire out of the hole of lack, as it were, and locates it in the drives. This is congruent with Kristeva's view of desire as activation or actualisation of the drives; a series of practices, bringing things together or separating them, making things, making reality, for desire does not take for itself a particular object whose attainment it seeks – rather, it aims at nothing above its own – metonymic – proliferation or self-expansion. It assembles elements out of singularities and breaks these into further singularities, which appears to conjure up the Deleuzian concept of 'disjunctive synthesis', except that, in the case of disjunctive synthesis, it is linear, chronological time that is most crucially undermined, time as a causal connector and developmental ground for both understanding and intervention. For Kristeva, time in the activation of the drives, and hence in poetic practice at work, is abolished. The time of the semiotic *chora* is past-present-future and this time-less-no-time knows no negation – yet. As the new becomes embodied, the new can emerge as a return to the newly informed and newly transgressed.

The relationship between these two approaches or paradigms is not obvious. It does not constitute a dialectical correlation, but rather an entanglement at the heart of 'experiential knowing' (Lakoff & Johnson, 1980: 19). It is as though, in the act of creating, we are haunted by a non-dialectical relationship between necessity and will, unconscious and rational processes. As such, it is not a 'disjunctive synthesis' (Deleuze & Guattari, 2004: 14), as is the case with Deleuze's conception of the 'vitality' of Being, which is a productive univocity, but rather a triangulation of two orders. One way of understanding how this triangulation works is, as I have suggested here, through understanding metaphor in a way that takes account of the reality of the unconscious via the semiotic *chora*, for 'human *thought processes* are largely metaphorical' (Lakoff & Johnson, 1980: 6): we do indeed describe things in terms of other things felt, heard or merely sensed – rhythms, images, affects, sounds, or words.

While I am convinced that this model throws light on the dream work of creative writing as research, I am acutely aware that it poses some problems for creative writers in the academy. My own use of metaphor, or writing through metaphor, as embedded in this performative book, illustrates some of these problems. The first problem is a purely structural one: the structure is not only labyrinthine, it is also subterranean. As such, it cannot be imposed from the outside. Some material will need to be discarded, as two chapters from this book were discarded. This also means that there are repetitions and contradictions, for one question, or set of related questions, is looked at from a variety of perspectives, creating a palimpsest of answers. Inevitably, some weaknesses or blind spots are uncovered, as Chapter 12 demonstrates. It is an unsettling process, this quest for a poetics, but one must go through it. If the act of writing is one of synthesis, its function is paradoxically one of separation and contrast. Creative writing research is the dramatisation of this hiatus.

Note

(1) Here, stop all poetic rapprochements, enticing though they were, for the terms 'methexis' and 'mathesis' are etymologically quite distinct. 'Methexis' is derived from 'metechô', for 'participation', while 'mathesis' comes from 'manthano', meaning 'I learn'. Thanks to Paul Magee for sharing his erudition in this regard.

10 Dramatic Encounters: Language, Craft, Theory

Every story we tell about ourselves can only be told in the past tense. It winds
backward from where we now stand, no longer the actors in the story but its
spectators who have chosen to speak. The trail behind us is sometimes marked
by stones like the ones Hansel first left behind him. Other times, the path is
gone, because the birds flew down and ate up all the crumbs at sunrise.
Siri Hustvedt

... meaning is never monogamous.
Susan Sontag

This chapter shows how theory can come to the rescue of creative writing, unbidden. It alternates between creative work ('Alabaster') and theory ('The grain of the voice and semblance'). 'Alabaster' is a short poetic text, itself split in two parts, which performs a moment of crisis experienced during the writing process. 'The grain of the voice and semblance' is a critical reflection on the resolution of this crisis. It exemplifies the concept of *Nachträglichkeit*, or the idea that an insight is attained after the fact. It does so by combining creative writing and theory as it explores the white space encountered on the brink of subjective dissolution and the role of both rhetoric and theory in preventing this dissolution. As such, it offers a subliminal dialogue with previous chapters while also elaborating on Lacan's concept of suppletion (Lacan, 2005 [1975–76]). It dramatises and analyses the limitations of the creative act and it shows how the knowledge gleaned from the discourses of criticism and theory may enhance the creative process and the recovery agency.

Any crisis is confronting. I therefore wish to caution the reader, for the fictional text addresses the idea of writer's block in the context of traumatic loss. The point is not to linger on an instance of the writing experience, but rather to invite reflections on the writing process in general, by highlighting the material dimension of lack. This, in turn, will open up avenues for more refined studies of writing and trauma.

Roland Barthes observes that actions such as writing are heavily charged with meaning. This is most obvious in his distinction between writing and authorship. Lacan's work shows how an unconscious and decentred discourse parallels conscious narration and imbues it with the voice of the Other. A decentred and topical discourse enables Barthes to write auto-biography in the guise of fiction. Barthes's work foregrounds the discourse of the Other while also deconstructing the text, as we saw briefly in Chapter 6. The fiction that follows, 'Alabaster', embeds poetry in a Lacanian matrix at a point in time when the narrator lost her mother tongue. The Oedipal connotations of the words embedded in this matrix are obvious, as Lacan's formulation of the Law referring to the constituting agency of what he calls the 'paternal metaphor' (Lacan, 2006 [1959a]: 465). As we have seen, for Lacan, the Name of the Father is a master signifier that ensures the structuring of the subject via the operation of the paternal metaphor, a kind of primary repression that breaks the fantasy of dual union with the mother and engages the subject in the symbolic order of language and culture by introducing the Law and regulating desire (Grigg, 1999: 55). What happens, then, when the speaker's filiation shifts to another language and when the form she chooses is poetry rather than the straightforward prose that has the imprimatur of the Law? This chapter combines creative writing and theory to scrutinise the lining of the voice at the moment of learning to speak again in another language and uncovers paler shades of white in the guise of a semblance, a concept we have encountered in our discussion of both Lacan and Badiou, but which could also be articulated in terms of Winnicott's false self. As such, it functions as an allegory of what happens as a result of our first encounter with trauma, that is to say, our encounter with the defiles of signifiers introduced by language.

The Kernel of the *In-Between*: Alabaster

Halfway through 1994, I believed the worst of the year was over. We lived in a rented house in the inner suburbs of Melbourne. It was a changeable house. Sometimes it felt safe as a church, and sometimes it shivered and cracked apart. A sloping slate roof held it down, pressing heat on us in summer, blowing cold in winter. What bounded the house was skin. Walls of cream gristle called *crépi*.

It was June 30th, an ordinary crisp winter day. Sunshine and magpies everywhere. After lunch, I took the children for a walk. His hands barely reaching the pram's handle, my first-born insisted on pushing his baby brother. Along the Merri Creek, there were egrets and ibises and ducks. Some turtles and tiny frogs. We sang duck songs and frog songs. I made up a magpie story as we passed a whole family of them. We bought quinces on the way back and I baked an upside-down quince cake. I was almost getting serious about planting winter vegetables, cornflowers and the last bulbs of irises, jonquils and ranunculaes before nightfall when I decided against it.

Nights close early in June. Everything seems to stand still, bleak, even gloomy by five. I bundled the children inside the house, drew the curtains and flicked on the lights. It felt safe despite the cold air curling at our feet.

When I turned off the light well after bed-time, I looked through the window. The roses looked dead but for a few white buds on their maimed limbs.

Why is white white?

Chalk, rice, zinc
    Crystal falls
        Limestone graves

Phosphorus
    Lightless body
        Alabaster

I woke up in the night, chilled as the whites in a Dutch still-life painting.
    A still-life belongs to time, and we to this stillness.
    In his cot, my baby's face was white wax.
    as if smothered by the moon itself.
    His lips were black.
    My voice died out in my scream.

(Hecq, 2010a)

The Grain of the Voice in the Realm of Semblants

'Alabaster', from which this excerpt comes, is the third chapter in 'Hush' (Hecq, unpublished), a book of fiction about cot death and the function of art-making in the work of mourning. I want to focus on this particular chapter because it highlights the generic hybridity of the text, namely the passage from prose to poetry and brief incursion into literary theory. As I wrote this difficult piece, my flight into poetry came out of the blue, *as if* to cover up the anxiety produced by the obscene fact I had to tell. Ironically, it produced a letter, which invokes some 'lip of the hole in knowledge' (Lacan, 2001 [1971]: 14). This flight into poetry constitutes a *semblant* (semblance), in the sense that it makes use of the signifier that covers over the hole in the real through the function of the letter, while at the same time locating a relation to *jouissance*. For Lacan, a semblant is an object of enjoyment that is both seductive and deceptive. As such, the signifier is the semblant *par excellence* (see for example Lacan, 2001 [1971]: 14; Lacan, 2006 [1971–72]: 14), for it sustains the field of desire through fiction, as a defence against the ravages of *jouissance*. Because the semblant covers a hole, or plugs it, the semblant comes to the place where something should be, but isn't, and where its lack produces anxiety. I will focus on 'Alabaster' with reference to Roland Barthes's intellectual autobiography, again, in order to explore the difference between prose and poetry as semblants in relation to the field of the Other. In particular, I will seek to explain how the semblant relates to the concept of voice as it is understood in psychoanalysis, and not necessarily in narratology.

A still-life belongs to time, and we, speaking beings, to the stillness that encompasses the experience of the unconscious. Thus, every text contains repressed material that structures a never-ending dialogue with the Other. But if all discourse, including autobiography, is a fiction (Lacan, 2001 [1971]: 19), in the sense that it is only a half truth, then poetry – a text that is written too fast to think – may be said to be a fiction that foregrounds unconscious disturbances in the field of the Other. It does so by projecting what we call a voice. To be more precise, it draws attention to what Roland Barthes has called 'The grain of the voice' in discourse (Barthes, 1977b). Such a discourse unveils the present absence of the Other by calling the reader's attention to it via signifiers, but also via blanks that stand in for silences, suppressed emotions or affects. I want to argue here that writing poetry foregrounds the unconscious by shifting registers from the imaginary to the symbolic. Further, I will argue that writing poetry in a language other than one's mother tongue gestures towards the letter, namely the material, though meaningless, support of the signifier (Lacan, 1998 [1972–73]: 30) and thus foregrounds a hole in knowledge due to a radical break with the mother tongue. The reason why I say that the register that takes precedence in this case is the symbolic, not the imaginary, refers to my own experience of writing 'Alabaster': resorting to poetry was an act that prevented the un-ravelling of the subject. Thus, the second language may be said to function as prosthetic tongue, *qua* symbolic anchor, and the medium of poetry as double semblant. The semblant in this case covers and covers up nothing, that is to say, it covers the void left by the loss of the primary object and it also covers up the fact that the Name of the Father is a semblant (Lacan, 2006 [1971–72]: 15), indeed, the semblant *par excellence* in any language.

For Lacan, the act of writing entails the reliving of a process by which an affective charge is released from its generating sources. The writer, and eventually the reader, directs this charge, imbuing it with the real that both brings it into being and attracts it. Fiction, autobiography and poetry therefore make it possible to link the conscious and unconscious registers, which, in turn, constitute the discourse of the subject. The writer's need to repeat, rather than simply remember, repressed material illustrates the need to reproduce and work through painful events of the past as if these were present. Like psychoanalysis, writing repeats the displeasure of what never took place during that time-event usually referred to as the primal scene, or repeats the trauma of what took place at a particular point in time. Fantasies of desire, incest, castration, death and repression re-enact not what took place, but rather what did not. Fantasies of reparation brought about by mourning, on the other hand, re-enact both what did and did not take place. These scenes are replayed and re-enacted on the stage of discourse as writers make up their personas, put on their masks, sharpen their pencils and perform their rituals. This discourse of the subject is a discourse of desire: 'we write with our desire', says Barthes, 'and I have never stopped desiring' (Barthes, 1977a: 98). What the desiring subject seeks is to retrieve some lost object, which is primarily the mother. However, because language manifests the presence of the mother tongue, writing does recover an absence. When one writes in another language, though, one denies this absence in an omnipotent gesture of self-creation, perhaps the ultimate narcissistic act, as one pretends to be both father and mother of oneself. Perhaps here is some indication of how *suppléance* comes into being as a stand-in for the ego, for, in this light, writing is more than a crutch: it is the ego itself (Lacan, 2005 [1975–76]: 152). In other words 'Alabaster' may give us a clue as to how the ego comes into being through a knotting of the real, the symbolic and the imaginary, for the text performs the knotting of the three registers, as opposed to Barthes's autobiographical text, which merely uses visual cues to highlight their disjunction.

Barthes alludes to the mother tongue as the language with which he has an incestuous relationship: 'The French language is for him', he says, referring to himself in the third person, 'essentially the umbilical language' (Barthes, 1977a: 119), perhaps fully aware that he has just cut off this umbilical cord by using 'he' instead of 'I'. For *Roland Barthes by Roland Barthes* (1977a) is an event of the body: it is Barthes striving to reconstitute an identity out of the textual fragments that compose it. By using the third-person pronoun, Barthes is, in fact, writing the symbolic mOther.

This Lacanian neologism plays on his concept of the Other as specifically referring here to the mother. Lacan's concept of the Other refers to radical alterity. As such, it is the index of the symbolic order, assimilated as it is with language and the Law: the (big) Other is the symbolic insofar as it is particularised for each individual subject. The Other is thus both another subject, in its radical alterity and unassimilable uniqueness, and also the symbolic order which mediates the relationship with that other subject. However, the meaning of 'the Other as another subject' is subordinate to the meaning of the other as symbolic order, for the Other is first and foremost 'the locus in which speech is constituted' (Lacan, 1993 [1955–56]: 274). It is therefore possible to speak of the Other as a subject in a secondary turn only in the sense that a subject may occupy this position and thereby 'embody' (Lacan, 1991 [1960–61]: 202) the Other for another subject. To complicate matters, the child's first encounter with the Other is mediated by the mother and there is at times a slippage between the two. The neologism mOther clears up this confusion. Bruce Fink explains why:

> The very expression we use about it – 'mother tongue' – is indicative of the fact that it is some Other's tongue first, the mOther's tongue, that is, the mOther's language, and in speaking of childhood experience, Lacan often virtually equates the Other with the mother. (Fink, 1997: 7)

The fragments that constitute Barthes's autobiography are indeed connected by the impersonal pronoun 'he', thus flaunting both the incestuous intermingling of his body with the mother tongue and his desire to disentangle from it. The fragments of text are the body of the text (Roland Barthes) without the father and beyond the Law, yet bearing the mark of the Law through the use of the third person. 'The fragment', says Barthes, 'implies immediate jouissance: it is a fantasy of discourse, an opening of desire' (Barthes, 1977a: 89). This gap in the text, this interstice of silence, is the focus of desire unable to speak its name, and the presence of the alien third-person pronoun signals the symbolic cut the writer Barthes performs upon his text in an attempt to ward off the mother's desire, thereby performing the paternal function and inscribing himself in the mOther's discourse.

This wilful symbolic inscription is further evidenced by overt references to Lacan's work. Barthes uses a photograph of himself as a baby in his mother's arms with the caption 'The mirror stage: "this is you"' (Barthes,

1977a: 25). Opposite from a drawing of the human circulatory system titled 'Anatomie' ('Anatomy'), Barthes's caption reads: 'To write the body. Neither the skin, nor the muscles, nor the bones, nor the nerves, but the rest: a clumsy id, fibrous, fluffy, and frayed, the cloak of a clown' (Barthes, 1977a: 182). The text is, literally, the body of the Other that struts and frets on the stage of language while being aware and in control of its own performativity.

Barthes's writing, in addition to its theoretical thrust, has a fictional component firmly embedded in the metonymic register through the use of the third-person narration. This has the effect of drawing the narrative away from the real and thereby from the hole in knowledge. In contradistinction, the excerpt from 'Alabaster' above shifts the register away from the literal towards the metaphorical. It might thus be said to be even more overtly fictional, and although it also struts and frets on the stage of language, it is not consciously aware of its theoretical thrust, but rather performs it through disturbances of language in a kind of *bricolage* that links the real, the symbolic and the imaginary through the letter 'o'. But the thrust is towards poetry and knowledge, and paradoxically reveals something about the truth of the subject via a symptom we call voice.

The Kernel of the *In-Between*: Alabaster (*continued*)

My voice died out in my scream.

Life goes on, they say. Life goes on leaving
me – a hiatus.

I became the copula between life and death.
An object with no voice.

Mère echo ooo ooo ooo

'Literature is like phosphorus', Barthes says in Writing Degree Zero.
'It shines with its maximum brilliance at the moment when it attempts to die.'
For Barthes, literature is always already a posthumous affair.
And so he tricked himself to write out the white into brilliance –
White paint comes from many things – chalk, rice, zinc, quartz, alabaster, lead. Vermeer
made some of his luminescent whites from alabaster and quartz –
in lumps that took the light into the painting and made it dance.

White is white because it reflects light off.

The price white pays for this sheer purity is that it absorbs no light into its own body –

and for lead white, this means its own heart is black.

And so I tricked myself to write out the white into glitter from the black of my heart.

> Chalk, rice, zinc
>   crystal falls
>   Limestone graves

> Phosphorus
>   Lightless body
>   Alabaster

From my limestone grave, a foreign voice came out.

In-crypted, I wrote myself out into a make-believe.

For the impossibility of saying nothing.
Of not saying anything.
Of not saying.
Of saying.

For the sheer possibility of putting death to death.

(Hecq, 2010a)

The Grain of the Voice in the Realm of Semblants (*continued*)

Roland Barthes by Roland Barthes (1977a) and 'Alabaster' (Hecq, 2010a) re-enact ongoing acts of desire in which the Name of the Father is deconstructed and reconstructed in the service of the author's ego. Both texts invite the reader to read them as fiction: 'All this must be viewed as spoken by a character in a novel', says Barthes in his epigraph on the inside cover of *Roland Barthes*, a crucial statement, as he repeats it later (Barthes, 1977a: 123); 'Alabaster' sets up the writer herself as mere *make-believe*, despite the deeper, even mythical aspect of *'mère echo'* (mother echo). Thus, each work projects the discourse of the Other as fiction into the text, where the play of characters, pronouns and signifiers foregrounds the Other's presence. Barthes's autobiography is written in the third person, whereas 'Alabaster' interweaves biographical events and imaginary happenings that blur the boundaries between the two, while clearly establishing the presence of the Law in the field of the Other in the prose passages. But the presence of the Law is not a given in this particular text, as the flights into poetry performatively demonstrate, and as the citation from Barthes's *Writing Degree Zero* (Barthes, 2010) attests. Indeed, the citation functions as a desperate call for the Name of the Father in an attempt to fend off the *jouissance* attached to the world of the mOther and to echoes of the mother tongue encapsulated in the bilingual pun *'mère echo'*, as well as in the nonsensical repetition of the phoneme 'o'. The citation may be said to cut across some ambient noise or noisy silence – the world of the mother, the noise that covers the dark presence of *Das Ding*, the latent index of the mother's murderous desire, nonetheless made manifest in ringing echoes.

It is, I believe, to silence these funereal echoes that I intuitively changed tack during the writing process. On the brink of some inevitable void, indeed, of some encounter with the real, I abandoned the 'sense full' of the metonymic law of prose for the 'sense blank' of poetry. I drew away from sense to play with the whiteness of words and with the blanks on the page, the blanks themselves functioning as stopgaps to meaning. I moved away from the metonymic axis of language to approach with extra care some truth I sensed to be inscribed along its metaphorical axis. It strikes me as utterly ironic that this shift occurred by way of free associating on the word 'white'. This flight into poetry was valuable. It uncovered 'nothing' and thereby it produced self-knowledge. It also enabled me to bypass the crippling anxiety that foreshadows an encounter with the real of madness. It may, indeed, have prevented such a horrific encounter. Thus Jacques-Alain Miller is right when he says that the function of semblants is 'to veil nothing' and also to make this nothing into something (Miller, 1997: 8). This definition of the semblant highlights its double function, which is of veiling and of drawing our attention to this veiling.

As Hebé Tizio observes, a semblant occurs only in a discourse. It takes the empty place that allows the element that is found there to take the place of the agent. The discourse is founded in place of the semblant (Tizio, 2009), because it is the agent that specifies the way *jouissance* is treated. In every discourse, the semblants are supported in different ways and each has its foundation: S1 appears as the semblant of mastery of the signifier; S2 as the semblant of knowledge; and the object as a semblant of *jouissance*. Thus, each one has a status as important as that of the other. However, these semblants are different by way of their specific relationship to *jouissance*, and hence to our intimate relationship with writing, whether it is fiction or poetry. Thus, semblants can manifest through the different forms of rejection or deferral, as Lacan shows when he says that *jouissance* 'is not challenged, is not evoked, is not tracked down, is not elaborated, other than through a semblant' (Lacan, 1998 [1972–73]: 85). Perhaps the semblants we choose or those that choose us are the signature of our work writ in white ink.

That is, no doubt, a paradoxical formulation, because this place of the agent is in all cases marked by the impossibility to act on what escapes discourse. One must not forget that, for psychoanalysis, a discourse is a mechanism that finds its main partner in *jouissance*, which is to say that it has a civilising function, but that it cannot render this kernel conscious, which, although foreclosed, and therefore real and unconscious, struggles for articulation. We are dealing with some other umbilicus of discourse, the one Freud discovered in dreams, that is resistant to interpretation: it is the letter as material support of the signifier. To be more precise, it is the letter in its phonetic guise, or the phoneme as grain of the voice. It would thus seem that both the use of a foreign tongue and the medium of poetry in 'Alabaster' function as semblants. The question is now: What 'nothing' do these cover? The answer to this question will be broached in the next chapter, which focuses on the sustaining aspect of theory, we might say, its maternal antecedents and paternal function.

Ironically in the light of the role of the Other in the definition of the imaginary order, and in the attempt to define the self in terms of what it means to be a mother, there is no mention of any maternal tradition in 'Alabaster'. There is an eloquent silence here in terms of the genetic family connection which the piece seems on the surface to be seeking. The comparisons are all based on the connections between inanimate objects and components of voice though, as well as on the shared activity of writing. On closer inspection, the lack of any mention of the physical maternal connection would seem to undercut the familial link, which, of necessity, requires women to give birth to succeeding generations. This deconstructs the familial connection I was trying to construct, or at least reconstruct in some absurd teleological gesture, and puts more stress on the shared activity of writing as an imaginary bond. However, on inspection, that activity is, in fact, dissimilar as opposed to similar, a point underlined by the admission that 'I' is a 'hiatus', a 'copula between life and death', a 'make-believe' in the making. Here is an index of the progression from the imaginary to the symbolic, as willed images of similarity are deconstructed by the very linguistic matrix through which they are expressed. The Other with which the 'I' of the text will define herself has changed radically from the context of the family evoked in the opening paragraph, with its evocation of acts of nurturing, to the more lettered context of a poet, with her literary productions. The thrust of the writing is from blood relations to semblant, from *sang rouge* to *sang blanc* (red blood to white blood).

As in 'The grain of the voice' (Barthes, 1977b), the voice is here multilayered. However, it is not experienced in the throat as 'pulsional incidents', as 'the language lined with flesh, a text where we can hear the grain of the throat, the patina of consonants, the voluptuousness of vowels, a whole carnal stereophony' (Barthes, 1977b: 71–82) in the throat, but in the ear: 'ooo' repeated three times. As a trope, the repetition of the phoneme 'o' has a more sinister ring. Indeed, instead of signalling the jubilant experience of speaking, it signals that death is lurking somewhere in the background. Death is not evoked by any process of reification which equates one thing with a signifier; rather, it is brought about by the voice, specifically by the voice speaking to itself, and repeating the vowel 'o' like a mantra in three sets of three.

It is the phonetic properties of the letter as spoken by the voice which evokes here the deathly quality of the mother tongue. In Lacanian terms, the voice, of course, is a symptom of what is left over from speech, an uncanny object that exceeds symbolisation. In other words, it is a thing without a body, for it also exceeds speech's capacity to make sound meaningful (Dolar, 2006: 15). But what the voice in the fiction that is poetry in a second language insists on is the gap between the repetitive, reminding nature of desire and the warning, the death that will finally close the gap that desire produces. The difference is in the excess, the irrational element that makes the presence of the voice all the more mysterious. The voice appears to be intensely personal and yet, as Barthes reminds us in his own work, even in the consistency of its message it expresses nothing of its message (Barthes, 1977b: 182). What it expresses is the real of trauma, with all its deathly intonations and connotations.

The voice here belongs with death. The voice is both inside and outside. It accompanies an anxiety that warns against the death of the subject. The speaker is attempting to escape the truth of the chilling desire or thrill produced not by the message, but by the voice without trace or body. The anxiety about the source of the voice is predicated on a logic similar to what Lacan calls 'the agency of the letter', or the repetition of the signifier 'Remember you must die' that continues to insist – traumatically hectoring and reminding 'me' despite her attempts to confer meaning on it (Lacan, 2006 [1959c]: 356). What the semblant covers is nothing. However, the anxiety this nothing gives rise to is the anxiety that surrounds the truth of death. It is the truth of being as make-believe, of life as artefact bought on credit.

At least this is, it seems to me, what writing means when the writer's filiation shifts to another language and when the form she chooses is poetry rather than the straightforward prose that has the imprimatur of the Law. For the writer, though identified with the dead one, does not assume the place of death, only the place of the cadaver. If I were to write in my mother tongue, the story would be different. It is the impossible. It is the ultimate blank. The incandescent fusion with the *mère mortifère* (the death-inducing mother), not the *mère echo* (mother echo/mere echo).

Why is white white?

Chalk, rice, zinc
   Crystal falls
      Limestone graves

Phosphorus
   Lightless body
      Alabaster.

(Hecq, 2010a)

By way of conclusion, though both texts discussed above are fictions of sorts, one stays firmly embedded in the imaginary by relying on the scopic drive while the other shifts to the invocatory drive, thus highlighting two different ways of relating to the signifier and to the letter, and thereby to *jouissance*. *Roland Barthes by Roland Barthes* (Barthes, 1977a) invokes the gap between expectation and desire, reality and fantasy, speech and writing. 'Alabaster', on the other hand, invokes this gap with regard to its intimate proximity to the lip of the hole in the real. Here, the voice is not simply the medium of linguistic communication, but rather an enigmatic object of desire that resists symbolisation. The voice as an object of desire is thus revealed as the layering of that which produces articulated speech; it is an index of the gap at the intersection of the real, and the imaginary must be filled by the symbolic for reality to be constituted by way of writing. The narrative drive is shaped by a questing that attempts to match the known with an unknown. If it is true that this text was written to put death to death, then writing in English may simply be a means of avoiding the sorrow, uncanny anxiety and fascination incited by its real presence, and writing poetry the very last resort before subjective dissolution.

Although I am now aware of a vast body of theory on writing trauma, some of which actually addresses techniques that may deflect any adverse effect on both writer and reader, I doubt that mere exposure to such theory would have helped me at the time of writing. I had to learn my lesson by going through it and by reconstructing theory from the inside out. This said, I cannot dismiss that the writing through of trauma is a highly recognised therapeutic device that humans have gravitated towards since we first used mechanical means to communicate. Drama therapist Robert Landy reminds us that the dramatising of events 'persists as a natural form of healing and has existed as a ritual healing process for thousands of years' (Landy, 2010: 7). Academic Brendan Stone, from the UK, whose work focuses on the relationship between narrative and human identity, with a specific focus on experiences of trauma as described in first-person autobiographical writing, extensively attests to this (e.g. Stone, 2004a, 2004b, 2006, 2008). Stone has written about autobiography and fiction from a personal viewpoint and is now extending his finding to collective bodies (Stone *et al.,* 2014). Meanwhile, a relatively new genre of fiction writing known as the 'trauma novel', of which *'Hush'* (Hecq, unpublished) may be an exemplar, has recently been identified. Theorist Michelle Balaev tells us that these are works that represent profound loss or intense fear on individual or collective levels (Balaev, 2008). Novels of this ilk include examples by Anne Michaels (1998), Toni Morrison (1988) and Alice Sebold (2002). Perhaps this subgenre would, in fact, include most postcolonial novels if one accepts that individual or collective loss is at the heart of the postcolonial project. But this is just a caveat. According to Whitehead:

> trauma fiction relies on the intensification of conventional narrative modes and methods. There are, however, a number of key stylistic features which tend to recur in these narratives. These include the use of intertextuality, repetition and a dispersed or fragmented narrative voice. (Whitehead, 2004: 84)

This allows for a disruption of linear chronology just as the recourse to metaphor and disruption of syntax do. These are techniques which enable representations of chaos. A trauma text provides a 'coherent view of reality that is necessarily reorganised through a painful process of reorientation' (Balaev, 2008: 163). 'Trauma knowledge', therefore, 'cannot be fully communicated or retrieved without distortion' (Whitehead, 2004: 84). The need to externalise and thereby relieve the inner tension with the above observation in mind gives the representational systems their function, through the use of metaphor and other figures of speech – including interference with narratorial pronouns, grammar and syntax and the recourse to silence, signified or not. What trauma theories have in common with psychoanalytically inflected approaches to writing informed by reader-response criticism is the problem of ethics in representations of pain, which necessarily escapes the literality of purely mimetic approaches to art. This is tackled, again from the inside out, in the next chapter.

11 Food for Thought: Investigating Aesthetic Care

> *'We' ... composed of many different things ... all life, all art, all waifs and strays – a rambling capricious but somewhat unified whole.*
> Virginia Woolf

This chapter talks back to Chapters 2 and 5. It combines creative work and the discourses of criticism and psychoanalysis to explore the relationship between writing and food in the work of mourning. As such, it is about grief, withholding grief, anorexia and writing. It describes the protagonist's confronting the death of a child and, in flashbacks, the evocation of a pre-existing psychological condition that flares up at this moment of crisis. Loss of speech is hinted at as a possible consequence of the crisis and writing as a way of piecing the self together. In so doing, it finds that criticism, and reader-response criticism in particular, may sustain the livelihood of the writer as subject. Like melancholia, writing entails dealing with loss but, as Lacan has shown, writing may also fulfil the function of an elaborate symptom – suppletion (Lacan, 2005 [1975–76]). In this personal work of fiction, the narrator's relationship with food adumbrates the creative writer's relationship with writing as a work of mourning that reconstitutes selfhood. By specifically addressing the enigma of *suppléance* with reference to anorexia, the creative work 'Blue like an orange' (Hecq, 2012d) gives us the key to one of its *pivotal* agents: anxiety. Just as the anorexic who fantasises about food cooks continuously and dishes it out to others, yet *will not* eat, the writer writes to sustain her own desire by choosing strategies for the delight of the other, namely, her reader. Thus, both writing and anorexia are shown to partake of the same economy, as they are both ways of negotiating anxiety from the position of melancholia.

'Blue like an orange' is the central chapter in *'Hush'*, a work in progress introduced in the previous chapter. At this juncture, it is important to mention why there were a number of generic changes made to this work. It has been written from the perspective of a memoir, a novel and now what may be called a polygeneric book of fiction. To me, the last version is the most satisfying. First, because it conveys to readers the full experience of bereavement in a social context while imparting the sense of loss this entailed without oppressing them. Second, because it highlights how the writing process is integral to the mourning process. Third, the last version has a performative element that brings out the playfulness of art-making, which was lacking in the first two discarded versions. Although this performative element came intuitively to me at a moment of crisis, when anxiety became overwhelming in the writing of 'Alabaster', reflecting upon what had happened when the stream of consciousness process was abruptly interrupted enabled me to find a form perfectly fitted to my subject. It also occurred to me then that I might learn from this lesson in re-reading myself to anticipate my readers' feelings at the point of tackling emotionally taxing passages.

This insight was retroactive. It came to me while reflecting on the way I had handled my own anxiety halfway through writing the previous chapter, enacting as it were the process of analytical discovery through association and *Nachträglichkeit* ('deferred action') (Freud, 1991 [1896]: 229). As pointed out in the Introduction to this book, Freud uses the term *nachträglich* constantly, often underlining it to signify its importance. The noun *Nachträglichkeit* also keeps recurring in his work. Although Freud never offered a precise definition of the notion of 'deferred action', it was undeniably part of his conceptual framework and research method. This concept is particularly useful, not only for understanding the creative process, but also for elucidating creative writing research. At the risk of repeating myself, most of the discoveries we make occur after the fact, that is, after the writing is done. In light of this comment, I offer the reader the creative work first and the exegetical component second.

Blue Like an Orange

We are two abysses – a well staring at the sky.
Fernando Pessoa

After the funeral I looked for sustenance in the sky. But the light was out to blind me. It fell though the branch of gum trees like numb fingers thumbing through clouds for words to name the wind. All it found were synonyms for blue as though nothing comforts the eye but light and shade pacing through hues and meanings of blue. Lapis-lazuli azure cobalt and navy and sapphire and cerulean. Tearful blue, sad, low, dejected, melancholy, desolate. But most of all lapis-lazuli whose veins yield azure and ultramarine. Azure light enough to allow the sun to flood through. Cobalt, harsh and sharp. Indigo. And ultramarine, a word that tastes of the sea, smooth, salty and warm. Ultra deep. The veined mingling of violet and green, a purple that is almost red, a green that is almost yellow and a yellow that is orange. What I saw in the sky when the rays of the sun lay flat upon my hand was a black sea I dipped into. And ducked out of.

The Mother, for lack of a proper name, formerly myself, listened for the click of the latch in the frame of the front door. She listened for the voice that would ask her a question. She listened and heard a voice.

The wind. The wind yowling.

No words.

What are words for, you ask.

She felt as though she had forgotten what it was like to lift her tongue, what it was like to lick her lips unstuck, what it was like to outlive the cold. To live.

It all seemed to have blown away from her, out of reach of her body, her memory, cut loose. This, she thought, is what it feels like to be dead.

Dead.

The word entered the Mother's head. It took up residence there and multiplied.

How a single word can kill.

My feet pushed her away and across the room, across the passage and into the corridor. Out onto the verandah. Carried her back into a time before that now time. She sniffed the air and fell in a cloud of musty dust. Vanished in the sky.

I could have screamed, but willed her eyes open. It just couldn't be true. The mother was going to wake up to the call of her baby, tune her ear to the sound of people talking in the street, the muffled roar of motorcars passing her window, the clamour of schoolchildren hurrying to school, all in one clap out of this room and into the cold of a brand new morning.

Today – yes, she thought, she will bake a cake, a lemon and almond cake, with lemons and almonds from her trees to celebrate the promise of the brand new day. Today – yes! She will be frivolous. She will dress up and dress the children in matching clothes the way they do in children's books and women's magazines. She will go to the market and buy flowers and food. They will listen to market music from the Andes. She will buy bunches of tulips, irises and jonquils as bright and lush as she can find. And she will buy oranges and chestnuts, cherry tomatoes and golden spuds, swedes and parsnips, a tiny pumpkin, asparagus, perhaps. Tarragon and thyme, garlic and ginger. And today – yes! She will surprise them all. Her family.

He will come home at six and he will say *hmm whatever it is it smells fantastic* and he will ask what did our little king do today? And he will kiss the first-born and the Mother and perhaps listen to the answer and then he will open his violin case and play something, something soft and crisp by Paganini and the new baby will look at his father and give him his first smile so that he too can delight as the Mother did in something as fleeting and precious as that. Then they will eat.

What I saw in the sky when the rays of the sun lay flat upon my hand was a black sea I dipped into. And ducked out of, for it was cold.

I ducked out of the black sea of blue for in this life meant to be starting all over again there was an endless series of things to be done, meals to be cooked. All in an endless time of grief not to be done. On hold. Grief in ashes for life's sake. For the first-born's sake, the sleeping boy who now refused to speak his mother tongue, the one to whom I'd said *I have you and we'll get through this* when the night fell on the day of the funeral and our voices hushed and in the immense sweetness of the blue night all I heard was the child, the first one, breathing.

It was a matter of existing within that polarity between the deep centre and the vast periphery. But time would not flow. Time was hard honey. Amber. Ambergris. *Gris* not blue.
Blue-grey.

I was a time bomb waiting to explode. Longed for food. Warmth. I felt so cold. At night my want was so strong I stared at the corner between the ceiling and wall, and a single, giant eye would appear. I could not or would not move that gigantic eye. I could not make it blink. My body lay cold and rigid and empty. Apart from me. I was hollow, and in the hole was that eye, endlessly staring.

I stared into the void in my life. Into the hole in my heart. I devoured books on cot death, filled my ears with interviews of professionals and parents who had been *touched* by it. I read to the child and helped him draw his own story of loss in a ledger adorned with stars. I cooked.

There were pancakes and French toast and brioche. Lemon pudding and orange cake and rhubarb pie and apple crumble. Poppy seed cake.

Marzipan. Blueberry muffins. Roasted chestnuts and peppers and egg-plants we called aubergines still. Artichoke hearts were preserved, for the child liked the leaves. There were cats' tongues and profiteroles and jalousies. Gingerbread men and gingerbread stars.

I longed for food, in whatever form. I felt so greedy, and yet it cut me off from the child and from his father too. I would not eat. There was no room for me. I rose and fell. Flailed around me in a sea of black. Lack. Living and wanting to die. I fell into the waterfall of my mind. I had been there before. Eating and I. Smoking and I. These had been the staples of my life. I had made them my life. One after the other. One the other side of the other. I had blown them up into huge bunches of flowers: irises and daffodils arranged alternately, gerberas arranged in incremental hues of lemon, orange, crimson, scarlet, sienna. Cambridge bells, bluebells, corn flowers, periwinkle and gypsophile. Hollyhocks. Red roses. Petals of blood. Asphodels and lilies and jonquils and hyacinths. Now that part of me had died for real, it felt more difficult to sort out the irises from the hyacinths, the daffodils from the jonquils. Spellbound and sickened by the smells, I almost forgot life in the process.

The fear of eating was huge. Palpable. Time would not flow. Time was rock hard. Amber. I was cold and empty. I could not eat lest I implode with guilt or explode with anger.

All meaning disintegrated and hit me hard where my heart should have been.

The fear of smoking was thin, like a mist that would surface in dreams.

Loving that disposal of greed. Loving that being painted into a corner, you see.

I listened to music. Or tried to. Thought it would fill the hole. I listened to Kinchela's 'Mourned by the wind' and nearly cried. It was a solace as tangible as if some other sentient being had been affirming my own sorrow. But I could not listen. Would not take any risks. No, not then. I asked myself what if I entered down into the numb emptiness of my life. But saw I couldn't go there, for the sake of the child. I sensed there was another dimension there. Movement. Space. And absolute nothingness.

Hunger was the obvious answer, like an atheist's prayer.

I tried writing. Words came in bursts and spurts. Made no sense. I had lost my alphabet in the night sky.

What did I want?

Misprint.

A copyist's error.

Never before had I asked myself that question.

I was a ghost on a ghost train. Had been on it for so long. It was the story of my life. I knew the terror. Knew the uncanny creatures and their accoutrements, those that spring out at you, always at the same place, same time. Here. Gossamer, the scent of jonquils and hyacinths, diaphanous bodies, ghosts that will knife you in the back. Dead stars dancing before your eyes. Strings of pearls. Fog steaming up. The old woman pushing her cart, not even hiding her scythe. And the fear, always the fear.

I would not cry. The wind blew through the house like in a book I read as a child about a girl who was lost. The wind. Perhaps, I thought, it would crack the lemon tree, the one whose lemons I make lemonade with. The one where ghosts rest and whisper, the wind would crack. Expose the back of the leaves, polish their dust off. All you could hear was the wind.

Words lost. Voice gone.

All had broken with the voice of the dead.

How dare the phone ring.

Consistency, the structures you get used to, make us believe all lies as truth lies strangled by a telephone cord in the late afternoon.

The fear was so strong I bolted for the door and into the street. I ran to the park as fast as incipient thoughts ran through my mind. I ran oblivious to the traffic. Oblivious to time. Oblivious of the cold. I ran to the pond. The one you call a billabong. And stood. And saw the child, the first-born, chasing the ducks. His hair on fire. When the shadows merged with the waters in the cold pond, when the wind moaned in the branches of the gum trees, when the last ray of sunshine gilded with its mystery the white gardenias and hollyhocks I turned back home.

I did not know what my thoughts were, nor did I know why I had to go through this. All I knew then was that I needed to write for the sheer satisfaction of keeping fear at bay, of experiencing the vanity of meaning, even if words did not make sense.

Blue like an orange. The dark is stitched with points of light and all the threads at the back of the sky make the lining of the universe.

It is odd, this urge to write out of fear. Out of the fear of succumbing to sorrow. A sorrow with far more distant echoes than this.

Why do we think and speak?

This is a child's question, just like *why is the sky blue*. You should be able to answer it, but can only offer a reprint: *blue like an orange*.

This is a lie. It is the earth which is blue like an orange. For you can eat oranges as we do the earth. For alongside the hunger for food is a deeper hunger that is thwarted. That's why you lie. Use metaphors. Fast and write.

And you need to check your thoughts for we christened the stars without thinking they needed no names and the numbers that are comets do cross the dark and land on virgin vines like chains of red pepper that crawl in the wind that whistles soft and sad as a flute in the twilight.

As I wrote, compelled back to the black sea, I felt my heart expanding towards the sky and tears came to my eyes for the first time since death had been.

It is odd our tears, shed or unshed, do not speak, and yet we seem to understand them and the sound of a child scuttling through the front door is sweeter than words.

'Mummy, I'm hungry'.

(Hecq 2012d)

Like Unappeasable Hunger

> *Writing is a way to trace my hunger, and hunger is nothing if not a void.*
> Sriri Hustvedt

In this exegetical part I contend that writing and anorexia partake of the same economy as they both embody mourning put on hold. Further, they both constitute a mode of survival by way of negotiating the anxiety that loss provokes, as loss is bound to reactivate the memory of the loss of the primary object and circle round it. This would seem to illustrate Lacan's theorising of 'object a' (Lacan, 1986 [1964]: 17) as both the object of anxiety and the final reserve of the libido (Lacan, 2004 [1962–63]: 119). However, I suggest here that writing as suppletion fulfils the function of, or stands in for, this lost object and helps the ego cohere by way of keeping anxiety at bay. Another way of putting this is that writing facilitates the knotting of the imaginary and the symbolic by avoiding the lure of the real in the form of object a, the other side of what I have called 'the kernel of the *in-between*' in the previous chapter.

The problem of how to convey disturbing material such as the experience of grief and associated psychotic or pseudo-psychotic phenomena in literary discourse was part of my struggle when writing the central chapter of

'Hush'. Since writing 'Alabaster' (Hecq, 2010a), I had been keenly aware of the need for me to find a safe space to write from or, at least, a safe *style* that would provide a safe space. This style entailed breaking into poetry at moments of crisis, which meant steering away from the meaning inherent in the metonymic axis of language by interchanging narrating personas, breaking up the syntax and making full use of metaphors, fragments and blank spaces (Hecq, 2010a). What these devices had provided me with was some emotional distance from my material. In other words, I had found a way of creating an emotional distance through *aesthetic distance*, by way of tropes. Although this begs the question of the difference between *semblant* (Hecq, 2010a) and *suppléance* (Hecq, 2011a), it is beyond the scope of this chapter.

In 'Blue like an orange', I wanted to show how grief reactivates previous losses, conflicts, anxieties and thereby old symptoms such as, to take an extreme example of communicating loss, anorexia nervosa. Though anorexia is a symptom that may manifest itself in different structures (Zentner, 1986: 74), I wanted to present it as a symptom of melancholia, as I felt my own experience resonated with Freud's statement in his *Draft G* (1895). This made increasing sense, as describing the grieving process enabled me to show the origin and meaning of the anorectic symptom in all its rawness while highlighting the fantasy of the fragmented body at its core.

So, what is the anorectic symptom? The anorexic subject eats *nothing*. And this *nothing* eats her away. Thus, what the anorectic body presents to the world, even if it is not yet cadaverous, is this *nothing*, which Lacan has called 'lack' (Lacan, 1993 [1955–56]: 139). This lack is, however, that which causes desire to arise. It may therefore be said that the anorexic stubbornly denies her most basic need for food in order to sustain her desire – unto death. Further, although there are three forms of lack in Lacanian theory, namely castration, frustration and privation, the term 'lack' tends to be synonymous with symbolic castration in discussions of Lacan's work. It is therefore not for nothing that the anorexic woman frightens people away, since she flaunts the spectre of death for all to see. As a writer, though, I did not want to scare my reader away.

Aesthetic Care: Intuition, *Nachträglichkeit*, Narrative Strategies

Since symptoms may be seen as having the structure of metaphor (Lacan, 2006 [1957]: 431), I decided to keep using metaphor as a way of providing aesthetic distance with intent to discover the deeper meaning of the metaphor. In addition, I experimented with breaking up linear time and interchanging narrative pronouns to provide emotional relief and aesthetic control. Unbeknownst to me at the time of writing, I also used colours to warn the reader.[1]

Aesthetic distance in 'Blue like an orange' mainly results from the fact that events are related by a lyrical 'I' with brief incursions by a third-person narrator situated in past tense. This narrative style is counterbalanced by a further, second-person narrator, who identifies with the reader in the past historic and also briefly in the present and future anterior. I made these choices because no authoritarian and distancing narrative agency will ever be able to capture the contingencies involved in a writing process which, though actively facing the impact of self-reflexivity inherent in the writing process, gives rise to personal change. The conventionally told story in memoirs about grief and mental illness does not communicate the eventfulness of emotional progress, but rather depicts situations occurring along a way that has been clearly marked out. For the reader, this is likely to evoke the impression of stasis or sheer alienation and a sense of grief, of bewilderment, if not horror. A paradigm for this type of text has yet to be devised. It calls for two simultaneous yet divergent narrative agencies: to allow for the twofold structure of the self in the (re-)making process, based on some dialogue intent on expanding and structuring elements, progressive and regressive time axes; and the exchanges between a self and a second hypothetical person. Another, alien and alienating speech would have to be interpolated into the narrator's own, submerged into it, yet surfacing at odd times with momentum.

This chapter is about grief, withholding grief, withholding speech and struggling to keep a sense of connection to the world of the living. Loss of speech is a consequence of overwhelming grief and writing clearly a way of approaching mourning as a necessary process to the restoration of selfhood. Behind the protagonist's manifest symptoms lies a painfully achieved self-denial, an attempted suicide by starvation, in fact, that is evoked in sporadic flashbacks as part of the narrative procedure of this chapter, which is to intertwine two levels of representation. Interpolated into descriptions of a mother's emotional state on the day after her youngest child's funeral are acute flash-forwards of her wish fulfilments as well as flashbacks to key moments of a previous mental illness. The two time zones are intertwined in such a way as the chronology of events is constantly interrupted. The two time periods of representation are kept separate by the use of different verbal tenses and narratorial instances. The condensation of the poles of the author, narrator and protagonist into a single position in the text is, however, one of the factors that stabilise the narrative, as would a mediating text, namely, one that evokes a certain 'authenticity' by merging divergent narrative perspectives (author, narrator and protagonist) while defining, albeit at times defying, its reading public. This complex frame, I hoped, would have a stabilising effect.

This stabilising effect of the text is due to the ways in which the literary strategies employed make it possible to describe something which evades verbalisation by not presenting it mimetically. I was mindful to refrain from dismantling formal linguistic structures, as I have also refrained from presenting the dissolution of a clear conception of space and time in the narrator's mind. Both, however, are integral components of personality dissolution as experienced in acute moments of grief and psychotic crises that may be present in anorexia. Such dissolution is merely alluded to and what is foregrounded is the role that writing can play in preventing such dissolution.

The intertwining of two different levels of representation results in the opposition, characteristic of first-person novels, between a narrating ego and a participating ego, but 'Blue like an orange' breaks with one convention of the traditional first-person memoir, namely, the idea that it should be possible to discern a narrating ego, which now, looking back, presents itself more experienced. The retrospectively handled realm of the participating ego merges with psychic reality, which remains unchanged, and in which the narrating ego is still involved via flashbacks and metaphorical reverberations in the narrative. Both levels of representation, the retrospective level and the narrative embedding of the chapter, merely offer different perspectives on the narrating ego's unmediated and continuing crisis.

Thematically, this is manifested in the way the narrator's imagination circles constantly around her relationship with food and eventually on how this symptom is translated into her relationship with language. Her initial obsession with some painful rejection of food, far from being overcome on the level of narrative frame (witness the metaphorical overflow and lists of words), is turned into its opposite, expressing itself as an anxiety-ridden insistence on eating:

> I longed for food, in whatever form. I felt so greedy, and yet it cut me off from the child and from his father too. I would not eat. There was no room for me. I rose and fell. Flailed around me in a sea of black. Lack. Living and wanting to die. I fell into the waterfall of my mind. I had been there before.

The two levels of representation mirror one another; the narrating ego is neither more mature nor healthier than the participating ego. Indeed, the text performs linguistic and psychical upheavals from a subjective, interior perspective.

The tensions between the two levels of representation induce different illusions of a time continuum, a phenomenon which may influence the reader's responses to this chapter, even to the whole book. The retrospective level is marked by the exclusive and consistent use of the historic past tense, well suited to comprehensive accounts from a standpoint far removed in time. The writing is done from within the moment, the experiential, although it is in the past tense, which suggests selection and the process of *Nachträglichkeit* ('deferred action') at work (Freud, 1991 [1896]: 229). During the reading process, however, the reader has to produce mental images which, in turn, she or he needs in order to build consistency out of the contingent information offered by way of time or narrating persona shifts, metaphorical fugues, use of fragments or mere blanks. The reader's centre of orientation is of crucial importance for the quality and the amount of mental images produced and her or his centre of orientation is situated in the narrative frame. Thus, the flashback and flash-forward fragments appear, as one reads, to be already in the past, itself appearing as a surreal collage dominated by the sky imagery. An illusion of events occurring in a time continuum is evoked by the construction of a chronology, while the serial arrangement of the individual fragments of narration is instrumental in establishing the illusion of an inner reality akin to, yet divergent from, plot. In fact, the very possibility of plot development is undermined because the narrating ego is constantly being overtaken by her life and emotions. There is no narrative distance between the describing agency and what is described. Events arise and fade away; they are not brought to any conclusion, but coincide with the time required to depict them. In other words, the narrated time collapses into narrating time, only to be interrupted at the end of the chapter in the writing *itself* by the life-affirming words of the protagonist's child, who breaks the narrative frame by entering the story.

Thus, on the one hand, writing can be seen as a defensive operation, for defence mechanisms take on the obsessively repetitive form of primary processes. However, the attempt at articulation in this chapter is the condition for working something through even though it also represents the endeavour of an ego threatened by disintegration to save itself as it founders. Further, the device of different, interlocking levels of representation, the interchangeability of narrative fragments and the deliberate collage of narratorial pronouns means that the narrative structure does *not* collapse. The textual strategies are marked by a specific ambivalence. They are both rejection and communication of what cannot be said: rejection in that they are highly structured, and therefore are not a mimetic depiction of psychotic phenomena; communication in that integral components of psychotic phenomena are conveyed by the very nature of this structure. This ambivalence mimics the structural position of the melancholic anorexic who controls the *nothing* she eats.

The narrating ego's imagination circulates obsessively and repetitively around the rejection or intake of *anything* that is bound to remain *nothing*, that is, around those areas (and not only the intake of *food*) within which the symptoms of anorexia manifest themselves:

> Eating and I. Smoking and I. These had been the staples of my life. I had made them my life. One after the other. One the other side of the other. I had blown them up into huge bunches of flowers: irises and daffodils arranged alternately, gerberas arranged in incremental hues of lemon, orange, crimson, scarlet, sienna. Cambridge bells, bluebells, corn flowers, periwinkle and gypsophile. Hollyhocks. Red roses. Petals of blood. Asphodels and lilies and jonquils and hyacinths. Now that part of me had died for real, it felt more difficult to sort out the irises from the hyacinths, the daffodils from the jonquils. Spellbound and sickened by the smells, I almost forgot life in the process.

The symptoms are described in their capacity of setting boundaries, and thus endowing the contingent temporal flow of life with a structure that seems to invest it with meaning. In fact, it is embedded in the syntax and in the larger structure, including the disposition of paragraphs. The structuring element of the symptoms is at the core of the ensuing metaphorical language partly chosen for their colours, partly borrowed from nature mysticism: flowers are 'blown ... up into huge bunches'. An alienating optical impression is thus given an object which is in itself commonplace, food, since human nourishment, like flowers, may be classified as *natural*, yet cannot be eaten. The innate contradiction necessary to metaphors, not consciously perceived but taken subliminally, is the fact that flowers are natural products, but are not (all) edible. Incidentally, the words 'petals of blood' refers to the title of a novel by Ngugi Wa Thiong'o (2005), alluding thus to the narrating persona's allegiance to the symbolic order of wordsmiths.

The collision of images and the optically striking nature of the metaphor translates the ambivalence inherent in psychotic symptoms in discourse: the fascination that arises from the possibility of structuring the contingent flow of time is overshadowed by a sense of disgust evoked by the idea of having to eat flowers, particularly flowers whose colloquial names contain a reference to industrial products (Cambridge bells) or to death (asphodels and hyacinths). Food is here represented by the specific way in which it is expressed through language, as both fascinating and inedible, that is, as *nothing*.

Sensations of physical dissociation are integral parts of psychotic phenomena. Jacques Lacan has coined the term 'phantasm of the dis-membered body' (Lacan, 2006 [1949]: 77) to characterise them or, more precisely, to describe the fact that analysands often dream of dismembered parts of their bodies during phases of their analysis in which they regress far back into realms of indifferentiation. In this chapter the phantasm – fantasy – of the dismembered body surfaces in the protagonist's fantasies:

> It was a matter of existing within that polarity between the deep centre and the vast periphery. But time would not flow. Time was hard honey. Amber. Ambergris. *Gris* not blue. Blue-grey.
>
> I was a time bomb waiting to explode. Longed for food. Warmth. I felt so cold. At night my want was so strong I stared at the corner between the ceiling and wall, and a single, giant eye would appear. I could not or would not move that gigantic eye. I could not make it blink. My body lay cold and rigid and empty. Apart from me. I was hollow, and in the hole was that eye, endlessly staring.

The optical dimension, which plays a central part in metaphor, is here personified and condensed into a giant eye. However, what is highlighted is no longer the exchange between different sensory areas; instead, the nar-rator's sensitivity is undifferentiated, compressed and it encompasses all her physical feelings. As we have seen, for Freud, the eyes carry an unusually high affective charge (Freud, 2001 [1914–16]). Eyes regulate perception, our way of understanding and interpreting the world and, according to Lacan, access to the symbolic order of language (Lacan, 2006 [1949]). They are close to the brain, not only because of their location in the body; they are cerebral, they control and structure the secondary process. It is this very function which fails in the passage quoted above: any movement of the eye, which precedes perception, appears impossible.

The spontaneous, subliminal connotation of this image is a sense of paralysis, while paralysis, in turn, is an integral component of anxiety. In combination with the expansive openness prestructured by the textual strategies, the sense of paralysis and anxiety build up a communicational situation between text and reader which may propel the reader into a sense of oppression, of which I was mindful. Emotional reactions to the inter-action of topic, textual strategies and metaphors occur within the tensions between what is actually said and what is only subliminally understood, but is present by the very fact of its omission. Thus, the recipient reacts emotionally to something not explicitly verbalised in the text.

Anxiety, however, *is* itself verbalised in the text:

I was a ghost on a ghost train. Had been on it for so long. It was the story of my life. I knew the terror. Knew the uncanny creatures and their accoutrements, those that spring out at you, always at the same place, same time. Here. Gossamer, the scent of jonquils and hyacinths, diaphanous bodies, ghosts that will knife you in the back. Dead stars dancing before your eyes. Strings of pearls. Fog steaming up. The old woman pushing her cart, not even hiding her scythe. And the fear, always the fear.

Suddenness as a way of perceiving something unexpected, accidental, out of context, entirely new, entirely alien, outside of the planning of anticipation, is one of the forms in which anxiety surfaces in narratives. In this passage, suddenness is suggestively evoked in the metaphor of the fairground ghost train. The reader knows what such ghost trains are and what it is like to board one. Therefore, the reader can assimilate the semantic field in question, namely the impact of suddenness, by associating it with certain emotions with which she or he is familiar. At the same time, however, the emotional dimension of anxiety signalling some subjective dissolution is transferred to a semantic field alien to it. The horror thereby conveyed can be explained through recognition of the incidents that usually do occur in fairground ghost trains; it is thereby weakened and tolerable.

Anxiety phenomena are verbalised in a similar way elsewhere, that is to say, by way of transferring it to other areas:

The fear of eating was huge. Palpable. Time would not flow. Time was rock hard. Amber. I was cold and empty. I could not eat lest I implode with guilt or explode with anger. All meaning disintegrated and hit me hard where my heart should have been.

The fascination emanating from the rejection of food obviously consists in the opportunity of structuring time through the symptom. Simultaneously, however, there is an underlying dimension of anxiety (Recalcati, 2011). But what is anxiety? And why is it such a powerful affect?

Uncanny Affiliates: *Nach(t)* and Nigh(t)

According to Søren Kierkegaard (1944), anxiety threatens existence and is undirected, a feeling that overwhelms the person concerned, although no actual cause for it can be discerned; fear, on the other hand, is directed, related to a definite object which is perceived as frightening. In the above excerpt from 'Blue like and orange', what is expressed is not so much anxiety as fear to signal that 'anxiety is not without an object' (Lacan, 2004 [1962–63]: 98). Or, to put it differently, anxiety is transferred: modified, named and personified as the fear of breaking a self-imposed rule of abstinence, that is, as fear of something definite. Yet underneath this fear is the anxiety provoked by the desire of the Other (Lacan, 2004 [1962– 63]: 14), the one that threatens to annihilate the subject which the reference to the narrator *as* ghost anticipates. This ghost also signals the nature of the narrator's fantasy, which is no other than the fantasy of her own death. Thus, the text translates fear into literary discourse, rather than conveying the dimension of anxiety which threatens existence. Fear of something familiar and well known is more amenable to description than anxiety, which shatters all structures, forms and concepts.

More and more such metaphors are introduced: fear is represented in images; that is to say, anxiety is given an object while at the same time it can be felt as a strange undercurrent to the linguistic imagery. But this very transfer of anxiety to other areas means that no overall pattern will evolve. We are on safe ground.

Here, the difference between anxiety as an emotional dimension of human experience and anxiety as it is transformed via tropes for the very purpose of alleviating it shows up clearly; the use of imagery does not wholly solve this problem of incommensurability. Only such metaphors as relate to the symptoms of anorexia nervosa, and the fantasy of the fragmented or dismembered body, carry subliminal connotations of disgust and paralysis. These alien ideas are able to engender, through their interaction with the other textual strategies (shifts in narrating personas, use of fragments or mere blanks), the openness which can tip over into a sense of oppression, but doesn't. But perhaps each reader will experience the text in different ways. In which case, we are never on safe ground.

Although the discussion at the end of this chapter turns back to Lacanian concepts explained in Chapter 5, it needs to be noted that the exegetical work would not have been possible without some exposure to some of the strands of reader-response criticism encountered in Chapter 2, as well as some awareness of Roland Barthes's textual strategies. This demonstrates that a poetics as defined in the Introduction to this book is constantly evolving, adjusting as it does to the requirements of the creative work as well as to the writer's degree of familiarity with theories and concepts. Or, breaking away as it must do, from theories and concepts, ideologies and dogmas. As we near the ending of this book, we make the latter move, itself brought about by *Nachträglichkeit* and self-reflexivity.

Note

(1) Thanks to John Forrest, who reads and listens with a painter's heart, for pointing this out to me.

12 Poetics of Auto-Genesis: On Becoming and the Canon

> We make form and form makes us.
> Ali Smith

> This 'style', or 'writing', of women tends to put the torch to fetish words, proper terms, well-constructed forms. This 'style' does not privilege sight.
> Luce Irigaray

This chapter returns to the question of poetics in reactionary fashion. Having established a dialogue between creative writing and theory, including rhetoric and criticism, having pushed the boundaries of theory by addressing the place of emotion and embodiment, having gone through the mirror of representation, I now ask the question: is it possible for women writers – particularly poets – to embrace a female subject matter in their writing and still be taken seriously as writers within the 'masculine universal' sphere of literature? In seeking answers to this question, I use a creative work, *Out of Bounds* (Hecq, 2009b), which talks back to the discourses of criticism and theory. Of particular interest here is the subject matter of literal gestational birth, which I contrast with the metaphorical notions of self-reproduction, as brought to the fore by proponents of the canonical, such as Harold Bloom.

In the Western literary canon, myths of autogenesis mark the transition from a matriarchal economy to a patriarchal one through figuring poetic births which are essentially masculine. In Judeo-Christian discourses, genesis comes forth from the father's word rather than from the mother's body in the privileging of the patriarchal order (Daly, 1991). In the realm of literary theory, nowhere is this made more explicit than in Lacan's teaching, according to which the Name of the Father is that which structures subjectivity (Lacan, 2006). Metaphors of birth are central to the manoeuvres whereby poets define themselves and to the critical procedures whereby their work is recognised and either marginalised or canonised. Poetry itself is often referred to as a gestational space. This chapter investigates the gendered topos of this gestational space. It looks for the poetic seed that portends birth and becoming. And above all, it looks for the body that houses this process. It argues that poetry which deals with the materiality of motherhood is highly problematic in an economy that prizes euphemistic birth in linguistic and abstracted terms. This poetic economy masculinises voice and feminises form, that is, the body of the text. Within such an economy, a female poet's voice undermines the inertness of the matter and *Mater* considered necessary for the self-birthing of male poets. Whether the price for this voice is cultural still-birth remains to be ascertained.

In many ways, this chapter is a call to re-conceive the given tropes of poetry as 'birth', given a gendered economy of metaphors of autogenesis. This caveat is placed against the psychoanalytic structure of Lacan's Name of the Father as a law-giving mechanism that values the word and thereby defines the subject as a pre-linguistic particularity lost in the universalising structure of language. I suggest that a literal rendition of a poetics of birth is disturbingly familiar to audiences and set this experience as the keystone in exploring the possibility that this indicates the masculinised romantic standard of poetry that my own work undermines.[1] In order to make my point, I trace a brief history of metaphors of autogenesis as pertaining not only to the act of creating but also, more significantly, to how poetry is critically received and canonised. Arriving at the conclusion that this space is a masculinised womb prompts other questions, such as the question of whether poetry is a return to the womb, which situates poetry as a kind of regression that ties in with deeper psychoanalytic articulations made by Kristeva in relation to the *chora* (Kristeva, 1982, 1984) – and also by others, such as Ehrenzweig (1975) and Bollas (1987).

When a female writer uses tropes of birth in her work, she seems to be consigned by our culture to a distinctively female poetics. Given the ways in which masculinised concerns are valued as universal and representative (Cixous, 1976), and female concerns considered of interest to women only, then a female author writing from her own maternal experience appears to be disqualified from the sphere of serious literature.

Pregnancy, gestation, birth and motherhood are major events in my work. My first story, 'Magic' (Hecq, 1997b: 50–53), was about giving birth. My first poem, 'Grief' (Hecq, 1997a: 3), was about losing a child. The novel *The Book of Elsa* (Hecq, 2000a) is a book of autogenesis, where the main character recreates herself in 'the land of furphies' and eventually gives birth to a child and to the book she has just written in the tongue of a mythical father whose work she emulates, namely James Joyce. In a similar vein, *Out of Bounds* (Hecq, 2009b) has its protagonist reinvent herself across languages as a woman, mother and poet. Stories and poems revolving around those themes abound in *Magic and Other Stories* (Hecq, 2000b), *Mythfits* (Hecq, 1999), *Good Grief* (Hecq, 2002), *Noisy Blood* (Hecq, 2004) and *Couchgrass* (Hecq, 2006a). And my work in progress, 'Hush' (see Chapters 10 and 11 of the present volume) explores the relationship between mourning, mothering and creating. I have noted at launches of my books or public readings how the audience often looks bored or cringes when I read pieces that address these themes *literally*, especially if these were poems or prose poems.

Listening to stories or poems about mundane aspects of female experience, I thought, did not appeal to an audience expecting more traditional or less personal poetic subjects. It may have been culturally specific, I hypothesised, but changed my mind after reading the same pieces to Francophone ears. The audience's indifference or discomfort, I decided, probably stemmed from a belief that such subjective exploration of 'lived maternal experience' (Liss, 2009: xviii) had no general appeal, even for women. However, I will argue here, by singling out my latest book of poetry as a brief case study, that resistance to birth as a poetic theme does not result from such experience being too personal and remote from what is perceived to be fit as a literary topic, but that the explicit treatment of such experience overloads a universal poetics already deeply embedded in incarnatory metaphors. Perhaps the indifference or discomfort experienced by my audience had less to do with this being a site of difference and more to do with the fact that it is a site of too much sameness. Writing about aspects of maternity is challenging in an aesthetic economy that rewards euphemistic birth in figurative language. Such aesthetic presupposition inevitably masculinises voice and feminises form. Although this may be true of all literary genres, this is especially true of poetry. From within such a paradigm, a female voice undermines the conditions originally thought necessary for the self-birthing of male poets, suggesting that poets of both genders are all 'skinning Mummy' (Cixous, 2009: vii) or killing Mummy when they write.[2]

The incarnatory tendencies of romanticism have long been noted by critics, as have the autochthonic self-sufficiency tropes of much modernist literature (see, for example, Joyce's *A Portrait of the Artist as a Young Man*, published in 1916). In fact, modernist critical practices compound the legacy of the language of incarnation and self-sufficiency as an aesthetic standard, and this, combined in the Anglophone tradition with modernist reclamations of the metaphysical poets and Milton, has resulted in a poetics in which the achievement of canonical status in 20th-century tradition relied heavily on organicist metaphors of birth. A similar phenomenon can be traced in the Fancophone tradition, from romanticism to surrealism and existentialism. Metaphors of birth are central to the critical procedures whereby poets become canonised in 20th-century traditions of representative poetry, particularly as culturally significant poets, such as poet laureates – in the Anglophone world – or poets anointed by the Académic française – in the Francophone world.

The confluence of relations of birthing and midwifery to poetic practice, especially modernist poetry, determines not only the gender of the matter of poetry, but also the critical operations at work in the reception of poetry and its canonisation. For example, Christopher Ricks's *The Force of Poetry* (Ricks, 1984) demonstrates how incarnatory tendencies inform ideas of what poetry is and how it should perform. The 'force of poetry' here invoked as 'animating' poetry, and by extension criticism, is taken from Dr Johnson, and is understood as 'that force which calls new powers into being, which embodies sentiment, and animates matter' (Ricks, 1984: 6). The matter animated is feminine and the gestational space for the emerging voice of the poet. Ricks's influential style in poetry criticism repeatedly traces 'the relation between the turning of a phrase, the turning of someone into someone or something else, and the bodily act of turning' (Ricks, 1984: 21) as indicative of greatness in poetry. Ricks's turning body is like the baby turning in readiness for birth, and in one representative instance the 'division of the couplet' is such that it makes 'its second line swing open like a great door in the light' (Ricks, 1984: 22), like the opening of the cervix, or more violently, perhaps, the incision of a scalpel in a caesarean cut, before the rush of delivery into the world.

Perhaps in the context of the authority of canonicity in the 20th century, Harold Bloom also relies heavily on invocations of birth that result from man-to-man reproduction in his ideas of poetic genius. Bloom's (1975) template of 'poetic strength' has exerted considerable influence in the mapping of the Western canon, as echoes of his ideas reverberate powerfully through contemporary discourse on poetry. Individuation figured in Oedipal terms, and through man-to-man regeneration, thus underwrites the tradition into which female poets write and against which their work is assessed. Bloom claims that:

> Only a poet challenges a poet as poet and so only a poet makes a poet. To the poet-in-a-poet, a poem is always *the other man*, the precursor, and so a poem is always a person, always the father of one's Second Birth. (Bloom, 1975: 19)

The linguistic second birth is explicitly appointed as the origin of poetic identity and, as such, the pre-Oedipal period and the original material are, for the most part,[3] expunged from the symbolic landscape and relegated to silence. Bloom's argument that 'to live, the poet must *misinterpret* the father, by the crucial act of misprision' (Bloom, 1975: 19) is unable to see the more obvious misprision/mis-prision of the matter of the poem. This second birth becomes established as the origin of the poet's history, in which the first birth and pre-Oedipal experience become mythicised and mystified. Bloom describes the psychological pull the memory of the first birth and pre-Oedipal relating exerts in mythical terms when he writes:

Ocean, the matter of Night, the original Lilith or 'feast famished', mothers what is antithetical to her, the makers who fear (rightly) to accept her and never cease to move towards her. If not to have conceived oneself is a burden, so for the strong poet there is also the hidden burden: not to have brought oneself forth, not to be a god breaking one's own vessels, but to be awash in the word not quite one's own. (Bloom, 1975: 15)

Notwithstanding the extraordinary narcissism of such a comment, the 'burden' of being 'awash in the word not quite one's own' is kept 'hidden' by the insistence on the origins of the voice beginning with the second birth. The establishment of the linguistic birth as primary is achieved through a critical emphasis on poets having both conceived and brought themselves forth through the godlike breaking of their vessels or form. It could in fact be argued that the second birth *is* the literal birth, since a place is prepared in the symbolic order ahead of the child's physical arrival. However, to achieve representative status on these terms, a poet's heroic vocal struggle to be self-birthed from the 'body' of the poem must have a sympathetic critical circle to bear witness to this poetic birth. As Diana Tietjens Meyers argues, such authenticating criticism occurs in the tradition where the language related to midwifery and birth are 'used to symbolise the assistance men give to each other in their creative labours' and which goes 'back as far as Socrates' (Tietjens Meyers, 2001: 768). Thus, the unnamed, unsymbolised *his*-story of birth is the sublimated subtext of the most cathected and valorised literature in the Western canon – Wordsworth, Shelley, Keats, Tennyson, Browning, Whitman, Dickinson, Stevens, Warren, Ammons and Ashbery – and the pull that Bloom describes accounts for much of the seemingly inherent paradoxes that marks poetry as distinct from other genres of writing. For poetry, more than any other literary genre, retains a certain mystique, or sacredness, that tacitly places it at the apex of Literature's hierarchy. For the late Derrida, for example:

> The poet, in the very experience of his freedom, finds himself both bound to language and delivered from it by a speech whose master, nonetheless, he himself is.... In question is a labor, a deliverance, a slow gestation of the poet by the poem whose father he is. (Derrida, 1985: 65)

Even in deconstructive fashion poetry is a gestational space. In fact, this is a mere refashioning of modernism's take, whereby poetry is an autochthonic activity. For Derrida, too, the poet is master – a term that denotes objectivity and awareness – of the speech that 'binds' and 'delivers' him, and he is gestated by the very poem that he himself has 'fathered'. The inert matter of the poem is, as in Ricks's view, 'moved' by the poet to deliver himself from it. As it turns out, for both modernism and postmodernism, the poem is constructed as an 'ageless wound', without history or name, so that it can facilitate the poet's self-naming and historicisation. As Derrida emphasises, 'poetic discourse *takes root* in a wound' (Derrida, 1985: 66). However, naming the form, the matrix, the matter of poetry as a wound, does in fact give away that it has a specific moment in psychic history. The poem mother is the mOther,[4] after the castration implemented by the Name of the Father. It is woman as a site of loss – the loss coinciding with the movement of the child as phallus away from the desire of the mother into the symbolic of language. Hence the Oedipal fantasy of omnipotence can be seen here as retrospectively reconstituting the first birth in such a way that the child is recast as rewriting its own birth. In this way, the mother's agency, as well as both the child and the mother's materiality, are edited out in favour of language. As Madelon Sprengnether points out:

> From a feminist and psychoanalytic standpoint, post-structuralist theory suffers from a tendency to render the condition of biological motherhood either meaningless or irrelevant, thus repeating the repression of motherhood that Irigaray perceives at the heart of Western culture. (Sprengnether, 1990: 238)

Moreover, such elision also erases the ambivalence at the heart of motherhood (Almond, 2010), a sentiment which female writers often write about when it informs their subjectivity as both daughters and mothers.

In both modernist and postmodernist registers, the poem is then seen, however tacitly, as a masculinised womb, to which it is necessary to return, and to inhabit, in order to create. In his analysis of creative behaviour, Anton Ehrenzweig points out that the condition of 'artistic and scientific perception' is one in which 'retrogression can be considerable, where the child cannot even differentiate his own ego from the external world'

(Ehrenzweig, 1975: 170). Ehrenzweig likens this 'retrogression' to a return to intra-uterine experience:

> Plato's famous simile of the captive reflects a philosophical vision which has retrogressed to a pre-natal state; the captive, lying bound in a cave averted from the light of the external world, may symbolise the unborn child in the womb. Freud shows us that the mystic in his 'oceanic' feeling of union with the universe contemplates an infantile state of consciousness before the formation of a separate ego. (Ehrenzweig, 1975: 170)

A common prerequisite to the second self-birth of a poet is an imaginary journey of return. This return to the 'place' of writing in which male poets explore pre-, peri- and post-natal registers also functions as a testimony to the authenticity and the fecundity of their work, as explored, for example, in Seamus Heaney's *The Place of Writing* (Heaney, 1989). In a cultural imaginary where the mOther replaces the maternal body, then, the 'textualised' experience of being inside the mother's womb can be affirmed metaphorically by men and function as a touchstone of their 'inner' authenticity, and of their struggle to emerge from doors in the dark, from this creative but insensate state.

The cultural imaginary that valorises the mother as 'the place' of writing depends on a metaphor of creativity which recalls the state of being inside the womb, and this is available to men but seems to be forbidden to women. This is borne out by differing critical attitudes to female and male poets writing about incarnation. In contrast to the rescue operation performed on behalf of male poets, the practitioners of Oedipally configured criticism do not rush to the rescue of a woman who writes about birth, gestation and mothering, but might instead treat her work as inferior, too personal and self-obsessed. In other words, it would seem that first-hand rendering of 'lived maternal experience' (Liss, 2009: xviii) is, within the confines of poetry and poetics, not admissible as worthwhile human experience. The woman writing in and out of her own body seems too close to the denied condition of the poet as privileged in a post-Oedipal economy – writing *in* the mother's body, which is both invoked and disposed of as a matter of/ in myth.

Luce Irigaray notes that women's position with regard to the symbolic order is as its residue or waste (Irigaray, 1985b) and Julia Kristeva has famously devoted one book on the subject, *Powers of Horror* (Kristeva, 1982). Interestingly, Seamus Heaney observes that in Thomas Kinsella's work 'the place of waste, the place of renewal and the place of writing have become coterminous with the domain of poetry' (Heaney, 1989: 62).

The womb mother is consigned to a symbolic wasteland, and replaced by the matter of the poem and by the mothering–father 'poet', a theme that informs Heaney's own work, as his delightful poem 'Alphabets' makes all too symbolically clear (Heaney, 1987: 1–2). The lesser poet, who has not mastered the wealth of ancestry, is, in Bloom's terms, an epigone, which literally means 'to be born after'; that is, they fail because they have not sufficiently erased traces of the one who bore them and who was born before them. The hen woman who 'drops the egg' of 'poetry' in Kinsella's poem is therefore not fit for poetic vocation, not fit for the sort of mothering that only a male poet is fit for, and the lesson to be learned here is that woman must remain in 'place' as place (Heaney, 1989: 62). Moreover, Heaney argues that the Kinsella poem 'His father's hands' uses birth metaphors, but, these are, more importantly in terms of his argument, self-birthing metaphors that pertain to the father and son's autochthonic regeneration, and which disposes of woman as fit mother for poetry. The simultaneous representation of mother and child is one that is highly problematic in a culture that privileges an illusory autonomy, and which cannot admit the prior existence of the mother as mother. The maternal body has to become a wasteland, disposed of in the imaginary. Borsch-Jacobsen notes that the subject has to 'dispose of' the 'womb-mother', this *a priori* and 'external' presence, 'in order to constitute its myth of itself' (Borsch-Jacobsen cited in Brennan, 1992: 165). The possibility of representing the mother's perspective carries with it the threat of annihilation for the child, that is, the fear of the loss of the mother encoded in lethal pre-Oedipal symbiosis. This is annihilation in fantasy, which has become a cultural cliché in which the loss of the mother is repeatedly re-edited as part of the sacrosanct narratives of artistic birth. Thus, the view privileged in the drama of this poetics is that of the child, who fetishises the mother in her capacity as an object, and fantasises that they themselves are Mummy, skinning the mOther – hardly the fantasy of a mature woman.

But, at the risk of repeating myself, Ehrenzweig observes that the 'retrogression' involved in approaching a creative state 'can be considerable, where the child cannot even differentiate his own ego from the external world' (Ehrenzweig, 1975: 170). Here, I wish to make a clear distinction between the mother object and a woman's subjective difference from this object. The mother object is literally the use to which a pre-Oedipal child puts the mother. As the primary object, the mother is the representational limits of the world to the child, and indeed mediates the world for the child, who identifies with her to the extent of seeing through her. As psychoanalysis demonstrates, this erasure of the mother object is a psychical necessity. But, because no adequate cultural symbology exists to represent the separation of woman and mother object (Lacan, 1998 [1972–73]: 7), or woman *quoad matrem* (Lacan, 1998 [1972–73]: 35), this erasure also ensures both the representational sacrifice of woman's subjective difference as well as the deletion of the 'holding' environment of the mother object. Therefore, the most privileged cultural perspective is that of the pre-Oedipal child who mistakes the word/mother for themselves, and for whom the admission of mother as either woman or matter is tantamount to its own erasure. In this either/or model, identity politics is haunted by a fierce battle between mother and child for sheer representational space, indeed symbolic existence.

As a work in which 'lived maternal experience' (Liss, 2009: xviii) and the business of writing coalesce and collide, my work brings the mother back into the picture and within earshot. The avowal of the mother's subjective difference in terms of gender, culture and language may be bewildering to a critical economy that may read this work as 'cryptic' (Capp, 2000) or 'elliptical' at times (McHattan, 2003), but always, it would seem, outside the register of representationally admissible meaning, for the reader seems obliged to 'mine' the text, 'trying to identify – like her protagonist – this single, solid "thing itself"' (Gildfind, 2011). This may be because it makes present the mother and child as separate subjectivities, and as each other's objects in the same space, that is, in the space of the text, especially if this text is classified as poetry. Through signifying the mother's perspective with the child's perspective, the subject with the object, the text itself ceases to be matter/an object and becomes instead a transitional space, that is, the space of the text. The simultaneous representation of co-subjects and of one's own object use is substantially under-read by the interpretative frames that privilege the self-reflective birthing of the univocal subject. *Out of Bounds* (Hecq, 2009b), for example, in a psychic and symbolic act of *tmesis*, iterates a separation of the mother object and a woman's subjective difference, through expressing how it feels to be representationally restrained by the confines of the inside view. However, it does not involve a refuting of their psychic work; rather, it explores what it means to be needed and used in this way by others, while also ardently bringing the point of view of the woman watching herself in this role of the symbolic space of the poem. In doing so, it insinuates that doubleness is an appropriate and representative template for subjectivity that, at the very least, does not involve the suppression or appropriation of the mother.

The middle section of *Out of Bounds* in particular also connects the mother's lack of a language in which to name herself with the potentially lethal legacy her child contends with: 'Ghostly jumpy mummy hosting chaotic echoes' (Hecq, 2009b: 54). The text suggests that because of mysterious suppression of the name of mother, the culture will be haunted, as women are collapsed into an object, without adequate means to symbolise and recognise their individuality in the culture at large. The limits of the womb from within, and of the mother from the inside, her speech, are culturally taken as the sum of a woman, as all that can be represented: her 'disembodied body' (Hecq, 2009b: 54) has become a 'numb instrument' and her 'power of speech' (Hecq, 2009b: 37) an 'unarticulated, disarticulated scream' (Hecq, 2009b: 54). In this symbolic system, a woman's subjectivity must always be its un(re)presentable other. The mother's lack of language, and the haunting of remaining unconscious that it promotes, weaves itself into all the speaker/poet envisions. This provides a poetic template of naming the supposedly unnameable in order to tell 'her own tale' (Hecq, 2009b: 81).

Describing the supposedly unnameable is expressed here in terms of a desire for representing woman's subjective difference to be recognised as more than just a boundary for the subjectivity of man and child in a patriarchal and postcolonial world:

> In the distance sirens toll for a life, a black shape
> merging with the black of Spring street buildings
> and post-politics, merging with the blood drying
> in the open mouth of a tongueless child….
> (Hecq, 2009b: 79)

Here, the speaker, 'mother of poetry' (Hecq, 2009b: 79), expresses her desire to write herself into history, 'walk-writing the city with wild goat ink blending the dust in her veins' (Hecq, 2009b: 79). The image of the wild goat and the reference to the dust in her veins suggest two remainders, one being animal – and therefore banned from the city – the other symbolic. One evokes exile while the other signals a more fundamental site of loss; both refer to woman as the negative of man rather than as the fullness of her difference.

Recognising this difference rather than obliterating it in favour of a fantasy of an omnipotent self is critical for a female poet in a way that is not so urgent for a male poet. To erase the mother is to delete the self-same, she with whom you identify, and thus the important identification that allows mature individuation and development of a healthy self is disallowed. This is reflected in the seemingly confusing use of first- and third-person pronouns in the line 'She's lost the power of speech, I hear the man, my man sneer' (Hecq, 2009b: 61), or perhaps more literally in the cultural child's question: 'Anybody in he-eare?' (Hecq, 2009b: 61), inviting the mother back into representation. 'He-eare' denies hearing the woman who holds the representational matrix of the mother object, the 'instru-ment' (Hecq, 2009b: 61). It is only through writing, as occurs in the last section, which 'ends in song' (Hecq, 2009b: 81), that the speaker is brought into a mode of being that does not require self-denial.

The rapturous emergence of voice from a form that needs to be mastered and restrained or, at the very least, trained, has been powerfully invoked in various modes of criticism as a mark of poetic greatness and, as if in playful dialogue with this cultural prevail, the protagonist of *Out of Bounds* is gleeful at having *'penfected'* herself (Hecq, 2009b: 50). Perhaps somewhat scandal-ously, the voices that emerge in this work are the voices heard in Thomas Docherty's reading of *The Waste Land*, a poem prototypically considered the foundational poem of modernism. In his reading, the emphasis is on 'listening', on the aural labyrinth that is muted in favour of the spatial and visual emphasis that has attracted most modernist poets. He observes that the very 'scandal of the womanly voice/vote' which haunts the poem con-stitutes what might be thought of as its Orphic moment, and argues that 'it wants to hear a music, but this music is noise it cannot hear' (Docherty, 1990: 162). Noting that 'the text is about the difficulty of writing, speaking, composing at all' (Docherty, 1990: 1950), the struggle of poetry is linked here to the silencing of woman's voice, which is most profoundly the silencing of the mother's difference from her object use as the mediator of the child's voice in the world. Acknowledgement of this struggle is echoed in Bloom's claim that we know 'the true ephebe ... by hearing in his first voices what is most central in the precursors' voices' (Bloom, 1975: 13), but Bloom's analysis takes such an insight in a very different direction, in which the criticism itself colludes in not hearing the womanly voice haunting his theories. Ostensibly, Bloom alludes to the influence of the poetic fathers with whom the ephebe is in agon, but, equally, this means the muting of the mother's precursive and percussive voice, in order to persist with the fantasy that the child/poet *is* the mother/world. *Out of Bounds* chronicles the return of this repressed, foreclosed or denied, scandalous womanly voice, this 'blundering *babbelchose*' (Hecq, 2009b: 25).

The muting of the voice goes hand in glove with the abjection of the body that houses it. The term abjection – literally meaning the state of being cast off – refers to Kristeva's idea of the abject encountered in Chapter 6, namely that which is discarded or silenced by social reason precisely because it disturbs it. For Kristeva, the abject is located between the object and the subject; it is outside the symbolic order, and yet it may be said to stick to it as that which repulses us. In *Powers of Horror* (1982), she explains that her concern with the semiotic *chora* means that sexual desire refers as much to the maternal body as it does to the phallic signifier that constitutes the subject's lack. What she calls 'the abject' therefore refers directly to the body of the mother that we need to reject in order to become sane subjects. This necessary abjecting, argues Kristeva, is essentially traumatic: it is a 'violent, clumsy breaking away' (Kristeva, 1982: 13). Should this breaking away be incomplete, the consequences are far from benign, for in that fusion between object and subject is where madness lies.

Bloom notes that strong poets (or those who, within a privileging economy based on the cathexis of birth and gestation within the poem, have been designated as strong) 'tend to incarnate by the side of the ocean, at least in vision, if inland far they be' (Bloom, 1975: 13). The female protagonist in *Out of Bounds* speaks from a place beyond 'a sea of fire' (Hecq, 2009b: 47), one that is, as she realises only too painfully, 'a sea of concrete and concreted padlocks' which only masquerades for 'padded land' (Hecq, 2009b: 45). In this work the speaker speaks from the place of the woman above water and challenges the expunging of the woman who houses the sea by speaking about the birth of the inner sea culturally valorised as the creative space of the strong poet. The economy protecting the strong poet attributes hollowness and abjection to the woman's body – one that records 'the thump of things unsaid, the rumple and grumble of sounds echoing' and presents them as 'a rush of prickly things under [the] skin all ruffled up and gushing through' (Hecq, 2009b: 50), especially upon being asked for her hand.

The distance between the woman and that person who asks for her hand – aroused by rain and culminating in 'One ... "ailing smoothly in aquamarine waters"' (Hecq, 2009b: 50) – is only widened by her bringing forth a widening of time and space brought out by parturition as the bell's sounds are lost behind the torn edges of another's self-excited birth. She is ailing, not sailing. The birth by water is her male partner's birth, one called up in Bloom's description of the self-incarnation of the strong poet, who will convert the oceanic waves of the womb into the waters of the word:

> We move from ocean to land by a drying up of the oceanic sense, and we learn sublimation through our precocious memories of a glacial catastrophe. It followed that our most valued activities are regressive. (Bloom, 1975: 11)

Bloom here elaborates a theory of poetic incarnation in which regression is privileged, but the regressive activity of returning to the womb is culturally sanctioned as a return to the dry womb of the intent modernist imagination. His definition of poetic incarnation as: 'Desiccation combined with an unusually strong oceanic sense [as] the highly dualistic yet not

all paradoxical answer' (Bloom, 1975: 11), gestures towards the doubleness of the subject. However, it resists the limits of its representation to
name the woman whose difference from the matter represents the 'yet not
all'. The paradoxical dualism is prevented from 'answering the bell' that
exceeds it as 'yet not all', because of the insistence on the dry Oedipal birth
and on the autochthonic powers of the father that assure the refusal of
the maternal body. *Out of Bounds* represents the consciousness of the one
who is 'not whole – *pas-toute* – with respect to phallic jouissance' (Lacan,
1998 [1972–73]: 7) and the dualism this presupposes, the perspective of the
mother who births this 'not whole' (Lacan, 1998 [1972–73]: 7) and *not all*
and who, consequently, is represented as a hollowed out instrument and
abjected body, waste and wasted. The music of the 'bells' inherent in her
own name (Isabelle) is obscured by the function of birthing language. The
representational matrix of the 'strong poet' becomes here a condition of
unrecognised somatic memory: 'Dreams collect images collect words/from
the glaze of eyes/that shoot silence through the mouth' (Hecq, 2009b:66),
except when heard through the ears of poetry 'she is all ears' (Hecq, 2009b:
69): Ding Dong/Bells. Black-lipped spirit child – mother of poetry/Is A
Belle' (Hecq, 2009b: 79) and more importantly when the writing begins in
the protagonist's head, 'silencing the gaze' (Hecq 2009b: 79) that crosses
her out and music becomes seen through her eyes in incarnatory and representative poetry:

The secret of the wise

woman with yellow Moons for eyes –
Sunstruck Moons
is what she writes
as the twilight clamps
shut
on a twyborn tale
out of the crossed out gaze
fleshing spaces in between
here & beyond
inside outside
words –
splinters out of the skin
specks of sun squeezed out of paper
things from between being & non being between
the apnoea & the breath
the syncopation & the beat –

>   things short of worlds
>   where one feels
>   One is enough
>   through the WORID.

(Hecq, 2009b: 80)

'Things short of worlds' suggest objects in the womb and the experience of intra-uterine life that is, within our culture, mythicised as impossible and unbelievable. The mother of poetry is here the container of the imaginary which forbids and keeps the representation of her subjectivity without itself, the 'gaze' that needed to be 'crossed out' in order to flesh out 'spaces in between/here & beyond/inside outside/words'. It is as though she sees beyond the finite of lack, celebrating some 'Other jouissance' (see Lacan, 1998 [1972–73]: 9–13), one that is not written, but 'doesn't stop being written' (Lacan, 1998 [1972–73]: 94; 145).

In a similar vein, yet different register, Derrida writes that the:

> overabundance of the signifier, its supplementary character is thus the result of a finitude, that is to say, the result of a lack which must be supplemented. (Derrida, 1985: 281)

The mother here is not visible beyond the heaviness of the full womb. The 'woman with yellow Moons for eyes' (Hecq, 2009b: 80), it would seem, can no longer be seen. She is now like a sun-struck star outside of the male's imaginary, which she may well refashion in her own tale.

She, who carries something of the speaker, is but an unknown echo for which a word is being sought to move the 'twyborn tale' in a shared symbolic system. The speaker's relation to this 'woman with yellow Moons for eyes' is ambivalent, for the imaginary of this woman's womb, the world encompassing death and life is so well established that the poet's own attempts both to occupy this space for her own purposes, and to bring the mythical woman, whose eyes only we see above the womb, into represen-tational visibility and audibility may find themselves thwarted without recourse to claiming allegiance to a shared symbolic legacy evident in the quotations from Woolf's *Moments of Being* (1982) and Nietzsche's poem 'O Mensch' as immortalised in Mahler's Third Symphony on the last page of the book. Here, doubleness is affirmed alongside an illusory oneness. The speaker seeks to identify with her symbolic mOther but also to separate and leave the matter as she simply puts herself in the shoes of a woman she meets at the tram stop, ready to tell the tale that has just been told. This hiatus is also a starting point through which access to the memories of the pre-Oedipal relationship with the matter can be both accessed and left behind, in order to bring them into a symbolic register that currently resists their realisation. This symbolic field is one in which 'O Mensch' as 'the essence of man' is confirmed within the unrepresented woman, who is instead represented as haunting. The woman as instrument – Viola – is played upon, but unplayed, as it were, not brought into subjectivity through mere symbolic play, but functions as the body limit, the text limit.

Thus, *Out of Bounds* addresses pre-Oedipal and pre-natal relating and difference, the unwriteable that nonetheless 'doesn't stop being written' (Lacan, 1998 [1972–73]: 94, 145), the 'trace' of the impossibility of the sexual relationship and 'its mirage-like path in the being who speaks' (Lacan, 1998 [1972–73]: 145). Here, in fact, poetry becomes the site of play (Winnicott, 1971), not simply of matter. In *The Shadow of the Object: Psychoanalysis of the Unthought Known*, the psychoanalyst Christopher Bollas elaborates his provocative theory of an aesthetic of self, in which we internalise the sense of the mother long before we internalise the symbolic content of language. He writes that at 'the beginning of life, handling of the infant is the primary mode of communicating, so the internalization of the mother's form (her aesthetic) is prior to the internalisation of her verbal messages' (Bollas, 1987: 32). This in fact is reminiscent of Kristeva's conceptualisation of the *chora* (Kristeva, 1984), as encountered in Chapters 6 and 9, where I state that Kristeva argues for the critical role of pre-linguistic affectivity and perception in the human subject, two vital factors for the development of the creative imagination. In *Revolution in Poetic Language* (1984), for example, she disputes Lacan's privileging of the symbolic over the imaginary. As we saw in Chapter 6, borrowing from Plato's *Timaeus*, she alters the notion of *chora*, to denote an imaginary space where subjectivity begins through awareness of sounds, rhythms and bodily sensations with reference to the mother's body. This pre-linguistic 'semiotic' realm of experience is, she insists, not lost when the subject moves into the realm of language and remains an essential part of meaning-making. It is particularly significant in poetic language, which, Kristeva maintains, has the ability to disturb our tendency to take on fixed identities in language by enhancing our capacity as 'subjects-in-process' (Kristeva, 1984: 28).

Out of Bounds brings this aesthetic, this sense of the mother's handling forward into representation as well as in the relationship created between reader and poem, whereby the reader 'mines the text' to figure out the unwritten. It structurally plays with received notions of form, and actually illuminates the process whereby the child dispenses with early experiences of mothering in favour of his or her own myth of self-creation and singular self-handling.

Bollas describes how this aesthetic operates in term of replacing the infant's rage and hunger with the pleasure of fullness (Bollas, 1987: 33). Bollas also calls this the 'maternal aesthetic' (Bollas, 1987: 32), which is described as a structural experience, the template for which is 'the mother's idiom of care' (Bollas, 1987: 32). The pre-Oedipal mother–child dyad is at the centre of modernist aesthetics, the rage for order representing the child's need for the mother's material transformation of hunger. The relationship that exists between the modernist artist's rage for order and the idiom 'good enough' (Winnicott, 1971) to seek order is the same relational structure that prevails between child and mother. In Wallace Stevens's 'Of modern poetry', his manifesto poem of modernism, for example, the poet seeks 'the finding of a satisfaction', seeking 'what will suffice' (Stevens, 1967: 54). Here is the child seeking the 'good-enough mother' (Winnicott, 1971), the good-enough idiom of care, a search that can take on grandiose dimensions, especially when it is doubled with an appeal to the symbolic father at the ending of *A Portrait of the Artist as a Young Man* (Joyce, 1986: 228).

When read as the bringing forth of pre-Oedipal and pre-natal relating into representation on its own terms, then *Out of Bounds* makes pre-linguistic sense. As such, it challenges Bloom's critical admonition that:

> To know that we are object as well as subject of the quest is not poetic knowledge, but rather the knowledge of defeat, a knowledge fit for the pragmatist of communication, not for that handful who hope to fathom (if not to master) the wealth of ocean, the ancestry of voice. (Bloom, 1975: 16–17)

The defensive desire, long spoken in poetry, and expressed most eloquently by Bloom, to master the first ocean and the first voice, that is, the mother, has long been influential in setting standards for the weighting of 'strong' poetry. This means of aesthetically and quietistically encoding a child's fantasies of omnipotence and self-delivery needs radical reassessment in the light of a poetics that not only acknowledges the reality of the unconscious, but challenges approaches to the symbolic. In this chapter I have shown that metaphors of birth are central to the manoeuvres whereby poets define themselves and to the critical procedures whereby their work is received via incursions into the gendered topos of this gestational space. I have argued that poetry which deals with the materiality of motherhood is problematic in a discourse that privileges euphemistic birth in linguistic and abstract terms, and that this discourse masculinises voice while feminising form. I have shown that within the parameters of this discourse a female poet's voice undermines the inertness of the matter and *Mater* considered necessary for the self-birthing of male poets, while pointing to ways in which the gestures of female poets may be better understood and, perhaps, received. What I have not done is to analyse how female poets are subjugated to the status quo despite their wanting to break the mould. But this comes as an after-thought, which needs to be credited to Freud's concept of *Nachträglichkeit* ('deferred action') (Freud, 1991 [1896]: 229) – the irony of which is not lost on me as I finish this book.

Notes

(1) I do not, in any way, wish to suggest that my work is unique in this respect. It is just that a certain personal experience triggered reflection on this topic. There is much poetry around dealing with the issue of the birthing body, and this is an avenue I would like to further explore.
(2) The French *faire la peau*, literally 'to do your skin', means to kill.
(3) For Lacan, there is a pre-Oedipal real that remains after the letter.
(4) mOther: a play on mother and Mother as the mother is often the one who introduces the child into the symbolic order.

Afterword: Poetic (A)Topos

In the beginning, the woman was not like me, because if she had been, I could not have seen the story clearly. After a while, when I was more used to telling the story, I was able to make the woman more like me.

Lydia Davis

The story began with a touch of hubris. I began work on this book in 2012, out of frustration after writing a chapter on theory for Jeri Kroll and Graeme Harper's *Research Methods in Creative Writing* (Kroll & Harper, 2013a) because I felt that I had not done justice to all the theories I mentioned in that piece. I thought it would be great to write a book devoted to theories that are useful for creative writers, especially poststructuralist theories.

Because I believe that theories can be constructive only through a process of deep involvement, I soon became aware of my own limitations. Further, I had started with an epistemological challenge, one that opposed the discipline of creative writing studies with that of the visual arts. While I think that the basis for this challenge was well founded, I discovered in the rewriting of the manuscript that one element was missing – not only is sight privileged in Western culture, it is also gender biased. Had I immersed myself deeper in the work of Luce Irigaray, I would have been aware of this from the start. This demonstrates how crucial the *experience* of writing is for bringing about perspective, insight and knowledge in creative writing studies. The way I saw the 'research question' at the beginning of the project has been utterly transformed. Such is the nature of any literary act, but also of all creative writing research; the process is replete with insights, contradictions, obstacles and double binds. What is more, insights always seem to occur ... too late.

Thank you Freud; I have experienced in my bones what *Nachträglichkeit* means.

Now is the time for the reader to ascertain where the story of this book ends. And for the critic to evaluate its worth.

For my part, this is a new departure, not an ending. The question asked in the previous chapter – is it possible for women writers, particularly poets, to embrace a female subject matter in their writing and still be taken seriously as writers within the 'masculine universal' sphere of literature? – was, I now realise, prompted by a certain discomfort at having perhaps revealed too much of the autobiographical in this book. On closer inspection, it was also brought about by the shocking discovery that the book privileges male authors, even for the sake of sheer argument. How odd. All things considered it isn't that odd. Ideas take time to percolate and make a difference in the fabric of our imagination. Some ideas, topics or fields of research are held in check out of respect for colleagues or students whose area it is at the time.

Like Oedipus, I have arrived at a forking path. Not blinded so far, I look forward to revitalising my understanding of the work of Luce Irigaray and Hélène Cixous. I also trust doctoral students to pique my interest and accompany, or even guide, me through unmapped terrain and uncharted waters.

Bibliography

Achebe, C. (1958) *Things Fall Apart*. London: Heineman.

Agence d'évaluation de la recherche et de l'enseignement supérieur (AERES), accessed 5 May 2013. Available at: http://www.aeres-evaluation.fr/

Almond, B. (2010) *The Monster Within: The Hidden Side of Motherhood*. Los Angeles, CA: University of California Press.

Alvarez, A. (2005) *The Writer's Voice*. London: Bloomsbury.

Anderson, D. (2013) Dove descending. *Australian Book Review*, no. 350, 20.

Anonymous (1838) *The Sydney Gazette and New South Wales Advertiser*, 11 December, p. 2.

Anzieu, D. (1981) *Le Corps de l'oeuvre: Essais psychanalytiques sur le travail créateur*. Paris: Gallimard.

Aristotle (1960) *Metaphysics* (R. Hope, trans.). Ann Arbor, MI: Michigan University Press.

Aristotle (1991) *On Rhetoric: A Theory of Civic Discourse* (G. A. Kennedy, trans.). New York: Oxford University Press.

Aristotle (2008) *Poetics* (S.H. Butcher, trans.). New York: Cosimo.

Armand, L. (2007) *Contemporary Poetics*. Evanston, IL: Northwestern University Press.

Artaud, A. (2004) *Oeuvres*. Paris: Gallimard.

Ashcroft, B. (2001) *Post-Colonial Transformation*. London: Routledge.

Ashcroft, B. (2007) Critical utopias. *Textual Practice* 21 (3), 411–431. doi 10.1080/0950236 0701529051

Ashcroft, B. (2008) *Caliban's Voice: The Transformation of English in Post-Colonial Literatures*. London: Routledge.

Ashcroft, B. (2009a) *On Post-Colonial Futures: Transformations of Colonial Culture*. London: Continuum.

Ashcroft, B. (2009b) Remembering the future: Utopianism in African literature. *Textual Practice* 23 (5), 703–722.

Ashcroft, B., Tiffin, H. and Griffiths, G. (1989) *The Empire Writes Back: Theory and Practice in Post-Colonial Literatures*. London: Routledge.

Atherton, C. (2010) Sleeping with the enemy: Creative writing and theory in the academy. Paper presented at the 15th annual conference of the Australasian Association of Writing Programs: 'Strange Bedfellows or Perfect Partners', RMIT, Melbourne. http://aawp.org.au/files/Atherton.pdf

Attié, J. (2005) This mad play of writing. *Psychoanalytical Notebooks: A Review of the London Society of the New Lacanian School* no. 13, 179–199.

Atwood, M. (1972) *Surfacing*. Toronto: McClelland and Stewart.

Atwood, M. (2002) *Negotiating with the Dead: A Writer on Writing*. Cambridge: Cambridge University Press.

Auster, P. (1998) *The Art of Hunger: Essays, Prefaces, Interviews and The Red Notebook*. London: Faber and Faber.

Auster, P. (2012 [1982]) *The Invention of Solitude*. London: Faber and Faber.

Australian Research Council (2012) *Excellence in Research for Australia 2012: National Report*. Canberra: ARC. Available at http://www.arc.gov.au/era (accessed 5 May 2013).

Ayers, D. (2008) *Literary Theory: A Reintroduction*. Oxford: Blackwell.

Badiou, A. (1988) *L'Être et l'événement*. Paris: Éditions du Seuil.

Badiou, A. (1992) *Conditions*. Paris: Éditions du Seuil.

Badiou, A. (2003) *Handbook of Inaesthetics* (A. Toscano, trans.). London: Continuum.

Badiou, A. (2005) *Infinite Thought: Truth and the Return to Philosophy* (O. Feltham and J. Clemens, eds). London: Continuum.

Badiou, A. (2008) *The Century* (A. Toscano, trans.). Cambridge: Polity Press.

Baer, J. (2012) Domain specificity of creativity: Theory, research, and practice. *TEXT*, special issue no. 13, *Creativity: Cognitive, Social and Cultural Perspectives* 16 (1). Available at http://www.textjournal.com.au/speciss/issue13/Baer.pdf (accessed 21 March 2013).

Balaev, M. (2008) Trends in literary trauma theory. *Mosaic (Winnipeg): Journal for the Interdisciplinary Study of Literature* 41 (2), 149–166.

Barrett, E. (2007) Experiential learning in practice as research: Context, method, knowledge. *Journal of Visual Art Practice* 6 (2), 115–124. doi 10.1386/jvap.6.2.115_1.

Barrett, E. and Bolt, B. (eds) (2007) *Practice as Research: Approaches to Creative Arts Enquiry*. London: I.B. Tauris.

Barry, D. (2013) Wrestling with Aristotle. *TEXT* 17 (2). Available at http://www.text journal.com.au/oct13/barry.htm (accessed 12 June 2013).

Barth, J. (1988) *Lost in the Funhouse*. New York: Anchor Books.

Barthes, R. (1973) *The Pleasure of the Text* (R. Miller, trans.). New York: Hill and Wang.

Barthes, R. (1975) *Roland Barthes*. Paris: Éditions du Seuil.

Barthes, R. (1977a) *Roland Barthes by Roland Barthes*. New York: Straus et Giroux.

Barthes, R. (1977b) *Image, Music, Text* (S. Heath, trans.) London: Fontana Press.

Barthes, R. (2010) *Writing Degree Zero: Elements of Semiology*. London: Vintage Classic.

Basu Thakur, G. (2013) Reading Bhabha, reading Lacan. In S. Biswas (ed.) *The Literary Lacan – From Literature to 'Lituraterre' and Beyond* (pp. 240–259). Chicago, IL: Seagull Books.

Bate, J. (2012) Foreword: On criticism and creativity. In D. Morley and P. Neilsen (eds) *The Cambridge Companion to Creative Writing* (pp. xv–xviii). Cambridge: Cambridge University Press.

Baudelaire, C. (1989 [1867]) *The Poems in Prose* (Introducion & trans. F. Scarfe). London: Anvil Press.

Beardsworth, S. (2004) *Julia Kristeva: Psychoanalysis and Modernity*. Albany, NY: State University of New York Press (SUNY).

Beckett, S. (1965) *Murphy*. Paris: Les Éditions de Minuit.

Beckett, S. (1968) *Watt*. Paris: Les Éditions de Minuit.

Benvenuto, B. (1999) Once upon a time: The infant in Lacanian theory. In B. Burgogne and M. Sullivan (eds) *The Klein–Lacan Dialogues*. New York: Other Press.

Bernold, A. (1992) *L'Amitié de Beckett: 1979–1989*. Paris: Hermann.

Bernstein, B. (1975) *Codes, Class and Control*. London: Routledge and Kegan Paul.

Bettelheim, B. (1987) *A Good Enough Parent: A Book on Child-Rearing*. New York: Knopf, Distributed by Random House.

Bhabha, H.K. (1994) *The Location of Culture*. London: Routledge.

Biggs, M.A.R. and Büchler, D. (2007) Rigor and practice-based research. *Design Issues* 23 (3), 62–69.

Biggs, M.A.R., Karlsson, H. and Riksbankens, J. (eds) (2012) *The Routledge Companion to Research in the Arts*. London: Routledge.

Blanchot, M. (1974) *L'Espace littéraire*. Paris: Gallimard.

Bloom, H. (1975) *A Map of Misreading*. Oxford: Oxford University Press.

Boileau-Despréaux, N. (1966) *L'Art poétique, suivi de l'épitre aux pisens (Art poétique) d'Horace et d'une anthologie de la poésie pré-classique en France, 1600–1670*. Paris: Union Générale d'Éditions.

Bollas, C. (1987) *The Shadow of the Object: Psychoanalysis of the Unthought Known*. London: Free Association Books.

Bolt, B. (2004) *Art Beyond Representation: The Performative Power of the Image*. London: I.B. Tauris.

Bolton, G. (2010) *Reflective Practice: Writing and Professional Development*. Los Angeles, CA: Sage.

Booth, W.C. (1961) *The Rhetoric of Fiction*. Chicago, IL: University of Chicago Press.

Borges, J.L. (1970) *Labyrinths: Selected Stories and Other Writings* (D. A. Yates, J. E. Irby and A. Maurois, eds). Harmondsworth: Penguin Books.

Borges, J.L. (2000) *Selected Poems* (A. Coleman, ed.). New York: Penguin Books.

Bos, G. (2014) The night-shift ending. An 80,000-word novel and accompanying exegesis. PhD dissertation, Swinburne University of Technology, Victoria, Australia.

Bosteels, B. (2002) Alain Badiou's theory of the subject: The re-commencement of dialectical materialism? Part II. *Pli* (13), 172–208. Available at http://www.scribd.com/doc/62381642/Bosteels-Bruno-Alain-Badiou-s-Theory-of-the- Subject-Part-2-the-Re-Commencement-of-Dialectical (accessed 6 September 2012).

Boulter, A. (2007) *Writing Fiction: Creative and Critical Approaches*. Basingstoke: Palgrave Macmillan.

Bourdieu, P. (2000) *Pascalian Meditations*. Cambridge: Polity Press.

Bourriaud, N. (2002) *Relational Aesthetics* (S. Pleasance and F. Woods, trans.). Paris: Les presses du réel.

Bowie, M. (2000) Psychoanalysis and art: The Winnicott legacy. In L. Caldwell (ed.) *Art, Creativity, Living* (pp. 11–29). London: Karnac Books.

Bracher, M. (1994) On the psychological and social functions of language: Lacan's theory of the four dimensions. In M. Bracher, M.W. Alcorn Jr, R.J. Corthell and F. Massardier-Kenney (eds) *Lacanian Theory of Discourse: Subject, Structure, and Society* (pp. 107–128). New York: New York University Press.

Bracher, M. (1999) *The Writing Cure: Psychoanalysis, Composition, and the Aims of Education*. Carbondale, IL: Southern Illinois University Press.

Bracher, M. (2006) *Radical Pedagogy: Identity, Generativity, and Social Transformation*. New York: Palgrave Macmillan.

Brennan, T. (1992) *The Interpretation of the Flesh: Freud and Femininity*. London: Routledge.

Brook, S. (2012) Introduction. Part 2: The critiques of practice-led research. *TEXT*, special issue no. 14, *Beyond Practice-Led Research* 16 (2). Available at http://www.textjournal.com.au/speciss/issue14/Brook%20%28Intro%202%29.pdf (accessed 21 March 2013).

Brophy, K. (2009) *Patterns of Creativity: Investigations into the Sources and Methods of Creativity*. Amsterdam: Rodopi.

Brousse, M-H. (1998) Hysteria and sinthome. *Psychoanalytical Notebooks of the London Circle* no. 1, 65–73.

Brown, F. (2006) *Flaubert: A Biography*. Cambridge, MA: Harvard University Press.

Brown, L. (ed.) (1993) *The New Shorter Oxford English Dictionary*. Oxford: Clarendon Press.

Burgoyne, B. and Sullivan, E.M. (eds) (1999) *The Klein–Lacan Dialogues*. New York: Other Press.

Burke, K. (1966) *Language as Symbolic Action: Essays on Life, Literature, and Method*. Berkeley, CA: University of California Press.

Calder, J. (2001) *The Philosophy of Samuel Beckett*. London: Calder Publications.

Caldwell, L. (ed.) (2000) *Art, Creativity, Living*. London: Karnac Books.

Campbell, M.M. (2014) *Poetic Revolutionaries: Intertextuality and Subversion*. Amsterdam: Rodopi.

Candy, L. (2006) *Practice Based Research: A Guide*. Available at http://www.creativityand cognition.com/wp-content/uploads/2011/04/PBR-Guide-1.1-2006.pdf   (Creativity and Cognition Studios website, accessed 21 March 2013).

Capp, F. (2000) Review of: 'The Book of Elsa'. *The Age*. Available at http://www.theage. com.au/books/20000731/A39860-2000Jul30.html (accessed 31 July 2000).

Carey, J. (2005) *What Good Are the Arts?* London: Faber and Faber.

Carroll, L.T.J. (1992) *Alice's Adventures in Wonderland and Through the Looking-Glass* (illustrated by John Tenniel). London: David Campbell.

Carroll, S. (2013) *A World of Other People*. Sydney: HarperCollins.

Carter, P. (1996) *The Lie of the Land*. London: Faber and Faber.

Carter, P. (2004) *Material Thinking: The Theory and Practice of Creative Research*. Carlton: Melbourne University Publishing.

Cavell, M. (2006) *Becoming a Subject: Reflections in Philosophy and Psychoanalysis*. Oxford: Oxford University Press.

Chalmers, D.J. (1996) *The Conscious Mind: In Search of a Fundamental Theory*. New York: Oxford University Press.

Chodorow, J. (2006) Active imagination. In R.K. Papadopoulos (ed.) *The Handbook of Jungian Psychology: Theory, Practice and Applications* (pp. 215–243). London: Routledge.

Chodorow, N. (1978) *The Reproduction of Mothering: Psychoanalysis and the Sociology of Gender*. Berkeley, CA: University of California Press.

Cicero, M.T. (1952) *Brutus. Orator* (G. L. Hendrickson, trans.). Cambridge, MA: Loeb Classical Library, Harvard University Press.

Cixous, H. (1976) The laugh of the Medusa (K. Cohen and P. Cohen, trans.). *Signs: Journal of Women in Culture and Society* 1 (4), 875–893. doi 10.2307/3173239

Cixous, H. (1981) Castration or decapitation (A. Kuhn, trans.). *Signs: Journal of Women in Culture and Society* 7 (11), 41–55.

Cixous, H. (2009) *Hyperdream* (B.B. Brahic, trans.). Cambridge: Polity Press.

Cixous, H. and Clément, C. (1986 [1975]) *The Newly Born Woman*. Minneapolis, MN: University of Minnesota Press.

Clemens, J. (2002) Platonic meditations: The work of Alain Badiou. *Pli* (11), 200–229.

Clemens, J. (2013) *Psychoanalysis is an Antiphilosophy*. Edinburgh: Edinburgh University Press.

Clément, C. and Kristeva, J. (2001 [1998]) *The Feminine and the Sacred*. New York: Columbia University Press.

Clifford, J. and Marcus, G.E. (eds) (2010) *Writing Culture: The Poetics and Politics of Ethnography*. Berkeley, CA: University of California Press.

Cocteau, J. (1999 [1926]) *Orphée*. Paris: Éditions J'ai lu.

Colebrook, C. (2006) *Deleuze: A Guide for the Perplexed*. New York: Continuum.

Csikszentmihalyi, M. (1997) *Creativity: Flow and the Psychology of Discovery and Invention*. New York: Harper Perennial.

Culler, J.D. (1975) *Structuralist Poetics: Structuralism, Linguistics, and the Study of Literature*. Ithaca, NY: Cornell University Press.

Culler, J.D. (1982) *On Deconstruction: Theory and Criticism After Structuralism*. London: Routledge.

Cunningham, V. (2005) *Reading After Theory*. Oxford: Blackwell.

Daly, M. (1991) *Gyn/ecology: The Metaethics of Radical Feminism*. London: Women's Press.

Damasio, A.R. (1989) Concepts in the brain. *Mind and Language* 4 (1–2), 24–28. doi 10.1111/j.1468-0017.1989.tb00236.x.

Damasio, A.R. (2000) *The Feeling of What Happens: Body, Emotion and the Making of Consciousness*. London: Vintage.

Das, B.K. (2005) *Twentieth Century Literary Criticism*. New Delhi: Atlantic.

Davis, L. (2004) *The End of the Story*. New York: Picador/Farrar, Straus, and Giroux.

Dawson, P. (2003) Towards a new poetics in creative writing pedagogy. *TEXT* 7 (1). Available at http://www.textjournal.com.au/april03/dawson.htm 172 (accessed 8 April 2013).

Dawson, P. (2005) *Creative Writing and the New Humanities*. London: Routledge.

Dawson, P. (2008) Creative writing and postmodern interdisciplinarity. *TEXT* 12 (1). Available at http://www.textjournal.com.au/april08/dawson.htm (accessed 8 April 2013).

De Klerk, E. (2009) *Subject to Reading: Literacy and Belief in the Work of Jacques Lacan and Paulo Freire*. Newcastle upon Tyne: Cambridge Scholars.

De Lauretis, T. (1984) *Alice Doesn't: Feminism, Semiotics, Cinema*. London: Macmillan.

Deleuze, G. and Guattari, F.I. (2004) *Anti-Oedipus: Capitalism and Schizophrenia* (R. Hurley, M. Seem and H. R. Lane, trans.). London: Continuum.

Derrida, J. (1976 [1967]) *Of Grammatology* (G. Spivak, trans.). Baltimore, MD: Johns Hopkins University Press.

Derrida, J. (1978) Speculations – On Freud (I. McLeod, trans.). *Oxford Literary Review* 3 (2), 80–98.

Derrida, J. (1980) The law of genre. *Glyph* 7, 202–232.

Derrida, J. (1985) *Writing and Difference* (A. Bass, trans.). London: Routledge and Kegan Paul.

Derrida, J. (1995) *Points…: Interviews, 1974–1994* (P. Kamuf, trans., E. Weber, ed.). Stanford, CA: Stanford University Press.

Derrida, J. (2001) *The Work of Mourning* (P-A. Brault and M. Naas, eds). Chicago, IL: University of Chicago Press.

Descartes, R. (1974) *Discours de la méthode: Suivi des méditations*. Verviers: Marabout Université.

Docherty, T. (1990) *After Theory: Postmodernism/Postmarxism*. London: Routledge.

Dolar, M. (2006) *A Voice and Nothing More*. Cambridge, MA: MIT Press.

Donnelly, D. (2012) *Establishing Creative Writing Studies as an Academic Discipline*. Bristol: Multilingual Matters.

Donnelly, D. and Harper, G. (2013) *Key Issues in Creative Writing*. Bristol: Multilingual Matters.

Doolittle, H. [H.D.] (1985) *Tribute to Freud*. New York: New Directions.

Dravers, P. (2005) Joyce and the sinthome: Aiming at the fourth term of the knot. *Psychoanalytical Notebooks: A Review of the London Society of the New Lacanian School* no. 13, 93–117.

Durack, M. (1959) *Kings in Grass Castles (On the Durack Family of Australia with Plates, Including Portraits)*. London: Constable.

Duras, M. (1984) *L'Amant*. Paris: Les Éditions de Minuit.

Duras, M. (1993) *Écrire*. Paris: Gallimard.

Duras, M. and Gauthier, X. (1974) *Les Parleuses*. Paris: Les Éditions de Minuit.

Duras, M. and Porte, M. (1977) *Les Lieux de Marguerite Duras*. Paris: Seghers.

Dyer, R. (1988) White. *Screen* 29 (4), 44–64.

Eagleton, T. (1978) *Criticism and Ideology: A Study of Marxist Literary Theory*. London: Verso Editions.

Eagleton, T. (2003) *After Theory*. New York: Basic Books.

Eagleton, T. (2008) *Literary Theory: An Introduction*. London: Blackwell.

Eagleton, T. (2012) *The Event of Literature*. New Haven, CT: Yale University Press.

Earnshaw, S. (ed.) (2007) *The Handbook of Creative Writing*. Edinburgh: Edinburgh University Press.

Easthope, A. (2003) *Poetry as Discourse*. London: Routledge.

Ehrenzweig, A. (1975) *The Psychoanalysis of Artistic Vision and Hearing: An Introduction to a Theory of Unconscious Perception*. London: Sheldon Press.

Elbow, P. (1998) *Writing with Power: Techniques for Mastering the Writing Process*. New York: Oxford University Press.

Evans, D. (1996) *An Introductory Dictionary of Lacanian Psychoanalysis*. London: Routledge.

Fanon, F. (2002) *The Wretched of the Earth*. London: Penguin.

Fazioni, N. (2012) Real and political: Badiou as a reader of Lacan. *International Journal of Badiou Studies* 1 (1), 51–77. Available at http://badioustudiesorg.ipower.com/cgi-bin/ojs-2.3.6/index.php/ijbs/article/view/14/0 (accessed 3 September 2012).

Felman, S. (1982) Psychoanalysis and education: Teaching terminable and interminable. *Yale French Studies* 63, 21–44. doi 10.2307/2929829.

Fink, B. (1996) Alain Badiou. *Umbr(a)* 1, 11–12. Available at http://www.umbrajournal.org/pdfs/articles/1996/alain_badiou-bruce_fink.pdf (accessed 2 July 2013).

Fink, B. (1997) *The Lacanian Subject: Between Language and Jouissance*. Princeton, MA: Princeton University Press.

Fish, S.E. (1980) *Is There a Text in This Class?: The Authority of Interpretive Communities*. Cambridge, MA: Harvard University Press.

Fisher, J. (2012) Forward to an academic discipline! [Book review: *Establishing Creative Writing Studies as an Academic Discipline* by Dianne Donnelly]. *TEXT* 16 (2). Available at http://www.textjournal.com.au/oct12/fisher_rev.htm (accessed 12 March 2014).

Foucault, M. (1961) *Folie et déraison: Histoire de la folie à l'âge de classique*. Paris: Presses Universitaires de France.

Foucault, M. (1966) *Les Mots et les choses: Une archéologie des sciences humaines*. Paris: Gallimard.

Foucault, M. (1975) *Surveiller et punir: Naissance de la prison*. Paris: Gallimard.

Frege, G. (1977) *Logical Investigations* (R. H. Stoothoff, trans., P.T. Geach, ed.). Oxford: Basil Blackwell.

Freiman, M. (2001) Crossing the boundaries of the discipline: A post-colonial approach to teaching creative writing in the university. *TEXT* 5 (2). Available at http://www.textjournal.com.au/oct01/freiman.htm (accessed 16 December 2013).

Freiman, M. (2003) Dangerous dreaming: Myths of creativity. *TEXT* 7 (2). Available at http://www.textjournal.com.au/oct03/freiman.htm (accessed 16 December 2013).

Freiman, M. (2006) Postcolonial creativity and creative writing. In N. Krauth and T. Brady (eds) *Creative Writing: Theory Beyond Practice* (pp. 81–99). Teneriffe: Post Pressed.

Freire, P. (1970) *Pedagogy of the Oppressed* (M. B. Ramos, trans.). Harmondsworth: Penguin.

Freud, S. (1896) L'Hérédité et l'étiologie des névroses. *Revue neurologique* 4 (6), 161–169. Available at http://www.psychanalyse-paris.com/1275-LHeredite-et-l-etiologie-des. html (accessed 28 January 2014).

Freud, S. (1940 [1932]) *Gesammelte Werke Bd. 15: Neue Folge der Vorlesungen zur Einführung in die Psychoanalyse.* London: Imago Publishing.

Freud, S. (1991 [1896]) *Gesammelte Werke Bd. 1: Weitere Bemerkungenüber die Abwher-Neuropsychosen.* London: Imago Publishing.

Freud, S. (2001 [1886–99]) Draft G. In J. Strachey (ed.) *The Standard Edition of the Complete Psychological Works of Sigmund Freud, Vol. I: Pre-psychoanalytic Publications and Unpublished Drafts* (pp. 200–206). London: Vintage, Hogarth Press and Institute of Psycho-analysis.

Freud, S. (2001 [1893–95]) *The Standard Edition of the Complete Psychological Works of Sigmund Freud, Vol. II: Studies on Hysteria* (J. Strachey, ed.). London: Vintage, Hogarth Press and Institute of Psycho-analysis.

Freud, S. (2001 [1900]) *The Standard Edition of the Complete Psychological Works of Sigmund Freud, Vol. IV: The Interpretation of Dreams (First Part)* (J. Strachey, ed.). London: Vintage, Hogarth Press and Institute of Psycho-analysis.

Freud, S. (2001 [1900–01]) *The Standard Edition of the Complete Psychological Works of Sigmund Freud, Vol. V: The Interpretation of Dreams (Second Part)* (J. Strachey, ed.). London: Vintage, Hogarth Press and Institute of Psycho-analysis.

Freud, S. (2001 [1901])*The Standard Edition of the Complete Psychological Works of Sigmund Freud, Vol. VI: The Psychopathology of Everyday Life* (J. Strachey, ed.). London: Vintage, Hogarth Press and Institute of Psycho-analysis.

Freud, S. (2001 [1901–05]) *The Standard Edition of the Complete Psychological Works of Sigmund Freud, Vol. VII: A Case of Hysteria. Three Essays on Sexuality and Other Works* (J. Strachey, ed.). London: Vintage, Hogarth Press and Institute of Psycho-analysis.

Freud, S. (2001 [1906–08]) Creative writers and daydreaming. In J. Strachey (ed.) *The Standard Edition of the Complete Psychological Works of Sigmund Freud, Vol. IX: Jensen's 'Gradiva' and Other Works* (pp. 141–154). London: Vintage, Hogarth Press and Institute of Psycho-analysis.

Freud, S. (2001 [1911–13]) *The Standard Edition of the Complete Psychological Works of Sigmund Freud, Vol. XII: Case History of Schreber, Papers on Technique and Other Works* (J. Strachey, ed.). London: Vintage, Hogarth Press and the Institute of Psycho-analysis.

Freud, S. (2001 [1914–16]) *The Standard Edition of the Complete Psychological Works of Sigmund Freud, Vol. XIV: On the History of the Psycho-Analytic Movement, Papers on Metapsychology and Other Works* (J. Strachey, ed.). London: Vintage, Hogarth Press and Institute of Psycho-analysis.

Freud, S. (2001 [1915a]) On narcissism: An introduction. In J. Strachey (ed.) *The Standard Edition of the Complete Psychological Works of Sigmund Freud, Vol. XIV: On the History of the Psycho-Analytic Movement, Papers on Metapsychology and Other Works* (pp. 67–104). London: Vintage, Hogarth Press and Institute of Psychoanalysis.

Freud, S. (2001 [1915b]) The unconscious. In J. Strachey (ed.) *The Standard Edition of the Complete Psychological Works of Sigmund Freud, Vol. XIV: On the History of the Psycho-Analytic Movement, Papers on Metapsychology and Other Works* (pp. 159– 215). London: Vintage, Hogarth Press and Institute of Psycho-analysis.

Freud, S. (2001 [1915–16]) *The Standard Edition of the Complete Psychological Works of Sigmund Freud, Vol. XV: Introductory Lectures on Psychoanalysis (Parts I and II)* (J. Strachey, ed.). London: Vintage, Hogarth Press and Institute of Psycho-analysis.

Freud, S. (2001 [1916–17]) *The Standard Edition of the Complete Psychological Works of Sigmund Freud, Vol. XVI: Introductory Lectures on Psychoanalysis (Part III)* (J. Strachey, ed.). London: Vintage, Hogarth Press and Institute of Psycho-analysis.

Freud, S. (2001 [1917–19a]) *The Standard Edition of the Complete Psychological Works of Sigmund Freud, Vol. XVII: An Infantile Neurosis and Other Works* (J. Strachey, ed.). London: Vintage, Hogarth Press and Institute of Psycho-analysis.

Freud, S. (2001 [1917–19b]) The uncanny. In J. Strachey (ed.) *The Standard Edition of the Complete Psychological Works of Sigmund Freud, Vol. XVII: An Infantile Neurosis and Other Works* (pp. 217–256). London: Vintage, Hogarth Press and Institute of Psycho-analysis.

Freud, S. (2001 [1923–25]) *The Standard Edition of the Complete Psychological Works of Sigmund Freud, Vol. XIX: The Ego and the Id and Other Works* (J. Strachey, ed.). London: Vintage, Hogarth Press and Institute of Psycho-analysis.

Freud, S. (2001 [1928]) Dostoevsky and parricide. In J. Strachey (ed.) *The Standard Edition of the Complete Psychological Works of Sigmund Freud, Vol. XXI: The Future of Illusion, Civilisation and Its Discontents and Other Works* (pp. 173–196). London: Vintage, Hogarth Press and Institute of Psycho-analysis.

Freud, S. (2001 [1932–36]) New introductory lectures on psycho-analysis. In J. Strachey (ed.) *The Standard Edition of the Complete Psychological Works of Sigmund Freud, Vol. XXII: New Introductory Lectures on Psycho-Analysis and Other Works* (pp. 7–182). London: Vintage, Hogarth Press and Institute of Psycho-analysis.

Frye, N. (1957) *Anatomy of Criticism*. Princeton, NJ: Princeton University Press.

Gaut, B.N. and Lopes, D.M. (eds) (2005) *The Routledge Companion to Aesthetics*. New York: Routledge.

Genette, G. (2005) *Essays in Aesthetics* (D. Cohn, trans.). Lincoln, NE: University of Nebraska Press.

Genoni, P. (2009) The global reception of post-national literary fiction: The case of Gerald Murnane. *Journal of the Association for the Study of Australian Literature. Special Issue: Australian Literature in a Global World*. Available at http://www.nla.gov.au/openpublish/index.php/jasal/article/view/857/1746 (accessed 12 April 2014).

Ghiselin, B. (1985) *The Creative Process: A Symposium*. Berkeley, CA: University of California Press.

Gildfind, H. (2011) Incarnadine words and incarnate worlds. Review of: 'Out of Bounds' by Dominique Hecq. *TEXT* 15 (1). Available at http://www.textjournal.com.au/april11/gildfind_rev.htm (accessed 30 May 2013)

Glover, S. (2012) Creative writing studies, authorship, and the ghosts of Romanticism. *New Writing: The International Journal for the Practice and Theory of Creative Writing* 9 (3), 293–301. doi 10.1080/14790726.2012.693097.

Goldberg, N. (1986) *Writing Down the Bones: Freeing the Writer Within*. Boston, MA: Shambhala.

Golding, W. (1982) *A Moving Target*. London: Faber and Faber.

Golding, W. (1984) *The Paper Men*. London: Faber and Faber.

Gray, C. (1996) *Inquiry Through Practice: Developing Appropriate Research Strategies*. Carole Gray website at http://carolegray.net/Papers%20PDFs/ngnm.pdf (accessed 19 July 2013).

Greenfield, S. (2003) *Tomorrow's People: How 21st-Century Technology Is Changing the Way We Think and Feel*. London: Allen Lane.

Grenville, K. (2005) *The Secret River*. Melbourne: Text Publishing Company

Griffiths, M. (2012) Research and the self. In M. Biggs, H. Karlsson and J. Riksbankens (eds) *The Routledge Companion to Research in the Arts* (pp. 167–185). London: Routledge.

Grigg, R. (1999) Foreclosure. In D. Nobus (ed.) *Key Concepts of Lacanian Psychoanalysis* (pp. 48–75). London: Other Press.

Hagman, G. (2009) Art and self. *Annals of the New York Academy of Sciences* 1159 (1), 164–173. doi 10.1111/j.1749-6632.2008.04344.x.

Halliwell, S. (1998) *Aristotle's Poetics*. Chicago, IL: University of Chicago Press.

Hallward, P. (2003) *Badiou: A Subject to Truth*. Minneapolis, MN: University of Minnesota Press.

Hamadache, M. (2011) Algeria in language and Algiers. PhD thesis, Macquarie University, Sydney.

Harari, R. (2001) *Lacan's Seminar on 'Anxiety': An Introduction*. New York: Other Press.

Harari, R. (2002) *How James Joyce Made His Name: A Reading of the Final Lacan* (L. Thurston, trans.). New York: Other Press.

Harper, G. (2010) *On Creative Writing*. Bristol: Multilingual Matters.

Harper, G. and Kroll, J. (eds) (2008) *Creative Writing Studies: Practice, Research and Pedagogy*. Clevedon: Multilingual Matters.

Harpham, G.G. (2005) Beneath and beyond the 'crisis in the humanities'. *New Literary History* 36 (1), 21–36. doi 10.2307/20057872.

Harris, M. (2008) Are writers really there when they're writing about their writing? and can we theorise about what they say and do? Paper presented at the 13th conference of the Australian Association of Writing Programs (AAWP): 'Creativity and uncertainty', University of Technology, Sydney, 27–29 November. Available at http://aawp.org.au/files/Harris_2008.pdf (accessed 16 October 2012).

Harris, M. (2009) Escaping the tractor beam of literary theory: Notes towards appropriate theories of creative writing – and some arguments against the inappropriate ones. *TEXT* 13 (2). Available at http://www.textjournal.com.au/oct09/harris.htm (accessed 16 October 2012)

Harris, R. (1986) *The Origin of Writing*. LaSalle, IL: Open Court.

Harris, W. (1960) *Palace of the Peacock*. London: Faber and Faber.

Harris, W. (1983) *The Womb of Space: The Cross-Cultural Imagination*. London: Greenwood Press.

Hart, J. (2013) *Textual Imitation: Making and Seeing in Literature*. London: Palgrave.

Haseman, B. (2006) A manifesto for performative research. *Media International Australia incorporating Culture and Policy*, theme issue *Practice-Led Research* 118, 98–106. Available at http://eprints.qut.edu.au/3999/1/3999_1.pdf (accessed 8 April 2013).

Hayes, J.R. and Flower, L.S. (1986) Writing research and the writer. *American Psychologist* 41 (10), 1106–1113. doi 10.1037/0003-066X.41.10.1106.

Heaney, S. (1980) *Preoccupations: Selected Prose, 1968–1978*. London: Faber and Faber.

Heaney, S. (1987) *The Haw Lantern*. London: Faber and Faber.

Heaney, S. (1989) *The Place of Writing*. Atlanta, GA: Scholars Press for Emory University.

Heaney, S. (1991) *Death of a Naturalist*. London: Faber and Faber.

Heaney, S. (1995) *The Redress of Poetry: Oxford Lectures*. London: Faber and Faber.

Heaney, S. (2001) *Electric Light*. London: Faber and Faber.

Hecq, D. (1997a) Grief. *SIDRF Newsletter*, no. 3.

Hecq, D. (1997b) Magic. *Woorilla* 8 (2), 50–53.

Hecq, D. (1999) *Mythfits: Four Uneasy Pieces*. Blackburn: PenFolk Publishing.

Hecq, D. (2000a) *The Book of Elsa*. Upper Ferntree Gully: Papyrus Publishing.

Hecq, D. (2000b) *Magic and Other Stories*. Macclesfield: Woorilla Publications.

Hecq, D. (2002) *Good Grief: And Other Frivolous Journeys into Spells, Songs and Elegies*. Scarsdale: Papyrus Publishing.

Hecq, D. (2004) *Noisy Blood: Stories*. Scarsdale: Papyrus Publishing.
Hecq, D. (2005) Uncanny encounters: On writing, anxiety and jouissance. *Double Dialogues: Anatomy and Poetics* 6 (winter). Available at http://www.doubledialogues.com/archive/issue_six/hecq.html (accessed 10 September 2012)
Hecq, D. (2006a) *Couchgrass*. Scarsdale: Papyrus Publishing.
Hecq, D. (2006b) The impossible power of psychoanalysis. In J. Clemens and R. Grigg (eds) *Jacques Lacan and the Other Side of Psychoanalysis: Reflections on Seminar XVII* (pp. 216–228). Durham, NC: Duke University Press.
Hecq, D. (2008) Writing the unconscious: Psychoanalysis for the creative writer. *TEXT* 12 (2). Available at http://www.textjournal.com.au/oct08/hecq.htm (accessed 2 March 2012).
Hecq, D. (2009a) Interactive narrative pedagogy as a heuristic for understanding supervision in practice-led research. *New Writing: The International Journal for the Practice and Theory of Creative Writing* 6 (1), 40–50. doi 10.1080/14790720802598647.
Hecq, D. (2009b) *Out of Bounds*. Prahran: re.press.
Hecq, D. (2010a) Alabaster: The grain of the voice and semblance. *Double Dialogues: In/Stead* no. 3. Available at http://www.doubledialogues.com/in_stead/in_stead_iss03/Hecq.html (accessed 23 March 2012)
Hecq, D. (2010b) Glitter: On writing and suppléance. *TEXT*, special issue no. 7, *The ERA: Creative Writing as Research* 14 (2). Available at http://www.textjournal.com.au/speciss/issue7/Hecq.pdf (accessed 23 March 2012)
Hecq, D. (2011a) 'Oranges and lemons': Art, therapy, subjectivity. *TEXT* 15 (2). Available at http://www.textjournal.com.au/oct11/hecq.htm (accessed 23 March 2012).
Hecq, D. (2011b) Theory. *TEXT* 15 (2). Available at http://www.textjournal.com.au/oct11/hecq_poetry.htm (accessed 23 March 2012).
Hecq, D. (ed.) (2012a) *The Creativity Market: Creative Writing in the 21st Century*. Bristol: Multilingual Matters.
Hecq, D. (2012b) Reading in Braille. *La Traductière* 30, 34.
Hecq, D. (2012c) Sunscapes: Subjectivity, creativity and the work of metaphor. Paper presented at the Refereed Proceedings of the 17th Conference of the Australasian Association of Writing Programs: 'Encounters: Place, Situation, Context', Deakin University, Geelong, Victoria, 25–27 November.
Hecq, D. (2012d) Blue, like an orange: On writing, mourning, and anorexia. In A. McCulloch and P. Radia (eds) *Food and Appetites: The Hunger Artist and the Arts* (pp. 152–166). Newcastle upon Tyne: Cambridge Scholars.
Hecq, D. (2013a) Towards a theory without credentials. In J. Kroll and G. Harper (eds) *Research Methods in Creative Writing* (pp. 175–200). Basingstoke: Palgrave Macmillan.
Hecq, D. (2013b) Tomorrow, the sun. *Meniscus* 1, 30. Available at http://www.meniscus.org.au/Meniscus%20-%20Volume%201,%20Issue%201%20[FINAL].pdf (accessed 21 December 2013).
Hecq, D. (2014a) Eventful metaphors: The event, the subject and writing. In A. McCulloch and R. Goodrich (eds) (pp. 88–101) *The Event: The Subject and the Artwork*. Newcastle upon Tyne: Cambridge Scholars.
Hecq, D. (2014b) Fabulations. *La Traductière* no. 32, p. 36.
Hinshelwood, R.D. (1991) *A Dictionary of Kleinian Thought*. London: Free Association Books.
Hoerni, U. (2009) Preface. In S. Shamdasani (ed.) *The Red Book: Liber Novus* (pp. viii–ix). New York: W.W. Norton.
Holland, N.N. (1975) Unity identity text self. *Publications of the Modern Language Association* 90 (5), 813–822. doi 10.2307/461467.

Hopkins, J. (2000) Psychoanalysis, metaphor, and the concept of mind. In M. Levine (ed.) *The Analytic Freud: Philosophy and Psychoanalysis* (pp. 11–35). London: Routledge.

Hopkins, J. (2004) Mind as metaphor: A physicalistic approach to the problem of consciousness. Unpublished paper, London Philosophy Papers, School of Advanced Study, Institute of Philosophy, University of London. Available at http://sas-space.sas.ac.uk/794/1/J_Hopkins_Mind.pdf (accessed 14 September 2012).

Hunt, C. and Sampson, F. (2006a) *Writing: Self and Reflexivity*. New York: Palgrave Macmillan.

Hunt, C. and Sampson, F. (eds) (2006b) *The Self on the Page: Theory and Practice of Creative Writing in Personal Development*. London: Jessica Kingsley.

Hunter, I. (2006) The history of theory. *Critical Inquiry* 33 (1), 78–112. doi 10.1086/509747.

Hustvedt, S. (2003) *What I Loved*. London: Sceptre.

Hustvedt, S. (2009) *The Sorrows of an American*. London: Sceptre.

Hutcheon, L. (1988) *A Poetics of Postmodernism: History, Theory, Fiction*. New York: Routledge.

Hutcheon, L. (1993) *The Politics of Postmodernism*. New York: Routledge.

Ingarden, R. (1973) *The Literary Work of Art: An Investigation on the Borderlines of Ontology, Logic, and Theory of Literature* (G. Grabowicz, trans.). Evanston, IL: Northwestern University Press.

Irigaray, L. (1973) *Le Langage des déments*. Paris: Éditions Mouton.

Irigaray, L. (1979) *Et l'une ne bouge pas sans l'autre*. Paris: Les Éditions de Minuit.

Irigaray, L. (1985a) *Speculum of the Other Woman*. Ithaca, NY: Cornell University Press.

Irigaray, L. (1985b) *This Sex Which Is Not One* (C. Porter, trans.). Ithaca, NY: Cornell University Press.

Iser, W. (1980) *The Act of Reading: A Theory of Aesthetic Response*. Baltimore, MD: Johns Hopkins University Press.

Jaccard, R. (1979) *La folie*. Paris: Presses Universitaires de France.

Janicaud, D. (2005) *On the Human Condition* (E. Brennan, trans.). New York: Routledge.

Jauss, H.R. (1982) *Aesthetic Experience and Literary Hermeneutics*. Minneapolis, MN: University of Minnesota Press.

Jay, M. (1993) *Downcast Eyes: The Denigration of Vision in Twentieth-Century French Thought*. Berkeley, CA: University of California Press.

Jimenez, J.R. (2012) *The Complete Perfectionist: A Poetics of Work*. Chicago, IL: Swan Isle Press.

Johnson, L. (2013) Literary subjectivity: A Lacanian approach to authority and 'Postcards from desolation – twelve stories'. PhD thesis, University of Technology, Sydney.

Johnston, A. (2010) This philosophy which is not one: Jean-Claude Milner, Alain Badiou, and Lacanian antiphilosophy. *S: Journal of the Van Eyck Circle for Lacanian Ideology Critique* 3, 137–158. Available at http://www.lineofbeauty.org/index.php/s/article/viewFile/43/108 (accessed 7 October 2013).

Jones, A. R. (1981) Writing the body: Toward an understanding of 'L'Ecriture feminine'. *Feminist Studies* 7 (2), 247–263. doi 10.2307/3177523.

Joyce, J. (1986 [1916]) *A Portrait of the Artist as a Young Man*. London: Grafton Books.

Joyce, J. (1986 [1922]) *Ulysses*. Harmondsworth: Penguin in association with Bodley Head.

Joyce, J. (1992 [1939]) *Finnegans Wake*. Harmondsworth: Penguin.

Jung, C.G. (1997 [1916]) *Memories, Dreams, Reflections*. London: Fontana Press.

Kaufman, J.C. (2001) The Sylvia Plath effect: Mental illness in eminent creative writers. *Journal of Creative Behavior* 35 (1), 37–50. doi 10.1002/j.2162-6057.2001.tb01220.x.

Kaufman, J.C. (2009) *Creativity 101*. New York: Springer.

Kaufman, S.B. and Kaufman, J.C. (eds) (2009) *The Psychology of Creative Writing*. New York: Cambridge University Press.

Keats, J. (1947) *The Letters of John Keats* (M. B. Forman, ed.). London: Oxford University Press.

Kierkegaard, S. (1944) *The Concept of Dread* (W. Lowrie, trans.). London: Blackwell.

King, S.E. (2000) *On Writing: A Memoir of the Craft*. New York: Simon and Shuster.

Kipling, R. (2008) *Something of Myself*. Ware: Wordsworth Editions.

Kitching, G.N. (2008) *The Trouble with Theory: The Educational Costs of Postmodernism*. Sydney: Allen and Unwin.

Klein, M. (1988a) *Love, Guilt and Reparation and Other Works 1921–1945*. London: Virago.

Klein, M. (1988b) The importance of symbol-formation in the development of the ego. In *Love, Guilt, and Reparation and Other Works, 1921–1945* (pp. 211–219). London: Virago.

Klein, M., Heimann, P., Isaacs, S. and Riviere, J. (1952) *Developments in Psycho-Analysis* (J. Riviere, ed.). London: Hogarth Press and Institute of Psycho-Analysis.

Krauth, N., and Brady, T. (eds) (2006) *Creative Writing: Theory Beyond Practice*. Teneriffe: Post Pressed.

Kristeva, J. (1969) *Σημειωτική: recherches pour une sémanalyse*. Paris: Éditions du Seuil.

Kristeva, J. (1974) *La révolution du langage poétique: l'avant-garde à la fin du XIXe siècle, Lautréamont et Mallarmé*. Paris: Éditions du Seuil.

Kristeva, J. (1980) *Desire in Language: A Semiotic Approach to Literature and Art* (T. Gora, A. Jardine and L.S. Roudiez, trans., L.S. Roudiez, ed.). Oxford: Blackwell.

Kristeva, J. (1982) *Powers of Horror: An Essay on Abjection* (L. S. Roudiez, trans.). New York: Columbia University Press.

Kristeva, J. (1984) *Revolution in Poetic Language* (M. Waller, trans.). New York: Columbia University Press.

Kristeva, J. (1986) Semiotics: A critical science and/or a critique of science (S. Hand, trans.). In T. Moi (ed.) *The Kristeva Reader* (pp. 74–88). New York: Columbia University Press.

Kristeva, J. (1987a) *Tales of Love* (L. S. Roudiez, trans.). New York: Columbia University Press.

Kristeva, J. (1987b) *In the Beginning Was Love: Psychoanalysis and Faith*. New York: Columbia University Press.

Kristeva, J. (2000) From one identity to another. In N. Lucy (ed.) *Postmodern Literary Theory: An Anthology* (pp. 69–91). Oxford: Blackwell.

Kristeva, J. (2002a) *The Sense and Non-Sense of Revolt: The Powers and Limits of Psychoanalysis* (J. Herman, trans.). New York: Columbia University Press.

Kristeva, J. (2002b) *Intimate Revolt: The Power and Limits of Psychoanalysis* (J. Herman, trans.). New York: Columbia University Press.

Kroll, J. (1999) Uneasy bedfellows: Assessing the creative thesis and its exegesis. *TEXT* 3 (2). Available at http://www.textjournal.com.au/oct99/kroll.htm (accessed 6 November 2013).

Kroll, J. and Harper, G. (eds) (2013) *Research Methods in Creative Writing*. Basingstoke: Palgrave Macmillan.

Kundera, M. (2002) *The Art of the Novel*. New York: HarperCollins.

Lacan, J. (1953) Some reflections on the ego. *International Journal of Psychoanalysis* 34 (1), 11–17. Available at www.ecolelacanienne. net/documents/1951-05-02.doc (accessed 8 December 2013).

Lacan, J. (1966) *Écrits*. Paris: Éditions du Seuil.

Lacan, J. (1974–75) Le Séminaire. Livre XXII: R.S.I. *Ornicar?* 2 (5), 87–108.

Lacan, J. (1975 [1953–54]) *Le Séminaire de Jacques Lacan, Livre I: Les écrits techniques de Freud* (J-A. Miller, ed.). Paris: Éditions du Seuil.

Lacan, J. (1978 [1954–55]) *Le Séminaire de Jacques Lacan, Livre II: Le moi dans la théorie de Freud et dans la technique de la psychanalyse* (J-A. Miller, ed.). Paris: Éditions du Seuil.

Lacan, J. (1980) Monsieur A. *Ornicar?* 21–22 (summer), 17.

Lacan, J. (1986 [1964]) *The Seminar of Jacques Lacan, Book XI: The Four Fundamental Concepts of Psycho-Analysis* (A. Sheridan, trans., J-A. Miller, ed.). Harmondsworth: Penguin.

Lacan, J. (1991 [1960–61]) *Le Séminaire de Jacques Lacan, Livre VIII: Le transfert* (J-A. Miller, ed.). Paris: Éditions du Seuil.

Lacan, J. (1992 [1957–58]) *The Seminar of Jacques Lacan, Book VII: The Ethics of Psychoanalysis* (D. Porter, trans., J-A. Miller, ed.). New York: W.W. Norton.

Lacan, J. (1993 [1955–56]) *The Seminar of Jacques Lacan, Book III: The Psychoses* (R. Grigg, trans., J-A. Miller, ed.). New York: W.W. Norton.

Lacan, J. (1994 [1956–57]) *Le Séminaire de Jacques Lacan, Livre IV: La relation d'objet* (JA. Miller, ed.). Paris: Éditions du Seuil.

Lacan, J. (1998 [1957–58]) *Le Séminaire de Jacques Lacan, Livre V: Les formations de l'inconscient* (J-A. Miller, ed.). Paris: Éditions du Seuil.

Lacan, J. (1998 [1972–73]) *The Seminar of Jaques Lacan, Book XX: Encore – On Feminine Sexuality, the Limits of Love and Knowledge* (B. Fink, trans., J-A. Miller, ed.). New York: W.W. Norton.

Lacan, J. (2001) Peut-être à Vincennes.... In J. A. Miller (ed.) *Autres écrits* (pp. 313–335). Paris: Éditions du Seuil.

Lacan, J. (2001 [1971]) Lituraterre. In J-A. Miller (ed.) *Autres écrits* (pp. 11–20). Paris: Éditions du Seuil.

Lacan, J. (2004 [1962–63]) *Le Séminaire de Jacques Lacan, Livre X: L' angoisse* (J-A. Miller, ed.). Paris: Éditions du Seuil.

Lacan, J. (2005 [1975–76]) *Le Séminaire de Jacques Lacan, Livre XXIII: Le sinthome* (J-A. Miller, ed.). Paris: Éditions du Seuil.

Lacan, J. (2006) *Écrits: The First Complete Edition in English* (B. Fink, H. Fink and R. Grigg, trans.). London; New York: W.W. Norton.

Lacan, J. (2006 [1949]) The mirror stage as formative of the *I* function as revealed in psychoanalytic experience (B. Fink, H. Fink and R. Grigg, trans.). In *Écrits: The First Complete Edition in English* (pp. 75–81). London: W.W. Norton.

Lacan, J. (2006 [1953]) The function and field of speech in psychoanalysis (B. Fink, H. Fink and R. Grigg, trans.). In *Écrits: The First Complete Edition in English* (pp. 237–268). London; New York: W.W. Norton.

Lacan, J. (2006 [1957]) The instance of the letter in the unconscious, or reason since Freud (B. Fink, H. Fink and R. Grigg, trans.). In *Écrits: The First Complete Edition in English* (pp. 412–444). London: W.W. Norton.

Lacan, J. (2006 [1959a]) On a question prior to any possible treatment of psychosis (B. Fink, H. Fink and R. Grigg, trans.). In *Écrits: The First Complete Edition in English* (pp. 445–488). London: W.W. Norton.

Lacan, J. (2006 [1959b]) Kant with Sade (B. Fink, H. Fink and R. Grigg, trans.). In *Écrits: The First Complete Edition in English* (pp. 645–668). London: W.W. Norton.

Lacan, J. (2006 [1959c]) The Freudian thing (B. Fink, H. Fink and R. Grigg, trans.). In *Écrits: The First Complete Edition in English* (pp. 334–363). London: W.W. Norton.

Lacan, J. (2006 [1960]) The subversion of the subject and the dialectic of desire in the Freudian unconscious (B. Fink, H. Fink and R. Grigg, trans.). In *Écrits: The First Complete Edition in English* (pp. 671–702). London: W.W. Norton.

Lacan, J. (2006 [1971–72]) *Le Séminaire de Jacques Lacan, Livre XIX: D'un discours qui ne serait pas du semblant* (J-A. Miller, ed.). Paris: Éditions du Seuil.

Lacan, J. (2007 [1969–70]) *The Seminar of Jacques Lacan, Book XVII: The Other Side of Psychoanalysis* (R. Grigg, trans.). New York: W.W. Norton.

Lakoff, G. and Johnson, M. (1980) *Metaphors We Live By*. Chicago, IL: University of Chicago Press.

Lamming, G. (1953) *In the Castle of My Skin*. New York: McGaw-Hill.

Lamott, A. (1994) *Bird by Bird: Some Instructions on Writing and Life*. New York: Pantheon Books.

Landy, R.J. (2010) Drama as a means of preventing post-traumatic stress following trauma within a community. *Journal of Applied Arts and Health* 1 (1), 7–18. doi 10.1386/jaah.1.1.7/1.

Lasky, K. (2013) Poetics and creative writing. In J. Kroll and G. Harper (eds) *Research Methods in Creative Writing* (pp. 14–33). Basingstoke: Palgrave Macmillan.

Leader, D. (1999) Interpretation. In B. Burgoyne and E. M. Sullivan (eds) *The Klein–Lacan Dialogues* (pp. 45–59). New York: Other Press.

Lecercle, J-J. (1990) *The Violence of Language*. London: Routledge.

Lehrer, J. (2007) *Proust Was a Neuroscientist*. Boston: Houghton Mifflin.

Lentricchia, F. (1980) *After the New Criticism*. Chicago, IL: University of Chicago Press.

Leonard, S. (2011) Creative writing as a contribution to critical thinking. Paper presented at the First Global Conference on Writing, 'Paradigms, Power, Poetics, Praxes', Prague, Czech Republic, 12–14 November.

Liss, A. (2009) *Feminist Art and the Maternal*. Minneapolis, MN: University of Minnesota Press.

Lloyd, G. (1984) *The Man of Reason: 'Male' and 'Female' in Western Philosophy*. London: Methuen.

Lobb, J. (2008) 'But if the author is dead, what are we doing here?' Teaching critical theory in a creative writing program. Paper presented at the 13th conference of the Australian Association of Writing Programs: 'Creativity and Uncertainty', University of Technology, Sydney, 27–29 November.

Lobb, J. (2012) 'They don't flinch': Creative writing/critical theory, pedagogy/students. Paper presented at the 17th conference of the Australian Association of Writing Programs: 'Encounters: place | situation | context', School of Communication and Creative Arts (SCCA), Deakin University, Waterfront Campus – Geelong, Victoria, Australia, 25–27 November.

Lodge, D. (1977) The novelist at the crossroads. In M. Bradbury (ed.) *The Novel Today: Contemporary Writers on Modern Fiction* (pp. 84–110). London: Fontana.

Lubart, T.I. (2009) In search of the writer's creative process. In S.B. Kaufman and J.C. Kaufman (eds) *The Psychology of Creative Writing* (pp. 149–165). New York: Cambridge University Press.

Lucy, N. (ed.) (2000) *Postmodern Literary Theory: An Anthology*. Oxford: Blackwell.

Lyotard, J.F. (1984) *The Postmodern Condition: A Report on Knowledge*. Minneapolis, MN: University of Minnesota Press.

Magee, P. (2008) Suddenness: On rapid knowledge. *New Writing: The International Journal for the Practice and Theory of Creative Writing* 5 (3), 179–195. doi 10.1080/1479072080 2245314.

Magee, P. (2009) Is poetry research? *TEXT* 13 (2). Available at http://textjournal.com.au/oct09/magee.htm (accessed 12 March 2012).

Magee, P. (2012) Introduction. Part 1: Beyond accountability? *TEXT*, special issue no.

14, *Beyond Practice-Led Research* 16 (2). Available at http://www.textjournal.com.au/speciss/issue14/Magee%20%28Intro%201%29.pdf (accessed 2 November 2013).

Mallarmé, S. (1973a) L'action restreinte. In B. Marchal (ed.) *Oeuvres complètes* (Vol. 2, pp. 214–218). Paris: Gallimard, Bibliothèque de la Pléiade.

Mallarmé, S. (1973b) Le mystère dans les lettres. In B. Marchal (ed.) *Oeuvres complètes* (Vol. 2, pp. 229–234). Paris: Gallimard, Bibliothèque de la Pléade.

Malouf, D. (2008) *On Experience*. Carlton: Melbourne University Press.

Manguel, A. (2010) *A Reader on Reading*. New Haven, CT: Yale University Press.

Marshall, J.D. (2009) Gavin Kitching's 'The trouble with theory: The educational costs of postmodernism'. *Educational Philosophy and Theory* 41 (3), 244–248. doi 10.1111/j.1469-5812.2009.00520.x.

Marty, É. (ed.) (2005) *Lacan et la littérature*. Houilles: Éditions Manuscius.

Masson, J.M. (ed.) (1985) *The Complete Letters of Sigmund Freud to Wilhelm Fliess, 1887–1904*. Cambridge, MA: Belknap Press of Harvard University Press.

McCulloch, A. (2008) There is nothing like a lie. *Double Dialogues: Art and Lies II* 9 (autumn). Available at http://www.doubledialogues.com/archive/issue_nine/mcculloch_overview.html (accessed 10 September 2012).

McCulloch, A. (2013) Existentialism: Ethics, the rupturing and continuing relevance of tragedy. In R. Lloyd and J. Fornasiero (eds) *Magnificent Obsessions: Honouring the Lives of Hazel Rowley* (pp. 148–159). Newcastle upon Tyne: Cambridge Scholars.

McHattan, C. (2003) Book review: *Good Grief* by Dominique Hecq. Australian Public Intellectual Network website. At http://www.apinetwork. com/main/index.php?apply=reviews&webpage=api_reviews&flexedit=&flex _password=&menu_label =&menuID=homely&menubox=&Review=5265 (accessed 8 January 2014).

Melrose, A. (2007) Reading and righting: Carrying on the 'creative writing theory' debate. *New Writing: The International Journal for the Practice and Theory of Creative Writing* 4 (2), 109–117.

Metevier, J. (2011) Discursive/psychical relations in the creative writing workshop. Paper presented at the First Global Conference on Writing, 'Paradigms, Power, Poetics, Praxes', Prague, Czech Republic, 12–14 November.

Meyer, M. (1993) *Questions de rhétorique: Langage, raison et séduction*. Paris: Éditions du Seuil.

Meyer Spacks, P.A. (2011) *On Rereading*. Cambridge, MA: Belknap Press of Harvard University Press.

Michaels, A. (1998) *Fugitive Pieces*. London: Bloomsbury.

Miller, J-A. (1993) Clinique ironique. *La Cause Freudienne* 23, 7–13.

Miller, J-A. (1997) Des semblants dans la relation entre les sexes. *La Cause Freudienne* 36, 8.

Miller, J-A. (1998) Le sinthome, un mixte de symptome et fantasme. *La Cause Freudienne* 39, 7–17.

Miller, J-A. (2003a) Lacan's later teaching (B. P. Fulks, trans.). *Lacanian Ink* 21. Available at http://www.lacan.com/frameXXI2.htm (accessed 4 March 2014).

Miller, J-A. (2003b) The written in speech. *Courtil Papers* 12. Available at http://www.ch-freudien-be.org/Papers/Txt/Miller.pdf (accessed 12 September 2013).

Miller, J-A. (2007) Jacques Lacan and the voice. In V. Voruz and B. Wolf (eds) *The Later Lacan: An Introduction* (pp. 137–147). Albany, NY: State University of New York Press (SUNY).

Milner, J-C. (1995) *L'Oeuvre claire: Lacan, la science, la philosophie*. Paris: Éditions du Seuil.

Milner, M. (1952) *A Life of One's Own*. Harmondsworth: Penguin Books, in association with Chatto and Windus.

Milner, M. (1971) *On Not Being Able to Paint*. London: Heinemann Educational.

Morley, D. and Neilsen, P. (eds) (2012) *The Cambridge Companion to Creative Writing*. Cambridge: Cambridge University Press.

Morris, M. and Patton, P. (eds) (1979) *Michel Foucault: Power, Truth, Strategy*. Sydney: Feral Publications.

Morrison, T. (1988) *Beloved*. London: Picador.

Mousley, A. (2010) The new literary humanism: Towards a critical vocabulary. *Textual Practice* 24 (5), 819–839.

Mullin, J. (2012) Rhetoric: Writing, reading and producing the visual. In M. Biggs, H. Karlsson and J. Riksbankens (eds) *The Routledge Companion to Research in the Arts* (pp. 152–166). London: Routledge.

Murnane, G. (2005) *Invisible Yet Enduring Lilacs: Essays*. Artarmon: Giramondo Publishing.

Murnane, G. (2012) *A History of Books*. Artarmon: Giramondo Publishing.

Murphy, M. (2000) Interview with Seamus Heaney. In M. Murphy and C. Ní Anluain (eds) *Reading the Future: Irish Writers in Conversation with Mike Murphy* (pp. 81–98). Dublin: Lilliput Press.

Naddaff, R. (2002) *Exiling the Poets: The Production of Censorship in Plato's Republic*. Chicago, IL: University of Chicago Press.

Nelson, C. (2008) Research through practice: A reply to Paul Dawson. *TEXT* 12 (2). Available at http://www.textjournal.com.au/oct08/nelson.htm (accessed 13 February 2013).

Ninacs, M. (2011) Critically writing cultural agency in the composition classroom. Paper presented at the First Global Conference on Writing, 'Paradigms, Power, Poetics, Praxes', Prague, Czech Republic, 12–14 November.

Noonuccal, O. (1964) *We Are Going: Poems*. Brisbane: Jacaranda Press.

Norris, C. (1982) *Deconstruction: Theory and Practice*. London: Methuen.

Oatley, K. and Djikic, M. (2008) Writing as thinking. *Review of General Psychology* 12 (1), 9–27. doi 10.1037/1089-2680.12.1.9.

Orbach, S. (2001) *Hunger Strike: Starving Amidst Plenty*. New York: Other Press.

O'Rourke, R. (2005) *Creative Writing: Education, Culture and Community*. Leicester: National Institute of Adult Continuing Education (NIACE).

Pappas, N. (2005) Aristotle. In B.N. Gaut and D.M. Lopes (eds) *The Routledge Companion to Aesthetics* (pp. 15–26). New York: Routledge.

Parker, M. (1993) *Seamus Heaney: The Making of the Poet*. Basingstoke: Macmillan.

Payne, M. and Schad, J. (eds) (2003) *Life.After.Theory*. London: Continuum.

Performance-Based Research Fund (PBRF) website. The Tertiary Education Commission – Te Amorangi Matauranga Matua. At http://www.tec.govt.nz/Funding/Fund-finder/Performance-Based-Research-Fund-PBRF- (accessed 8 April 2013).

Pessoa, F. (1994) *Je ne suis personne: Une anthologie vers et proses* (M. Chandeigne, F. Laye and P. Quillier, trans., R. Bréchon, ed.). Paris: Christian Bourgeois Éditeur.

Pessoa, F. (2001) *The Book of Disquiet* (R. Zenith, trans.). London: Penguin.

Plato (1982a) Phaedrus. In E. Hamilton and H. Cairns (eds) *The Collected Dialogues of Plato, Including the Letters*. Princeton, NJ: Princeton University Press.

Plato (1982b) *Philebus* (R. Waterfield, trans.). New York: Penguin.

Plato (2007) *The Republic* (D. Lee, trans.). Harmondsworth: Penguin.

Pope, R. (2005) *Creativity: Theory, History, Practice*. London: Routledge.

Popper, K.R. (1972) *Objective Knowledge: An Evolutionary Approach*. Oxford: Clarendon Press.

Prose, F. (2006) *Reading Like a Writer: A Guide for People Who Love Books and For Those Who Want to Write Them*. New York: HarperCollins.

Pruyser, P.W. (1983) *The Play of the Imagination: Toward a Psychoanalysis of Culture*. New York: International Universities Press.
Quintilian (1921) *The Institutio Oratoria of Quintilian* (H.E. Butler, trans.). Cambridge, MA: Loeb Classical Library, Harvard University Press.
Rabaté, J-M. (2001) *Jacques Lacan: Psychoanalysis and the Subject of Literature*. New York: Palgrave.
Ragland-Sullivan, E. (1987) *Jacques Lacan and the Philosophy of Psychoanalysis*. Urbana, IL: University of Illinois Press.
Ramey, L. (2007) Creative writing and critical theory. In S. Earnshaw (ed.) *The Handbook of Creative Writing* (pp. 42–53). Edinburgh: Edinburgh University Press.
Rancière, J. (2013) *Aisthesis: Scenes from the Aesthetic Regime of Art*. London: Verso.
Rasmussen, R. (2005) On Joyce and psychosis. *Psychoanalytical Notebooks: A Review of the London Society of the New Lacanian School* no. 13, 45–55.
Recalcati, M. (2009) The anorexic passion for the mirror. *Lacanian Ink* 9. Available at http://www.lacan.com/frameXXIV9.htm (accessed 13 July 2013).
Recalcati, M. (2011) Hunger, repletion, and anxiety. *Angelaki: Journal of the Theoretical Humanities* 16 (3), 33–37. doi 10.1080/0969725X.2011.621217.
Regnault, F. (1997) *L'Antiphilosophie selon Lacan, in Conférences d'esthétique Lacanienne*. Paris: Agalma.
Research Assessment Exercise (RAE) 2006 website. The Research Grants Council (RGC) Hong Kong. At http://www.ugc.edu.hk/eng/ugc/publication/press/2007/pr020320 07.htm (accessed 2 July 2013).
Research Assessment Exercise (RAE) 2008 website. Higher Education Funding Council for England (HEFCE), the Scottish Funding Council (SFC), the Higher Education Funding Council for Wales (HEFCW) and the Department for Employment and Learning, Northern Ireland (DEL). At http://www.rae.ac.uk (accessed 2 July 2013).
Research Excellence Framework (REF) website. Higher Education Funding Council for England (HEFCE), the Scottish Funding Council (SFC), the Higher Education Funding Council for Wales (HEFCW) and the Department for Employment and Learning, Northern Ireland (DEL). At http://www.ref.ac.uk (accessed 2 July 2013).
Rich, A. (1986) *Blood, Bread and Poetry: Selected Prose, 1979–1985*. London: Virago.
Ricks, C. (1984) *The Force of Poetry*. Oxford: Clarendon Press.
Ricoeur, P. (1970) *Freud and Philosophy: An Essay on Interpretation*. New Haven, CT: Yale University Press.
Riffaterre, M. (1971) *Essais de stylistique structurale*. Paris: Flammarion.
Rimbaud, A. (1966) *Complete Works, Selected Letters* (W. Fowlie, ed.). Chicago, IL: University of Chicago Press.
Riviere, J. (1929) Womanliness as a masquerade. *International Journal of Psychoanalysis* 10, 303–313.
Rodenbach, G.C.A. (1997 [1914]) *Le Rouet des brumes*. Paris: Séguier.
Rodman, F.R. (ed.) (1987) *The Spontaneous Gesture: Selected Letters of D.W. Winnicott*. Cambridge, MA: Harvard University Press.
Roe, S. (1994) Shelving the self. In S. Roe, S. Sellers, N.W. Jouve and M. Roberts (eds) *The Semi-Transparent Envelope: Women Writing – Feminism and Fiction* (pp. 47–92). New York: M. Boyars.
Royle, N. (2013) Composition and decomposition. *Times Higher Education*, 28 March. Available at http://www.timeshighereducation.co.uk/features/composition-and-decomposition/2002751.article (accessed 15 April 2013).
Runco, M.A. (2007) *Creativity: Theories and Themes, Research, Development and Practice*. Amsterdam: Elsevier Academic Press.

Said, E.W. (1979) *Orientalism*. New York: Vintage Books.

Saint Exupéry, A. (1946) *Le Petit prince*. Paris: Gallimard.

Salusinszky, I. (1993) *Gerald Murnane*. Melbourne: Oxford University Press Australia.

Sarrimo, C. (2010) Creative writing as a communicative act – An artistic method. *New Writing: The International Journal for the Practice and Theory of Creative Writing* 7 (3), 179–191. doi 10.1080/14790726.2010.509509.

Sartre, J-P. (1947) *The Roads to Freedom* (E. Sutton, trans.). New York: A.A. Knopf.

Sartre, J-P. (1957 [1943]) *Being and Nothingness: An Essay on Phenomenological Ontology* (H. Barnes, trans.). London: Methuen.

Sartre, J-P. (1964) *Les Mots*. Paris: Gallimard.

Sartre, J-P. (1965 [1938]) *Nausea* (R. Baldick, trans.). Harmondsworth: Penguin.

Sartre, J-P. (1970 [1939]) Intentionality: A fundamental ideal of Husserl's phenomenology (J.P. Fell, trans.). *Journal of the British Society for Phenomenology* 1 (2), 4–5. Available at http://www.mccoyspace.com/nyu/12_s/anarchy/texts/03-Jean-Paul_Sartre-Intentionality.pdf (accessed 4 December 2013).

Sartre, J-P. (1973) *L'Idiot de la famille; Gustave Flaubert de 1821–1857*. Paris: Gallimard.

Sartre, J-P. (1983) *Lettres au Castor: Et à quelques autres, tome 2, 1940–1963*. Paris: Gallimard.

Sartre, J-P. (1986) *The Age of Reason* (E. Sutton, trans.). London: Penguin.

Sartre, J-P. (2004 [1940]) *The Imaginary: A Phenomenological Psychology of the Imagination* (J. Webber, trans.). London: Routledge.

Sawyer, R.K. (2009) Writing as collaborative act. In S.B. Kaufman and J.C. Kaufman (eds) *The Psychology of Creative Writing* (pp. 166–179). New York: Cambridge University Press.

Schmid, W. (2013) Implied reader. In P. Hühn *et al*. (eds) *The Living Handbook of Narratology*. Hamburg: Hamburg University Press. Available at http://wikis.sub.uni-hamburg.de/lhn/index.php/Implied_Reader (accessed 2 July 2013).

Sebold, A. (2002) *The Lovely Bones*. London: Picador.

Siegle, R. (1986) *The Politics of Reflexivity: Narrative and the Constitutive Poetics of Culture*. Baltimore, MD: Johns Hopkins University Press.

Skrebels, P. (2007) 'Precisely this fragment of the past … precisely this present': An interventionist pathway towards the theorised exegesis. *TEXT* 11 (2). Available at http://www.textjournal.com.au/oct07/skrebels.htm (accessed 26 June 2013).

Skriabine, P. (2005) Does the father say knot? *Psychoanalytical Notebooks: A Review of the London Society of the New Lacanian School* no. 13, 148–161.

Smith, A. (2013) *Artful*. London: Penguin.

Smith, H. and Dean, R.T. (eds) (2009) *Practice-Led Research, Research-Led Practice in the Creative Arts*. Edinburgh: Edinburgh University Press.

Snow, C.P. (1963) The two cultures. In S. Weintraub (ed.) *C.P. Snow, A Spectrum: Science, Criticism, Fiction* (pp. 30–33). New York: Scribner.

Soler, C. (1989) Deux vocations, deux écritures. *La Lettre Mensuelle* 81, 30–57.

Soler, C. (1993) L'expérience énigmatique du psychotique de Schreber à Joyce. *La Cause Freudienne* 23, 50–59.

Sontag, S. (1966) *Against Interpretation and Other Essays*. New York: Farrar, Straus and Giroux.

Sontag, S. (ed.) (1993) *A Roland Barthes Reader*. London: Vintage.

Sparrow, J. (2012) Creative writing, neo-liberalism and the literary paradigm. In D. Hecq (ed.) *The Creativity Market: Creative Writing in the 21st Century* (pp. 78–96). Bristol: Multilingual Matters.

Spivak, G.C. (1999) *In Other Worlds: Essays in Cultural Politics*. New York: Methuen.

Sprengnether, M. (1990) *The Spectral Mother: Freud, Feminism, and Psychoanalysis*. Ithaca, NY: Cornell University Press.

Stallybrass, P. and White, A. (eds) (1986) *The Politics and Poetics of Transgression*. London: Methuen.

Stanford, W.B. (1984) *Greek Tragedy and the Emotions: An Introductory Study*. London: Routledge.

States, B.O. (1985) *Great Reckonings in Little Rooms: On the Phenomenology of Theatre*. Berkeley, CA: University of California Press.

Stevens, A. (1987) Clinique de la suppléance. *Ornicar?* 44, 65–76.

Stevens, A. (1990) Délire et suppléance. *Quarto* 42, 33–37.

Stevens, A. (1995) Aux limites de la psychose. *Quarto* 47, 47–79.

Stevens, W. (1967) *The Collected Poems of Wallace Stevens*. New York: Alfred A. Knopf.

Stock, B. (1983) *The Implications of Literacy: Written Language and Models of Interpretation in the Eleventh and Twelfth Centuries*. Princeton, NJ: Princeton University Press.

Stokes, A. (1978) *The Critical Writings of Adrian Stokes*. London: Thames and Hudson.

Stone, B. (2004a) Towards a writing without power: Notes on the narration of madness. *Auto/Biography* 12, 16–33.

Stone, B. (2004b) How can I speak of madness? Narrative and identity in memoirs of mental illness. In D. Robinson (ed.) *Narrative, Memory and Identity: Theoretical and Methodological Issues* (pp. 49–57). Huddersfield: University of Huddersfield Press. Available at http://eprints.hud.ac.uk/4973/2/Chapter_4_Brendan_Stone.pdf (accessed 3 December 2012).

Stone, B. (2006) Knowing, not-knowing, fiction: Remembering Ross David Burke. In *Narrative, Memory and Knowledge: Representations, Aesthetics, Contexts* (pp. 91–99). Huddersfield: University of Huddersfield. Available at http://eprints.hud. ac.uk/4904/2/Chapter_8_-_Brendan_Stone.pdf (accessed 3 December 2012).

Stone, B. (2008) Why fiction matters to madness. In D. Robinson (ed.) *Narrative and Fiction: An Interdisciplinary Approach* (pp. 71–77). Huddersfield: University of Huddersfield. Available at http://eprints.hud.ac.uk/4829/2/Chapter_8_Brendan_Stone.pdf (accessed 4 December 2012).

Stone, B., Wilson, A. and Beresford, P. (2014) *Madness and Distress: From Individual to Collective Narratives* (Narratives of Learning and Teaching about Mental Health). Lancaster: MHHE.

Stow, R. (1982) *To the Islands*. Harmondsworth: Penguin.

Strange, S. (2012) Creative research: A radical subjectivity? *TEXT*, special issue no. 14, *Beyond Practice-Led Research* 16 (2). Available at http://www.textjournal.com.au/speciss/issue14/Strange.pdf (accessed 21 November 2012).

Struever, N. (1998) Rhetoric: Historical and conceptual overview. In M. Kelly (ed.) *Encyclopedia of Aesthetics* (pp. 151–155). New York: Oxford University Press.

Sullivan, G. (2005) *Art Practice as Research: Inquiry in the Visual Arts*. Thousand Oaks, CA: Sage.

Taylor, A. (2006) Writing/theory: A personal view. In N. Krauth and T. Brady (eds) *Creative Writing: Theory Beyond Practice* (pp. 225–234). Teneriffe: Post Pressed.

TEXT (2012) Special issue website series no. 14, *Beyond Practice-Led Research* 16 (2). Available at http://www.textjournal.com.au/speciss/issue14/content.htm (accessed 21 November 2012).

Thurston, L. (2002) *Re-inventing the Symptom: Essays on the Final Lacan*. New York: Other Press.

Tientjens Meyers, D. (2001) The rush to motherhood – Pronatalist discourse and women's autonomy. *Signs: Journal of Women in Culture and Society* 26 (3), 735–773.

Tizio, H. (2009) The analyst and the semblants. *PAPERS: Electronic Journal of the Action Committee of the School One* 1. Available at http://semblantsandsinthome.wordpress.com/2009/12/12/text-the-analyst-and-the-semblants-h-tizio (accessed 1 February 2010).

Todorov, T. and Porter, C. (1983) *Symbolism and Interpretation*. London: Routledge and Kegan Paul.

Turcotte, G. and Morris, R. (2012) As good as it gets? National research evaluations. In D. Hecq (ed.) *The Creativity Market: Creative Writing in the 21st Century* (pp. 66–77). Bristol: Multilingual Matters.

Valéry, P. (1966) *Oeuvres, Vol. 2* (J. Hytier, ed.). Paris: Gallimard.

Vincent, T. (2000) *L'anorexie*. Paris: Éditions Odile Jacob.

Wa Thiong'o, N. (2005) *Petals of Blood*. New York: Penguin.

Walker, Y. (2013a) Letters to the End of Love (a novel) and the politics and poetics of the modern epistolary novel (an exegesis). PhD thesis, Curtin University, Perth.

Walker, Y. (2013b) *Letters to the End of Love*. St Lucia: University of Queensland Press.

Wallace, D.F. (1989) *Girl With Curious Hair*. New York: W.W. Norton.

Wallas, G. (1926) *The Art of Thought*. New York: Harcourt, Brace and Company.

Wallis, B. (ed.) (1984) *Art After Modernism: Rethinking Representation*. New York; Boston: New York Museum of Contemporary Art; David R. Godine Publishers.

Wandor, M. (2008) *The Author Is Not Dead, Merely Somewhere Else: Creative Writing Reconceived*. New York: Palgrave.

Webb, J. (2008) *Brief Notes on Practice-Led Research*. Australasian Association of Writing Programs (AAWP) website. At http://www.aawp.org.au/postgraduate_resources (accessed 14 December 2012).

Webb, J. (2009) Finding a fit: University writing courses and the publishing sector. *Creative Writing: Teaching Theory and Practice* 1 (1), 63–84.

Webb, J. (2012) Seeing, doing, knowing: Poetry and the pursuit of knowledge. *TEXT*, special issue no. 13, *Creativity: Cognitive, Social and Cultural Perspectives* 16 (1). Available at: http://www.textjournal.com.au/speciss/issue13/Webb.pdf (accessed 21 July 2012).

Webb, J. and Brien, D.L. (2008) 'Agnostic' thinking creative writing as practice-led research. *Working Papers in Art and Design* 5. Available at http://sitem.herts.ac.uk/artdes_research/papers/wpades/vol5/jwdobabs.html (accessed 15 October 2012).

Webb, J. and Brien, D.L. (2012) Addressing the 'ancient quarrel': Creative writing as research. In M. Biggs, H. Karlsson and J. Riksbankens (eds) *The Routledge Companion to Research in the Arts* (pp. 186–204). London: Routledge.

Webb, J., Brophy, K., Magee, P. and Biggs, M. (2013–15) 'Understanding Creative Excellence: A Case Study in Poetry.' Australian Research Council (ARC) Discovery Project (A$215,000, DP130100402). University of Hertfordshire, University of Melbourne, and University of Canberra.

Wellek, R. and Warren, A. (1956) *Theory of Literature*. New York: Harcourt, Brace and Co.

White, H. (1973) *Metahistory: The Historical Imagination in Nineteenth-Century Europe*. Baltimore, MD: Johns Hopkins University Press.

White, P. (1981) *Flaws in the Glass: A Self-Portrait*. London: Jonathan Cape.

White, P. (1986) *Memoirs of Many in One*. London: Jonathan Cape.

Whitehead, A. (2004) *Trauma Fiction*. Edinburgh: Edinburgh University Press.

Williams, P. (2013) Creative praxis as a form of academic discourse. *New Writing: The International Journal for the Practice and Theory of Creative Writing* 10 (3), 250–260. doi 10.1080/14790726.2012.754476.

Wimsatt, W.K. and Beardsley, M.C. (1972) The affective fallacy. In D. Lodge (ed.) *20th Century Literary Criticism: A Reader* (pp. 345–358). London: Longman.

Winnicott, D.W. (1945) Primitive emotional development. *International Journal of Psychoanalysis* 26, 137–143.

Winnicott, D.W. (1971) *Playing and Reality*. Harmondsworth: Penguin.

Winnicott, D.W. (1988) *Human Nature*. London: Free Association Books.

Wittgenstein, L. (1953) *Philosophical Investigations* (G.E.M. Anscombe, trans.). Oxford: Basil Blackwell.

Wolff, E. (1971) Der intendierte Leser. Überlegungen und Beispiele zur Einführung eines literaturwissenschaftlichen Begriffs. *Poetica* 4, 141–166.

Wolton, D. (2009) Globalisation and cultural diversity. Paper presented at the University of Melbourne, Melbourne, 7 May.

Woolf, V. (1931) *The Waves*. New York: Harcourt, Brace and Company.

Woolf, V. (1984) *The Diary of Virginia Woolf, Vol. V: 1936–41* (A.O. Bell, ed.). London: Hogarth Press.

Woolf, V. (1985) *Moments of Being* (J. Schulkind, ed.). San Diego, CA: Harcourt Brace Jovanovich.

Wright, A. (2007) *Carpentaria*. Artarmon: Giramondo.

Wright, A. (2013) *The Swan Book*. Artarmon: Giramondo

Wright, E. (1984) *Psychoanalytic Criticism: Theory in Practice*. London: Methuen.

Yeats, W.B. (1982) *Selected Poetry* (A.N. Jeffares, ed.). London: Pan Books, Macmillan.

Young, R. (1990) *White Mythologies: Writing History and the West*. London: Routledge.

Zentner, M.I. (1986) Che vuoi? Or some remarks on anorexia nervosa. *Papers of the Freudian school of Melbourne*, 63–77.

Žižek, S. (1999) *The Ticklish Subject: The Absent Centre of Political Ontology*. London: Verso.

Žižek, S. (2003a) *The Indivisible Remainder: An Essay on Schelling and Related Matters*. London: Verso.

Žižek, S. (2003b) *Lacan: The Silent Partners*. London: Verso.

Zurbrugg, N. (ed.) (2004) *Art, Performance, Media: 31 Interviews*. Minneapolis, MN: University of Minnesota Press.

Index